MERCER STREET

2017 - 2018

Program Director:
Dara Rossman Regaignon

Editor:
Stephen Donatelli

Senior Production Editor:
Richard Larson

Managing Editor:
Tara Parmiter

Production Editor:
Christopher Cappelluti

Development Editors:
Angelica Chong
Sam Holloway
Helena Keown
Olivia Loperfido

Program Manager:
Christine Jensch

***Mercer Street* Committee:**
Stephen Donatelli, Chair
Grant Ginder
Matthew Nicholas
Victoria Olsen
Jacqueline Reitzes

EXPOSITORY WRITING PROGRAM
NEW YORK UNIVERSITY
COLLEGE OF ARTS & SCIENCE

MERCER STREET

To the Class of 2021:

Welcome to New York University!

An NYU education begins, in part, with writing. This practice reflects the University's longstanding commitment to the centrality of written inquiry to undergraduate education.

It's a bit of a cliché to say that reading and writing are connected, but in 2017 it seems important to say it nonetheless. As information circulates more and more quickly—moving ever farther from its origin—we have to read critically and for context: *Who was the author? What were they trying to achieve? What is their evidence?* This is all the more urgent when we take up what we read, re-posting it or relying on it for insight or opinions of our own.

Over the course of the next four years, you have a wide range of courses open to you; alphabetically, they range from accounting to history to mechanical engineering to woodwind studies. No matter what field you choose, during your time here you will find yourself using writing to think, analyze, investigate, and create. And no matter what path or career you choose after you graduate (as a scholar, educator, health practitioner, entrepreneur, artist, performer, lawyer, engineer, or activist), you will find yourself using writing for those purposes and others: to propose, to investigate, to analyze, and to represent yourself and your work. Recent research shows that work in the twenty-first century involves more writing than ever before, regardless of the specific occupation. This writing ranges across genres (email, proposals, essays, reports, and more), and encompasses prose that is creative, technical, reflective, and persuasive. It's writing that seeks to make an impact on its readers, that seeks not only to make audiences see the questions and challenges that face us today in new ways but also to help them imagine new possibilities and perspectives.

The essays collected in this volume represent some of the best work written for Expository Writing Program or CAS First-Year Seminar courses over the course of 2016-17; most were written by first-year students. These essays are smart, moving, funny, analytic, imaginative, and—like us all, and like all written work—incomplete. They open up questions, problems, and puzzles that are not entirely solvable. The faculty of EWP hope that you will both enjoy and learn from them.

Take heart! College is a time to challenge yourself and to nurture your mind both in and out of the classroom. Your most surprising encounters—your most creative or insightful moments—may happen when you least expect them. Be interested. That is always the best way to begin.

With all best wishes,

Dara Rossman Regaignon
Director of the Expository Writing Program
Associate Professor of English

Editor's Note

Last year at this time the essayists published in this volume were reading, as you are now: with a purpose. What was it? Somehow, it was to build confidence and mastery in the writing of essays that explain, question, and engage sources thoughtfully and with a view to contending with them. Within the respectful environment of your expository writing course, guided by your writing teacher and through many productive encounters with your peers, giving and receiving equally, you'll have your turn at deepening an inheritance of writing practices that your predecessors have left for you.

By reading these essays with a technical or builder's eye, you and your instructor will often be talking about how to make essays worthy of serious thinkers. The structure of this kind of essay is not formulaic, but will become apparent each time out. Essays come in many forms, after all—an essay adapts itself to the questions and problems and evidence its author has chosen.

This work will help to prepare you for the writing you do in other classes, this semester and over the course of the next several years. To write well one must know how to size up the situation: *What community or audience am I writing to? What kinds of questions interest them? What kinds of evidence will surprise or persuade them?* Professors across the University recognize and honor writing that can reason closely with sources. For writers, the progress of our thought process will also bring an additional, unexpected pleasure, the pleasure of discovering what we ourselves had not known or thought or imagined before. Here, then, are twenty-seven essays that actually managed to surprise their own authors! Now you can study them for the way they draw you in.

Yes, the writers published here are going to show you a lot in a powerful way. It's true that the topics they have chosen are interesting in themselves: gender rights; environmental emergencies; empathy; the cinema. The fundamental lessons in your writing course will always be more mobile and not as fixed to a particular topical concern. These lessons are basic not because they are easy, but because they are foundational. Our concern is with certain deep denominational values such as how to structure arguments sensibly, how to project the character of your own mind, and how to keep an argument moving by continuing to feed hard questions to it, as your reader is going to be doing.

We hope that the essays presented here will help you to engage with some fundamental writerly practices, practices moreover in which your own peers have succeeded.

Readers may also find a short statement at the head of each text. Each of these snapshots captures a term or a practice that can then be followed into the essay proper.

Stephen Donatelli
Editor
Director of Writing in the Disciplines

Acknowledgements

The Expository Writing Program is grateful to G. Gabrielle Starr, Dean of the College of Arts and Science through Spring 2017, for her many years of support for this publication. Dean Starr's patronage has given *Mercer Street* the kind of stability needed for sustaining an intellectually satisfying dialogue between student writers and student readers.

The *Mercer Street* Committee—Jacqueline Reitzes, Victoria Olsen, Matthew Nicholas, Grant Ginder, and Richard Larson—and editorial staff are grateful to EWP Director Dara Rossman Regaignon for her ongoing commitment to student writers' success and achievement.

Denice Martone, EWP Associate Director, and EWP's other Directors—William M. Morgan and Benjamin Stewart—contributed shaping and guidance to this project. The *Mercer Street* editors are very grateful to them, as well as to Assistant Directors Nicole Callihan, David Cregar, Beth Machlan, Jono Mischkot, and Elizabeth Mikesell, and to the many Writing Program faculty members who read submissions. We are also grateful to the growing number of faculty from the CAS First-Year Seminars for directing students to this opportunity.

Richard Larson's technical wizardry with the manuscript is in evidence everywhere. We also thank Christine Jensch for the speed and professionalism she has devoted to making *Mercer Street* possible, year after year. And Managing Editor Tara Parmiter ensured the seamlessness of our operation. Her editorial expertise and decisive management style taught us what print production should be like.

Four talented and resourceful undergraduate student editors— Angelica Chong, Sam Holloway, Olivia Loperfido, and Helena Keown—brought intense editorial care to the 27 essays published here. And thank you, Chris Cappelluti, for special editorial assistance.

Cover Photograph and Title Page Transparency: Denice Martone
Jacket Design and Title Page Design: Lisa Klausing
Printing: GHP Media and Judy Zimmer

MERCER STREET

CONTENTS

Writing the Essay: Tandon School of Engineering

Writing the Essay: Art and the World

International Writing Workshop: Tandon School of Engineering

International Writing Workshop II

College of Arts & Science Freshman Seminars

The Advanced College Essay: Education and the Professions

The Advanced College Essay: Tandon School of Engineering

The Advanced College Essay: The World through Art

Burlaud raises a compelling problem in this essay on Joan Didion's "On Going Home": Why does revisiting a childhood home as an adult make people so uneasy? This problem goes beyond the question Didion raises in order to explore complex issues of memory, acceptance, and change.
(Instructor: Jacqueline Reitzes)

YOUR HOUSE IS NOT A HOME

Sandra Burlaud

But don't you know you can't go home again?" writer Ella Winter once asked American novelist Thomas Wolfe (qtd. in Godwin xii). If the title of his 1940 novel *You Can't Go Home Again* is any indication, we can assume that Wolfe found the idea particularly convincing. He's not alone: the theme of not being able to return home appears exponentially in literature, movies, and TV shows, making it a well-known trope. In these tales, characters are forced out of their homes, and the story revolves around them trying to make it back to where they came from, only to grimly realize that their home is no longer what it used to be ("You Can't"). But these tropes are primarily concerned with a physical separation from home. Sometimes home still appears to be within one's reach, but the issue takes a more psychological and emotional turn. Even when the scenery that framed our childhood remains untouched and familiar, what happens when something still feels *off*?

American novelist and literary journalist Joan Didion, in her essay "On Going Home," reflects on this uneasy sensation, recalling a trip back to her native California for the occasion of her daughter's first birthday. Aiming to reconnect with the home of her youth, Didion decides to closely examine old mementos and memories that she has kept so carefully. At first "paralyzed by the neurotic lassitude" of being assaulted by childhood memories, she is then determined to find an "answer" to these specific snapshots of her youth that she struggles to make sense of (200). However, Didion presents these various objects—a bathing suit, an aerial photograph, a teacup—and the memories associated with them as "ambushes," unexpected attacks

that throw her off-balance and shine light onto the seemingly contradictory situation of being home but not *feeling* home (201). Her
inability to find meaning in these items—or to see herself in them—
reminds her that she is unable to "go home again" (200). Tired and
vanquished, she sits with her mother, the two women both "veterans
of a guerilla war [they] never understood" (200). Didion's repeated
use of aggressive, warlike diction paints an uncommon portrait of
family life: a series of unexpected blows and attacks, a never-ending
emotional struggle that leaves its fighters resigned but still ignorant of
the battle's greater meaning. Didion implies that home is supposed to
be a safe haven, filled with reassuring memories and loved ones, but
the aggression her childhood home still generates reveals the underly-
ing difficulties that come with such a broad and nuanced concept.
Given the inconsistency between our idealized image of home and the
troublesome reality of it, how can we define *home*?

At the very beginning of the essay, Didion creates a clear distinction between the home in which she grew up and the house in which
she now lives with her husband and daughter—to her, this is "a vital
although troublesome distinction" (199). This need to separate the
two parts of her family stems in part from the impact Didion's childhood home has on her. She tends to "fall into [her family's] ways,"
which she describes as "difficult, oblique, deliberately inarticulate"
(199). This transformation is beyond her control and seems to frus-
trate her husband, who fails to understand Didion's family's idiosyn-
crasies. "Marriage is the classic betrayal," Didion writes (199). To her,
there now exist two distinct, almost unrelated parts of her family, and
the task of uniting the two fragments seems so colossal, and perhaps
even pointless, that she does not even bother trying. Instead, while her
brother refers to her husband as "Joan's husband," even in his presence, further complicating her pre-marital home's atmosphere, she
prefers to remain distant from the situation, analyzing from afar
(199). The meeting of these two opposing parts of her family, her two
homes, is at the source of Didion's anxieties and uneasiness: in
addition to being unable to connect to her childhood home, she is
torn between two families and her two identities that come along with
them.

As Didion goes to visit a family graveyard, her father's ranch, and her great-aunts, her emotional paralysis becomes apparent. At the graveyard, she stays in the car and only observes that some of the monuments are "broken, overturned in the dry grass" (201). During her conversation with her great-aunts, she does not bother correcting them when they mistake her for another cousin. "Questions trail off, answers are abandoned," and Didion seems to be stuck in a kind of incapacitating nonchalance (201). This paralyzing feeling seems to be echoed by the rest of the family members: she and her husband constantly "miss each other's points" and do not bother communicating, while her mother "shrugs" when she hears about the vandalized monuments in the graveyard (199, 201). This bizarre state of mind highlights the contradictory nature of going back home: family members all settle back into their old, ambiguous ways, yet no one can fully reconnect emotionally with their home. However, even when dealing with an emotional question, Didion's voice remains very analytical and detached, and her mere observations do not require the reader to identify with the story.

Didion's deliberately 'cold' choice of narrative style affects the way we read and understand the essay's problem, as we learn in Adam Gopnik's "The Corrections: Abridgement, Enrichment, and the Nature of Art." The *New Yorker* staff writer, in his 2007 essay, demonstrates that manipulating and modifying art can lead to an impoverished final product. Through various examples of "compact editions" of great literary classics or extended edition movies that aim to be "meaningful additions" to the original stories, Gopnik concludes that "art is a business not of clear narratives but of troubled narrators" (562, 566, 569). The narrator's presence is what separates "the compact from the achieved," the superficial from the complex, and "guarantees that . . . the viewer's mind will continue to divide, and multiply" (569). It is crucial to be able to clearly follow the plot or ideas of a story, but Gopnik suggests that a deeper understanding of a text's problem can only be achieved through the guidance of a narrator. After all attempts at abridging classics, cutting out seemingly superfluous details that "undercut" the "tensile strength of the narrative," we see that it is in fact all these details, thoughts, and uncertainties that make the narrator's voice such a driving force in a story and make these books into the great classics that they are (564).

Didion, in her essay, has a tendency to cut out the non-essential details and create an orderly story, including dates (we notice her journalistic influences) but omitting character names. Gopnik might suggest that she is presenting a "'taut, spare, driving' narrative" that makes her stories very clear and easy to follow for the reader but does not call for any emotional involvement (563). Moreover, the initial problem regarding the definition of home needs refining; the essay is not really primarily concerned with a definition, although Didion's sober style might warrant that conclusion. Through Gopnik's concept of the "troubled narrator" bringing a story to life, we can extract deeper meaning. In the first part of the essay, Didion habituates the reader to an almost absent narrator. However, she then suddenly paints a very contradictory picture: "I had by all objective accounts a 'normal' and a 'happy' family situation, and yet I was almost thirty years old before I could talk to my family on the telephone without crying after I had hung up" (200). For the first time in the essay, Didion makes her anxiety apparent in this destabilizing moment that throws the reader off guard. The reader's sudden realization that the author is in fact affected by the situation described in her story urges us to look deeper into the problem. Why does this contradictory sentence stand out? Why is the narrator so troubled? Through this unusual sliver of emotion, we gain insight into the full extent of Didion's thoughts: it seems to be an impossible task to reconnect to the homes of our youth, yet those homes are still the source of inexplicable anxieties that continue to shape us and our relationships.

At the end of her essay, Didion regretfully declares that she will not be able to give her daughter *home*, although she wishes she could (201). Didion has built a contradictory and anxiety-inducing portrait of home throughout her essay, yet she still wants to give her child home the way she experienced it. It seems like Didion sees this struggle as an obligatory side effect of a happy childhood. Moreover, in her brief discussion about generational differences regarding the importance of home, Didion implies that the concept of home might be irrelevant to younger people because it is not "the source of all tension and drama" anymore (200). But does this tension have to be a defining characteristic of home? It feels like an important part of the restlessness felt by Didion comes from her very fixed mental image of *home* and her lack of motivation when it comes to dealing with troubling family situations. Although it can be a difficult task, changing her expectations of what home should be could make it easier to raise her daughter and offer her a different version of home.

It is true that relationships tend to change and weaken over time when no active work is put into maintaining them. Our relationships with home and family are no exception. While it might be tempting to settle back into old, familiar, but problematic ways around our family, a conscious effort to communicate could perhaps help us grow out of this habituated state of apathy and free us of this "nameless anxiety" that underlies our relationships (Didion 200). Even though it might not be possible to ever truly reconnect to our childhood homes, making sure that our relationships are as open and comfortable as possible can perhaps make that truth less painful. As to offering a home to future generations, what makes the idea of home so special to us is that it is ours, a source of all that we are. This home may be initially created around a sense of "cousins, and of rivers, and of [our] great-grandmother's teacups" (Didion 201), or around a completely different experience, but it remains home nonetheless.

WORKS CITED

Didion, Joan. "On Going Home." *The Broadview Anthology of Expository Prose*, edited by Laura Buzzard et al., 3rd ed., Broadview Press, 2016, pp. 199-201.

Godwin, Gail. "A New Introduction." *You Can't Go Home Again*, by Thomas Wolfe, Scribner, 2011, pp. ix-xvi.

Gopnik, Adam. "The Corrections: Abridgement, Enrichment, and the Nature of Art." *The Broadview Anthology of Expository Prose*, edited by Laura Buzzard et al., 3rd ed., Broadview Press, 2016, pp. 562-569.

"You Can't Go Home Again." *TVTropes*, www.tvtropes.org/pmwiki/pmwiki.php/Main/YouCantGoHomeAgain.

Taking up Ursula Franklin's claim that without unprogrammed silence we are likely to lose spiritual connection, Hudson develops the nuanced argument that spirituality requires the experience of community and that such an experience can be found by sharing ritual moments in either silence or sound with others. (Instructor: Leeore Schnairsohn)

THAT WE MAY HEAR

Milo Hudson

Ursula Franklin, in her speech "Silence and the Notion of the Commons," worries that silence—which she views as integral to the spirituality and the common good of humanity—is being threatened by the harrowing effects of continually advancing technology (439). To Franklin, silence is comparable to any of Earth's unpolluted elements as an impending casualty of our "technologically mediated society" (440)—it faces annihilation unless we intervene (439).

Franklin harbors a conservative belief on how sound should rightly be perceived. She mourns a waning perception of sound as "ephemeral," as "coupled to its source," a view which has become obsolete with the technologically driven ability to establish sound permanently (440). The ephemerality of sound is central to Franklin's core beliefs. Without it, silence could not permeate the sound environment, or what she calls "the soundscape" (440). Previously, she explains, the soundscape was distinct from the landscape in that it could not be obstructed by unseemly, humanmade creations—sound was experienced, not manipulated. However, much to Franklin's perturbation, the dimensions of the soundscape have come to almost mirror those of the landscape: just as a landscape can be obstructed by "a horrible building somewhere in front of a beautiful mountain," the soundscape can be overwhelmed by "modern devices" that "separat[e] the sound from the source" (440).

Ultimately, Franklin's concern for sound is a smaller piece of her crusade for silence. In addition to being a research physicist and an activist, Franklin was a practicing Quaker. Her experience as a

provided external info. abaut avthor.

Quaker, along with her knowledge and understanding of Quaker history, gives her a unique perspective on the idea of silence as a human right and something integral to the common good. This perspective primes her argument that the silence we are entitled to is being ushered away without our consent. Common societal good, in both a functional and spiritual sense, requires an environment that allows for things to happen spontaneously, that allows for the "unappointed, unordained, unexpected, and unprogrammed" in order to develop and be maintained (441). Exactly how this process takes place is not so much explained or outlined but felt throughout the essay. At one point, Franklin describes her experiences in Quaker meetings as one in which thoughts would manifest themselves from the "*collective* silence" into the minds of individual participants, an exchange she senses as an "uncanny," "spiritual force" (441).

When I was a child, my own family attended Quaker meetings on a regular basis. I have not reflected on those experiences since our attendance dropped off when I was six or seven, but as I do now, through the lens of Franklin's values, several things strike me about the silent meditation that took place. I remember the old man with a yellow patch on his neck who struggled to speak (I later surmised this was the result of the surgical removal of his larynx), and yet speak he did, out of the collective silence. I remember that the other children and I remained quiet despite our young, excited vitality—even at that age, we could sense the intrinsic power of that silence. To me, that collective silence came to represent a certain wisdom that I aspired to one day obtain. I wanted to have the same connection to it that those old, enlightened few who spoke seemed to have. Communal silence embodies that inherently difficult-to-describe but immediately felt sense of power and knowledge, that unseen but alive substance that Franklin evokes in her writing, which can only and precisely be described as spiritual.

But the spiritual aspects of sound and silence cannot be said to resonate, in a benevolent way, with every individual. In "Salvation," Langston Hughes recounts a childhood experience in a spiritual soundscape that causes him to fabricate meaning rather than find it. As the members of his local church gather up the youth and consign themselves to "bring the young lambs into the fold," Hughes waits

[margin handwritten note: relates to her own life.]

faithfully for Jesus to reveal himself out of the silence—but to no avail (203). He writes, "The whole congregation prayed for me alone, in a mighty wail of moans and voices. And I kept waiting serenely for Jesus, waiting, waiting—but he didn't come. I wanted to see him, but nothing happened to me" (204). He seeks salvation not only from his own imperfections, but from the berating, chaotic voices that assault him: like Franklin, Hughes yearns for a spiritual force to reach out from the silence and deliver him from the tempest of the soundscape. However, unlike for Franklin, silence *fails* him. His religious experience starkly opposes Franklin's: instead of a communal silence, it is an individual silence battered by outside communal noise. In his inward search for an unprogrammed connection with Christ, while trying to resist the pressure of projecting a programmed and fake connection, he doesn't find spirituality. Instead, he is left with a silent shame, which festers into an agonized sound that escapes him in a lonely cry that he cannot stifle, ironically contrasting his congregation's "joyous singing" (205). Hughes's reaction evidences a distinct lack of spirituality; his having the faith to look inward in silence, to reach for the power and knowledge unseen, avails only emptiness. Franklin rages against the manipulation of the public soundscape by privatized elements and praises the virtues of a soundscape that belongs to "the commons" (443), but Hughes would contend that a community imposing its voice on an individual is as fundamentally wrong as a privatized voice imposed on a community. Depriving one's own senses as a religious experience in the silence, one can find something spiritual, but one can also find nothing. To understand why, perhaps we must know what spiritual meaning can be found, or not, by embracing one's senses instead.

Before technology allowed for aspects of the soundscape to be so easily made permanent, Mark Twain struggled to negotiate the loss of meaning within his personal landscape. In *Life on the Mississippi*, Twain reflects upon his close relationship with the Mississippi River, which he imagines as a grand, ever-evolving book written in its own unique language (76). He entertains no thoughts of restraint in consuming the river's words, stating that "there was never a page that was void of interest, never one that you could leave unread without loss, never one that you would want to skip, thinking you could find higher enjoyment in some other thing" (76). But tragically, as Twain masters the intricate language of the river, "the beauty, the grace, the poetry" cease to appear to him; he begins to see it only in the terms of its "use-fulness" to his profession (77). Twain reaches the same unmeaningful emptiness by exploring the seen that Hughes reaches by exploring the unseen.

Comparing the spirituality that Franklin and I could find in our experiences of silence with the tragic emptiness that awaited Twain and Hughes reveals a striking variable in these experiences: commu-nity. Hughes lacked a community to join him in silence, and Twain rejected input from his fellow humans in favor of what nature alone could express. Perhaps attempting to perfectly balance the embrace or the deprivation of one's senses is the wrong step, or an incomplete step, in the search for spiritual meaning. Instead, perhaps unity with one's community must be brought into harmony, be it in silence or not. What these experiences point to together, which they could not by themselves, is a need to not only look inwards to the self, but also outwards to the connectedness of the commons. We must draw spirit from the unseen and unheard through interconnected and communal experiences.

WORKS CITED

Franklin, Ursula. "Silence and the Notion of the Commons." *The Broadview Anthology of Expository Prose*, edited by Laura Buzzard et al., 3rd ed., Broadview Press, 2016, pp. 439-444.
Hughes, Langston. "Salvation." *50 Essays*, edited by Samuel Cohen, Bedford/St. Martin's, 2007, pp. 203-205.
Twain, Mark. "from *Life on the Mississippi*." *The Broadview Anthology of Expository Prose*, edited by Laura Buzzard et al., 3rd ed., Broadview Press, 2016, pp. 76-78.

In this essay, Kahan argues that Robert Putnam's emphasis on family circumstance and community norms to explain the education gap is incomplete. Drawing evidence from a wide range of scholarly and journalistic sources, she contends that responsibility for education needs to be understood in broader, more collective terms. (Instructor: Gerard O'Donoghue.)

THE POVERTY LINK:
SCHOOL, HOME, AND A LIFETIME
OF FINANCIAL HARDSHIP

Charlotte Kahan

Alabama's Livingston Junior High School is in a state of utter disrepair. The majority of the girls' bathroom stalls are out of order. The ceiling over one classroom leaks when it rains, leading to the spread of mold and the buckling of floor tiles. The room can no longer be used for classes; garbage buckets fail to catch all of the rainwater, and the mold poses a health hazard. Paint peels off the walls, and broken windows remain unfixed (Turner et al. "Money Problem"). The school district, which serves low-income and minority students, is unable to extract enough taxpayer dollars from the community to finance basic repairs, and the hundreds of students in the district suffer as a result (Turner et al. "Money Problem").

According to a 2015 study by the Southern Education Foundation, low-income children comprise the majority of students attending American public schools (Suitts). Students who experience financial hardship at home may attend local public schools that are severely under-funded and under-resourced. Failing schools constitute one of many factors that perpetuate cyclical, intergenerational poverty and low social mobility. The U.S.'s decentralized public schools are part of a system that contributes to widening class disparities and decreased opportunities for children to surpass the socioeconomic status of their parents.

The role of money in the success of schools is a surprisingly controversial research subject, and some academics propose that family traditions and home life are more influential in a child's educational success than well-funded schools. For example, parents who take time to read with their children and encourage intellectual growth will raise more highly achieving youth (Caucutt, Burtless). However, the school and the home are two crucial components of a community that are inextricably linked, typically either in relative wealth or in relative poverty. Poor neighborhoods are frequently plagued by failing public schools, because these schools rely, at least in part, on the revenue of district taxpayers for funding (Turner et al. "Money Problem"). The interconnectedness of this 'school-home link' creates a vicious cycle for low-income residents: taxpayers are unable to financially con-tribute to quality local schooling, and, as a result, poor children are educationally disadvantaged compared to their peers in richer dis-tricts. This double bind decreases the likelihood that poor children will be able to escape the financial hardship of their upbringings, since achieving the 'American Dream' requires at least a "good education—[one that is] good enough to command a job that pays a non-poverty wage" (AEI-Brookings).

The consequences of poverty are severe. Robert D. Putnam, political scientist and author of *Our Kids: The American Dream in Crisis*, explains the phenomenon of America's expanding inequality gap between the rich and poor by using specific children as case stud-ies. David, a young man from Port Clinton, Ohio, (Putnam's home-town), has endured an "obviously chaotic" family life: his father has served time in prison, his mother's perpetual absence from the home has been filled by several women his father has dated, and now he feels as though he is the sole responsible caregiver for his younger half-siblings (Putnam 859-860). David's academics and job prospects suffer as a result of his volatile home life. Putnam starkly contrasts David's difficult upbringing with that of Chelsea, who lives in the same city as David but hails from a considerably wealthier family. In addition to enjoying "fancy themed birthday parties" and nightly fam-ily dinners, Chelsea was privileged enough to attend a high school that offered her the opportunity to work as the editor-in-chief for the school yearbook, receive scholarship money, and serve as the student body president (Putnam 857-858).

Putnam places a great deal of focus on the erosion of social norms, family stability, and community ties after Port Clinton's manufacturing sector collapsed over the latter half of the twentieth century. He cites increasing rates of juvenile delinquency, single-parent households, divorce, and unwed births to help explain the stagnation of working class progress there (855-856). When describing David's life in the poorer area of Port Clinton, Putnam discusses the incarceration of David's father, the separation of his parents, the presence of drugs in his home, and his "diverse brood of younger half-siblings" (859-860). However, in a narrative of Chelsea's life in the wealthier part of Port Clinton, Putnam describes her protective mother Wendy, who cooks dinner in the kitchen while her children do their homework, encourages her children to "read, read, read, read," and installs a diner in the basement of the family home where Chelsea can socialize with friends (857).

Despite Putnam's heavy emphasis on family, a discrepancy in family behavior (as is evident in Chelsea's and David's stories) is not the only—or even the primary—culprit behind the widening divide between the rich and the poor. Poverty is cyclical, and its catalysts extend far beyond just family life and social norms. A critical factor in David's unstable upbringing is the lack of guidance he received in school:

> "I really want to get a higher education," he says. "I need one. It's hard to get a job without one anymore." But he has no idea how to get there. He can recall no helpful guidance counselor or teacher from his school years, and his parents are obviously useless. (Putnam 860)

Although Chelsea's supportive family was a significant factor in her academic success, with her mother constantly advocating for her when Chelsea was denied something she thought she deserved, her school in the wealthy part of Port Clinton offered her the opportunities and tools she needed to thrive. David may have experienced a better childhood if he had a more loving and encouraging family, but a higher quality school system could have mitigated his angst and anger, encouraged him academically, and paired him with guiding adults to help him succeed. Chelsea's need for these services was never as great as David's, because his chaotic home left a gaping hole in his life that needed to be filled by some positive force like school. To have a more comprehensive understanding of inequality, it is necessary to consider how inadequate public education systems, combined with low wages and high costs of living, keep people trapped in poverty and hardship.

Roughly 300 miles away from Putnam's hometown of Port Clinton, in Chicago, Illinois, is the Ridge School District, which serves predominantly low-income families. Ridge Superintendent Kevin Russell notes, "We don't have a lot of the extra things that other districts may have, simply because we can't afford them" (qtd. in Turner et al. "Money Problem"). However, the Rondout School, located just one hour north of Ridge, spends nearly three times as much money per student and boasts small class sizes, individualized student learning plans, freshly cooked lunches, and well-paid teachers (Turner et al. "Money Problem"). The funding discrepancy between Ridge and Rondout stems partly from differences in their tax bases: the successful businesses near Rondout contribute funding for the local schools via their tax dollars, while "Ridge simply has less to work with . . . fewer businesses, lower property values" (Turner et al. "Money Problem"). Whether a school like Ridge can provide students with new textbooks or specialized teachers depends "at least in part on the property wealth around them" (Turner et al. "Money Problem"). The state of Illinois provides some aid to Ridge and other struggling schools in an effort to compensate for the disadvantages faced by its poor students, but low-income schools have historically been denied adequate financial support by federal and state governments.[*]

Clearly, public schools in low-income areas are hard-pressed to find adequate sources of funding in order to maintain quality academic programs. The social woes of drugs, crime, and broken families that Putnam describes are symptomatic of larger issues that have tangled and deeply ingrained roots in poor communities. The deficit

---

[*] The unfair appropriation of school funding is often linked to racial bias and discrimination (see, for example, Gillian B. White). The role of race in perpetuating inequality is undeniable. It would be unjust, however, to hastily squeeze in an examination of racism and poverty; this paper will thus focus on economic factors that sustain the poverty cycle and the wealth gap in the U.S.

of tax-payer money in working class areas is a complex issue that is difficult to remedy because individuals who are struggling financially are often unable to simply 'lift themselves up by their bootstraps' and aggregate more wealth by 'trying harder' at work. To live in poverty is to grapple with daily expenses that can balloon into ever-more costly expenditures. Barbara Ehrenreich, author of *Nickel and Dimed: On (Not) Getting By in America*, decided to intentionally experience living in poverty by forsaking her comfortable life and working low-wage jobs to survive. She describes the stories of other people she has met who are struggling to financially stay afloat: "Gail is sharing a room in a . . . flophouse for $250 a week. . . . [T]he rent would be impossible alone. . . . [And] Joan . . . lives in a van parked behind a shopping center at night" (508-509). Ehrenreich explains how living in poverty—on a minimum-wage salary—is ironically *expensive*, creating a cycle of financial insecurity and stress that is difficult to escape. For example, "if you can't put up the two months' rent you need to secure an apartment, you end up paying through the nose for a room by the week. If you have only a room, with a hot plate at best, you can't save by cooking up huge lentil stews that can be frozen for the week ahead" (509). These are part of "a host of special costs" that the poor must pay, which Ehrenreich describes to assert that there are "no secret economies that nourish the poor" (509). The inability to pay larger expenses up-front ultimately costs poor people more in the long run, preventing them from aggregating wealth over time and breaking the cycle of poverty.

While Putnam describes how difficult it is for David to live in a state of poverty in Port Clinton, Ehrenreich's work expounds on the intricacies of financial and time management, proving to readers that the working poor face an economic system that is essentially rigged against them. With vivid language, she notes the "gross improvidence in some of these arrangements [in which the poor are forced to live]. . . . In poverty, as in certain propositions in physics, starting conditions are everything" (509). A few hundred dollars more in the bank—an amount of money that would likely seem trivial to a wealthier individual—makes a potentially life-changing difference to a person struggling to pay for rent or groceries. David, Putnam's case study, cannot expunge his juvenile record because he is unable to afford the "couple hundred dollars" required to do so, and thus he must cope with the difficulties of finding a well-paying job despite criminal charges against him (Putnam 860).

For author Linda Tirado, living paycheck to paycheck from multiple low-wage jobs in between bouts of unemployment creates an economically impossible and emotionally exhausting cycle of pain (ix). In *Hand to Mouth: Living in Bootstrap America*, Tirado asserts that "we [too often] look at academic problems of poverty and have no idea of the why," and thus she takes the burden upon herself to explain how she and other people living in poverty "know that the very act of being poor guarantees that [they] will never not be poor" (xvi). How could an individual in such a dire personal economic situation possibly be capable of providing an adequate sum of tax dollars to support her child's local school system?

Children who are raised in households struggling with perpetual poverty likely face long-term repercussions. A poor child's success is closely tied to the academic credentials of their parents. Caroline Ratcliffe of the Urban Institute explains: "Compared with ever-poor children whose parents do not have a high school education, ever-poor children whose parents have a high school education or more than a high school education are 11 and 30 percent, respectively, more likely to complete high school" (Ratcliffe). Furthermore, the Institute reports that the longer children live in poverty (labeled "persistently poor"), the greater the negative impact they will suffer:

> Although 93 percent of never-poor children complete high school, and 83 percent of ever-poor, nonpersistently poor children complete high school, only 64 percent of persistently poor children do so. . . . This disadvantage can erode employment prospects and wages *throughout a lifetime*. (Ratcliffe; emphasis added)

A lack of educational opportunity in low-quality schools contributes to the vicious 'school-home' cycle that perpetuates and exacerbates the status quo—poor taxpayers, poor schools, and poor children who become poor taxpaying adults—thus explaining how poverty can become intergenerational.

The effects of the 'school-home cycle' are evident in the personal stories of Putnam's case studies, Chelsea and David. Chelsea's maternal grandfather was a "prominent lawyer"; her mother Wendy has a graduate degree and works in private practice as a special educator; her father Dick is "a sales manager for a major national corporation," a position that no doubt requires a particular level of education, expertise, and competence in the field (Putnam 857). In contrast, David's father is a high school dropout and "tried in vain to make a living as a truck driver, like his own father, but as an adult has been employed only episodically" (858-859). It is no coincidence that Chelsea and her brother both attend a Big Ten university, with their parents paying full tuition, while David lives on paychecks from temporary jobs just to survive (860-861). Educational opportunity and relative wealth are clearly linked across generational lines.

A sudden increase in public school funding in low-income areas may not raise test scores or eliminate the achievement gap that can exist between poor and wealthy students. Some insist that the real indicator of schools' success is not how much money they have to spend, but how the schools spend what they have, and that families have greater influence over their child's success than do schools (Turner et al. "More Money"). These alternative theories legitimize Putnam's emphasis on family unity and values in the development of a successful, well-balanced child. Nevertheless, if extra funding for schools is used properly (for example, funneled primarily to the most needy students) and is steadily increased annually, data shows that money does indeed make a difference in education (Turner et al. "More Money"). A working paper published by the National Bureau of Economic Research supports this conclusion:

> Event-study and instrumental variable models reveal that a 10 percent increase in per-pupil spending each year for all twelve years of public school leads to 0.27 more completed years of education, 7.25 percent higher wages, and a 3.67 percentage-point reduction in the annual incidence of adult poverty. . . . Exogenous spending increases were associated with sizable improvements in measured school quality. (Jackson et al. 2)

Thus, although more money is not a cure-all for failing public schools, research shows that needy schools and students would benefit significantly from more educational funding. Better quality schools will help to dismantle at least part of the cycle of poverty and give children the opportunity to improve their socioeconomic status as adults.

Putnam portrays the widening gap between the rich and the poor as an issue fueled by differences in social values and family traditions. But more disturbing and pressing is the fact that low-income people are increasingly unable to escape the cycle of poverty, even through the avenue of education. Putnam's focus on seemingly self-destructive social norms in impoverished communities is not misguided, but it warrants a more comprehensive discussion of the relationship between cyclical poverty and failing schools. Ehrenreich, Tirado, and researchers from a variety of institutions corroborate the conclusion that upward mobility is difficult to achieve today in the U.S.—and public schools in poor neighborhoods can often do little to change that. The title of Putnam's book, *Our Kids*, refers to tight-knit community ties that motivate people to view their neighbors' children as their own. However, as a result of harsh economic realities and the structure of local school districts, it is simply not enough for families within the same public school district and of the same socioeconomic status to care for one another. Instead, the 'our' in Putnam's title needs to apply more broadly to counties and states wherein the rich and poor live together and care for *one another's* children. Only then can society strengthen inter-community ties, expand educational opportunities, and improve social mobility.

WORKS CITED

AEI-Brookings Working Group on Poverty and Opportunity. "Report: A Good Education Is Important to Achieving the American Dream." *The Brookings Institution*, 3 Dec. 2015, www.brookings.edu/research/a-good-education-is-important-to-achieving-the-american-dream/.

Burtless, Gary. *Does Money Matter?: The Effect of School Resources on Student Achievement and Adult Success.* Brookings Institution Press, 1996.

Carsen, Dan. "School Funding in Alabama: A View From Sumter County." *WBHM*, 22 Apr. 2016, news.wbhm.org/feature/2016/school-funding-alabama-view-sumter-county/.

Caucutt, Elizabeth. "The Real Reason Why Poor Kids Perform Worse in School—and in Life." *The Washington Post*, 28 Apr. 2015, www.washingtonpost.com/posteverything/wp/2015/04/28/the-real-reason-why-poor-kids-perform-worse-in-school-and-in-life/?utm_term=.d21b7200cf78.

"Child Poverty." *National Center for Children in Poverty*, 2016, www.nccp.org/topics/childpoverty.html.

Ehrenreich, Barbara. "from *Nickel and Dimed: On (Not) Getting By in America.*" *The Broadview Anthology of Expository Prose*, edited by Laura Buzzard et al., 3rd ed., Broadview Press, 2016, pp. 508-510.

Jackson, C. Kirabo, et al. "The Effects of School Spending on Educational and Economic Outcomes: Evidence from School Finance Reforms." *The National Bureau of Economic Research*, 2015-2016, www.nber.org/papers/w20847.

"More Than 40% of Low-Income Schools Don't Get a Fair Share of State and Local Funds, Department of Education Research Finds." *U.S. Department of Education*, 30 Nov. 2011, www.ed.gov/news/press-releases/more-40-low-income-schools-dont-get-fair-share-state-and-local-funds-department-.

Putnam, Robert D. "from *Our Kids: The American Dream in Crisis.*" *The Broadview Anthology of Expository Prose*, edited by Laura Buzzard et al., 3rd ed., Broadview Press, 2016, pp. 852-862.

Ratcliffe, Caroline. "Child Poverty and Adult Success." *Urban Institute: Low-Income Working Families Initiative*, Sept. 2005, www.urban.org/sites/default/files/alfresco/publication-pdfs/2000369-Child-Poverty-and-Adult-Success.pdf.

Suitts, Steve. "A New Majority Research Bulletin: Low Income Students Now a Majority in the Nation's Public Schools."

Southern Education Foundation, 2015, www.southerneduca-
tion.org/Our-Strategies/Research-and-Publications/New-
Majority-Diverse-Majority-Report-Series/A-New-Majority-
2015-Update-Low-Income-Students-Now.

Tirado, Linda. *Hand to Mouth: Living in Bootstrap America.*
Penguin/Berkley, 2014.

Turner, Cory, et al. "Why America's Schools Have a Money
Problem." *National Public Radio*, 18 Apr. 2016,
www.npr.org/2016/04/18/474256366/why-americas-schools-
have-a-money-problem.

—. "Can More Money Fix America's Schools?" *National Public
Radio*, 25 Apr. 2016, www.npr.org/sections/ed/2016/04/25/
468157856/can-more-money-fix-americas-schools.

White, Gillian B. "The Data Are Damning: How Race Influences
School Funding." *The Atlantic,* 30 Sept. 2015, www.theat-
lantic.com/business/archive/2015/09/public-school-funding-
and-the-role-of-race/408085/.

Analyzing essays from James Baldwin and Claudia Rankine, Louder develops a compelling problem: Why do white Americans fail to mourn properly the violence against black bodies? She argues that as long as black Americans are perceived as strangers and outsiders in their own nation, the tragedy will persist. (Instructor: Beth Machlan)

WE GON' BE ALRIGHT

Christina Louder

August 28, 1955: fourteen-year-old Emmett Till is brutally beaten and murdered for allegedly whistling at a white woman. Beaten nearly to death, tied with barbed wire, eyes gouged out, and shot in the head, Till's naked body was thrown into the Tallahatchie River and left to be found three days later. Unidentifiable: that was the state of his body. He could only be recognized by a ring on his finger. However, despite the brutality of the situation, the two men responsible were declared not guilty ("Death"). Over sixty-one years later, on October 15, 2016, a visitor to the spot where Till's body was found posts a picture on Facebook of Till's memorial sign riddled with bullet holes (Wilson).

The disrespect and disregard for black bodies has not disappeared over time. There is something intrinsic about this disrespect; it is in the fabric of our country, in the nuances of our laws, and in the everyday actions of Americans everywhere. Black Americans can relate: we have all experienced the many forms racism takes, yet, somehow, we all know that we must persevere. Somehow, in the words of Kendrick Lamar, we all know that "we gon' be alright." Perpetual disregard sparks a question, though, that is essential to understanding how Emmett Till can be subjected to hateful bigotry even in death: what does it mean to be black in America, and how do we, as black people, deal with this identity?

In "Stranger in the Village," James Baldwin discusses how his own identity as a black American was called into question. Comparing his experience in America to his experience in a small, all-white Swiss town, Baldwin reflects on how black people are treated as "living wonder[s]" by white observers in both countries (148). Though the landscape, demographics, and interactions may differ, Baldwin's identity remains the same. He is regarded as a stranger in Switzerland and as a familiar yet unwelcome outsider in America, an outsider whose existence has created not only a "new black man" but "a new white man, too" (156). Baldwin illuminates how blackness shapes not only how you fit into the world, but also how others react to your presence in it. Blackness is not a mask that can be taken off and put on at will; it is an identity that cannot be shed for your convenience. Blackness is who you are. To Baldwin, blackness is an involuntary commitment to living your life as less than human.

Baldwin ascribes this involuntary commitment in part to white supremacy and the hold it continues to have over this country. At its core, white supremacy functions to deny human beings their humanity and to uphold false ideologies that place white men as the "creators of civilization" and the supreme judges of whose identities are acceptable and whose are not (154). Surrounded by a culture that has both controlled and created you, and the realization of what this means, instills in black people what Baldwin calls an "absolutely inevitable" rage (150). His solution, his means of coping with what his blackness means in America, is a hopeful acceptance. However, in Baldwin's terms, acceptance does not equal complacency. Instead, he posits that as a black man, he "must accept the status which myth, if nothing else, gives [him] in the West before [he] can hope to change the myth" (155). He believes in finding the pockets of progress that exist in the history of the black man in America. In acknowledging that progress, we gain clarity that although the history of black people in this country is difficult and "shameful," to say the least, "it is also something of an achievement" (156). Baldwin believes that these moments can provide us with the hope we need to continue to work for our own upliftment and achievement. We are angry, and understandably so, but Baldwin advocates for the channeling of this frustration into turning our "peculiar status in the Western world to [our] own advantage" (155). Only through becoming aware ourselves and informing others of our inescapable presence in this country will we be able to acknowledge the fact that "this world is white no longer, and it will never be white again" (156). "Stranger in the Village" was written in 1953; it is now 2016, and this country is still not okay with its multifaceted racial identity. This country is still trying to deny its differences rather than learning to live with and embrace them.

At the New York Hall of Science, I witnessed an exhibit called *Reverse Masks*, in which a mold of a face is placed beside a cast made of it, both of which are backlit against a dark background. The two plaster masks are identical, except that one is the negative of an image and one is the positive (Phelps). However, as the viewer observes the piece from different angles, it appears as if one mask is following their every movement—this is not the mold, though; it is the cast. The cast, which caves inward, appears to protrude outwards towards the viewer as if the two are identical, despite the viewer's explicit knowledge that they are not. This perception of difference, or lack thereof, implies that what we see is not always under our own control. Confronted by this phenomenon, I shied away. I had to physically move away from the exhibit because interacting with it became disturbing. Why is difference so jarring?

We, as Americans, have yet to figure out how to live with the differences staring us in the face—the racial differences upon which this country is based—but, unlike with the reversed masks, we do not have the option of ignoring those differences. Let me rephrase: perhaps white people have the option of ignoring differences, but that option, once employed, is detrimental to American progress. After all, "people who shut their eyes to reality simply invite their own destruction, and anyone who insists on remaining in a state of innocence long after that innocence is dead turns himself into a monster" (Baldwin 156). Racial differences are ingrained in American life, and all of us come face to face with them every day, whether we want to or not. Baldwin's hope relies on a certain optimism that implies that time is all that is needed for progress or for people to stop running away. *Give it some time, make them keep seeing us, and soon they will understand. They will be forced to accept us as human and to accept our contributions to this country.* Time has passed since Baldwin's essay, though—more than sixty years' worth—and black people across the country still face willful and deliberate ignorance daily. Remaining optimistic through our frustration is nice in theory, but it doesn't do much in practice. There are still Emmett Tills all across the country, but now their names are Michael Brown and Eric Garner, Tamir Rice and Rekia Boyd.

In "The Condition of Black Life Is One of Mourning," Claudia Rankine states: "Anti-black racism is in the culture" (781). For Rankine, racism is undeniable and inescapable when every day we see slain black bodies on the streets and on the news. "We live in a country where Americans assimilate corpses in their daily comings and goings," she says. "Dead blacks are a part of normal life here" (779). We, as Americans, are desensitized now to the sight of disfigured and disrespected black bodies. According to Rankine, being black in America means living with an omnipresent sense of grief, a grief that comes with the knowledge that "on any given day it can be open season on any black person"—the knowledge that next time it could be any one of our daughters, sons, husbands, wives, mothers, or fathers (784). Rankine posits not only that "the condition of black life is one of mourning," but also that this condition is commonplace. Almost always, it is accompanied by an awareness that your worth in this country is decided by a justice system that views you no differently than the rest of the country does—as an 'other,' and with contempt (779, 781). We mourn when we lose something that meant a lot to us, when we realize that we will now be left without someone or something important. Black people live in a state of mourning because black lives matter to us. But do they matter to the rest of the American people? Rankine believes that the path to progress must be paved first with a national recognition of black issues (782). She states that "history's authority over us is not broken by maintaining a silence about its continued effects" (784). It is of the utmost importance to recognize the effects history continues to have on America's present climate, specifically with regard to race. For example, the never-ending attacks on black bodies cannot be contextualized without an understanding of how America has viewed black people since it built an entire nation on our backs. Ignoring that does us more harm than good—it allows us to continue to live under the control of the past and inhibits us from moving towards a livable future.

To Rankine, there should be no qualms about making a few people uncomfortable for the sake of a good cause. What cause could be better? Black people have been fighting to be seen as innately valuable—to *matter*—for far too long. Perhaps, then, we do need to mourn together. Perhaps Mamie Till Mobley, mother of Emmett Till, had the right idea in "insisting we look with her upon the dead," thus reframing "mourning as a method of acknowledgment" (Rankine 780). In allowing an open casket at her son's funeral, Mobley forced Americans to see her son and to see what their systems had wrought. She forced them to take a position and claim some kind of ownership over their role in atrocities like Till's murder. By forcing the world to see what she saw—"by placing both herself and her son's corpse in positions of refusal relative to the etiquette of grief"—Mobley hoped to make them feel even a sliver of what she felt (Rankine 780). It is clear that this did not galvanize or even change the minds of all Americans. However, Mobley still made an important point: upon seeing the image of Till's mangled body, "a person had to decide whether his dead black body mattered enough to be mourned" (Rankine 781). This is the call to recognition for which Rankine advocates. We must establish national responsibility for what happens to black lives and for what actions we take when they are prematurely ended.

White people, though, are *already* forced to see us. This perpetual presence means that they cannot ever have a world without us. White people in America are not allowed that blissful ignorance once afforded to white people in small Swiss villages. They see us everywhere they go and are therefore forced to see our differences and react to them. Baldwin believed that having to live with and see black people would cause white people, and in turn all Americans, to open their eyes. He believed that this would allow for steps forward in black people's fight for racial upliftment. Baldwin spoke with an optimism that Rankine, sixty-two years later, no longer has, despite the world being "white no longer" (Baldwin 156). Seeing us has not been enough. White people see our slaughtered bodies on the television and their newsfeeds every day; videos of cops shooting black men, women, and children proliferate; and yet, black people are still being murdered at the hands of police officers who walk free.

Rankine claims that the present climate only deepens the divide between black and white people, making it harder to meet that "perpetual challenge" (Baldwin 156). Yes, whiteness in America cannot exist independent of blackness, but does that necessarily mean any-thing more than that? Does it mean there will be more empathy from white people for the black experience? Yes, "the white liberal imagination" can try to "feel temporarily bad about black suffering," but this short-lived and easily escapable empathy is not equal to the experiences of black people (Rankine 779). Sympathy and empathy are two different things; you can feel bad for someone without ever feeling *for* them. Sympathy is what has allowed the American people to look briefly at the decimation of black bodies with sadness, maybe even regret. Their discomfort is what keeps them from moving on to empathy.

The ability to detach yourself from what is happening and not see yourself in a victim is powerful; because you view someone as an 'other,' you suddenly do not have to, and will not, mourn. You do not have to and will not make yourself change for the sake of making progress. Perhaps this is the core issue: this detachment white Americans allow themselves. Our bodies are not the same, so we do not grieve the same way. Being black in America is not an experience that can be defined by one person or one mindset. It is a state of being that I know I can never fully explain accurately because it is so complex. There is no perfect answer; no one, not even Rankine or Baldwin, can tell you how to cope with your black life. Discovering what blackness means today is of the utmost importance, but believing that any one of us has the complete right answer will prove more detrimental than beneficial. What I can tell you is that some serious soul-searching needs to occur in America if we are to move forward. The state of race relations here is far too dangerous for things to continue the way they are. Emmett Till was murdered over sixty years ago, yet I can directly relate to the anguish, disgust, fear, and grief that comes with seeing a body, just like mine, destroyed and ignored. Till's death occurred before Trayvon Martin, Tamir Rice, and Michael Brown were even born. Yet the vandalism of his memorial occurred after all their deaths; this is sadly indicative of little, if any, progress in American race relations. Black people are still not seen as Americans, or even as people. Perhaps if our grief was taken up by all, we would all feel the sense of urgency for substantial change. Perhaps if

American life, and not just black life, was riddled with endless mourning, something would have changed by now.

WORKS CITED

Baldwin, James. "Stranger in the Village." *The Broadview Anthology of Expository Prose*, edited by Laura Buzzard et al., 3rd ed., Broadview Press, 2016, pp. 146-156.

"The Death of Emmett Till." *History.com*, 2010, www.history.com/this-day-in-history/the-death-of-emmett-till.

Lamar, Kendrick. "Alright." *To Pimp a Butterfly*, Top Dawg Entertainment, Aftermath Entertainment, and Interscope Records, 2015.

Phelps, David L. *Reverse Masks*. 1980, Sculpture, New York Hall of Science, New York.

Rankine, Claudia. "The Condition of Black Life Is One of Mourning." *The Broadview Anthology of Expository Prose*, edited by Laura Buzzard et al., 3rd ed., Broadview Press, 2016, pp. 778-784.

Wilson, Kevin, Jr. "I'm at the exact site where Emmett Till's body was found floating in the Tallahatchie River 61 years ago. The site marker is filled with bullet holes. Clear evidence that we've still got a long way to go." *Facebook*, 15 Oct. 2016, www.facebook.com/Imagine2LifeFilmworks/posts/10154009542402717.

Patton examines Leslie Jamison's book The Empathy Exams *and notes the difficulty of defining "empathy" conclusively. Centering this essay on the investigation of that key term, she compiles evidence from critics and scientists in outlining Jamison's efforts to use writing as a means of connecting her own pain with that of others. (Instructor: Gerard O'Donoghue)*

BLOOD, INK, AND PAIN: AN EXCAVATION

Emma Patton

Leslie Jamison's ex-boyfriend called her a "wound dweller" ("Grand" 186). The young essayist was offended. She wrote to a friend, "I've got this double-edged indignation about my bodily ills and ailments . . . On the one hand, I'm like, Why does this shit happen to me? And on the other hand, I'm like, Why the fuck am I talking about this so much?" (187). Jamison goes on to explore her physical and emotional ills, as well as the pain of others, through eleven essays compiled in her 2014 book *The Empathy Exams*. She dwells on wounds and, in the process, thoroughly reckons with the concepts of pain and empathy, seeking out pain to compile varying levels of visibility and intimacy. Her essays range from the personal confession of a journal entry to the cold analysis of a medical file. Jamison's attempt to tackle pain and empathy becomes an exploration of her own relationship with anguish.

Why did Jamison devote 218 pages of text to exploring empathy? Empathy eludes definition. According to Karen E. Gerdes, a professor of social work, "between 1957 and 1967 there were twenty-one different definitions of empathy offered in the social work literature" (2328). Researchers struggled to even categorize empathy, labeling it an "ambient interpersonal process," a "specific skill," or a purely physiological response, among other titles (2328). This lack of complete definition or categorization stems from its abstract nature. According to the *Oxford English Dictionary*, empathy is "the ability to understand and appreciate another person's feelings" ("empathy, *n.*"). However, it is immensely difficult to measure a person's feelings.

Though this definition sounds succinct, it fails to give full shape to the concept of empathy. In 2007, neuroscientists Jean Decety and Yoshiya Moriguchi made significant progress in defining empathy, or at least its broad characteristics. They identified four major components of empathy: "affective sharing," "self-awareness," "mental flexibility and perspective taking," and "emotion regulation" (Gerdes 2331-32). Their study found that all four components must be present for a person to have a "complete experience of empathy" (2331-32). Based on these criteria, Jamison is a deeply empathetic person. However, while all four components act in Jamison's work, her propensity for each varies greatly.

Jamison effectively shares in other people's emotions, often mirroring their perceived feelings: crying when they cry, flinching when they flinch. This sharing is largely due to her adeptness in the field of "mental flexibility and perspective taking" (Gerdes 2332). She frequently imagines what it would be like to be in another person's position. While visiting a friend in prison in her essay "Fog Count," she ponders the families of the other prisoners, thinking of their weekly visitation routines. She writes, "There's a certain heartbreak to knowing the minutia so well: the inmate number, the plastic bag of quarters, the jeans and the hard chairs and the faces of the guards" ("Fog" 144). However, this ability to dive into other people's worlds often makes it difficult for Jamison to draw boundaries between herself and the person or persons she observes; she "erases the perceived boundary between self and other," struggling with the "self-awareness" detailed by Decety and Moriguchi (Gerdes 2332). This tension often leads to a lack of "emotion regulation" (2332)—Jamison tends to become overwhelmed by the emotions that arise in reaction to others' feelings.

However, Jamison detaches herself in order to combat her tendency to mirror the emotions and pain of others and submerge herself in their minutiae. It is difficult to call this disassociation "emotion regulation," because Jamison oscillates between extremes. When she allows herself to feel pain, it is an intense, vivid experience. When she analyzes that pain, her analysis is cold and unyielding. Jamison frequently applies both approaches to the same experience. Mark O'Connell, a critic for *The Slate Book Review*, observes this uncanny ability: "she flinches, and then she explores that flinch with a steady gaze." Jamison herself once wrote that she "looked back at [her] own life like text" (qtd. in McAlpin). This type of analysis is evident when Jamison applies the methodology of the Russian formalist Vladimir Propp to examine the time she was attacked in Nicaragua. In the essay "The Morphology of the Hit," she classifies each part of her experience getting mugged according to Propp's *Morphology of the Folktale*: "a map for storytelling" consisting of thirty-one functions, or plot points, that can be rearranged and applied to any story ("Morphology" 70). Though she breaks down each part of the experience according to one of Propp's functions, the content under each function contains the raw language of a woman reliving a painful experience—it's full of blood, pain, and vulnerability.

One of the most vulnerable points in this essay occurs when Jamison reflects on the visibility of her wounds to the local townspeople. She writes: "Everything was visible to them—swollen face, bloody arms, bloody legs, bloody clothes. These were the only things I was composed of, and everyone saw them—everyone understood them—as well as I could" ("Morphology" 73-74). The visibility of pain is an ongoing concern for Jamison. In this particular instance, her pain has a distinct physical manifestation—after being punched, her face is swollen and she is covered in blood. The Nicaraguan townspeople can tell that a trauma has just taken place. However, pain does not always elicit such gruesome wounds. In "The Empathy Exams," Jamison reflects on the emotional toil of an abortion she underwent some years before writing the essay. Much of the pain of the abortion was invisible to the outside eye. Jamison's "sadness about the abortion was never a convulsion" ("Empathy" 12). Had the same Nicaraguan citizens seen her leaving the abortion clinic, they wouldn't have paused their daily activities and registered the trauma. She admits, "Part of me has always craved a pain so visible—so irrefutable and physically inescapable—that everyone would have to notice" (12). To Jamison, tangible pain legitimizes her internal strife. When she began experiencing severe cramps three days after her abortion, she was relieved because "at least [she] knew what [she] felt" (12). Because of the pain, she could explain her distress easily to an outsider and, perhaps most importantly, to herself.

Jamison's concern over visible and tangible pain makes it difficult for her to reckon with both emotional and physical pain, as emotional pain rarely has a physical manifestation. The official definition of pain, according to the International Association for the Study of Pain, is "an unpleasant sensory and emotional experience associated with actual or potential tissue damage, or described in terms of such damage" (Wrigley and Siddall 31). However, the term "pain" is often applied to purely emotional struggles, removed from the fear of damaged tissue. For instance, the pain of loneliness is real, or at least commonly accepted as real, yet it does not necessarily have a physical component; Jamison's anguish in the aftermath of her abortion was certainly real before she experienced cramps. This may be due to the fact that emotional pain activates the same region of the brain, the dorsal anterior cingulate cortex, as physical pain (Eisenberger 190). Despite similarities in neural activity, physical pain, which is chiefly exterior, is still visible, or at least easily understandable, to the outside viewer, while emotional pain is not.

Jamison craves visible pain because she wants identifiable verification of suffering. She is not alone. In "Grand Unified Theory of Female Pain," Jamison briefly examines the concept of 'cutters,' people who purposefully cut their own skin as an expression of inner pain. Jamison herself confesses to cutting because she wanted to give physical shape to her own unhappiness. She understands that "bleeding is . . . excavation, interior turned out—and the scar remains as residue, pain turned proof" ("Grand" 192). People who cut don't wish for blood; they, like Jamison, wish for evidence.

In her essay "Devil's Bait," the group of people Jamison encounters at a Morgellons convention in Austin, Texas, is different: they are hunting for visibility. These individuals firmly believe in the physicality of their pain, believing fibers grow out of their skin, causing irritation and discomfort. Their self-diagnosis of Morgellons disease is not, however, recognized in the scientific community; their fibers are barely visible to those who aren't "Morgies" ("Devil's" 28). Jamison interviews several Morgies at the convention. Her interviews are deeply personal—she hears from Dawn, a nurse who fears that Morgellons will affect her future relationships, and Paul, a Texan who has been battling with Morgellons for eight years. He called his disease "the devil's fishing bait" before he had heard of Morgellons (43). The name sprung partially from the fateful fishing trip, during which he believes he contracted the disease, and partially from being "lured into response" (43). Paul's battle with the disease is apparent: his skin is pockmarked and his ear mangled. Jamison observes these are likely self-inflicted wounds, made in attempts to purge the disease. His motivation was different than that of 'traditional' cutters, but the excavated results are the same.

Paul's scars echo the lines Jamison carved into her own skin in the sense that both are visible manifestations of an otherwise indiscernible pain. *The Empathy Exams* achieves a similar effect: pain is made visible to readers via ink on a page. Jamison expresses internal and external pain through the countless experiences she shares in the eleven essays that make up the collection. These accounts, personal and otherwise, effectively make the book a compilation of anguish. This compilation is reminiscent of the poetry constructed by a friend Jamison met at a writers' retreat in Mexico, an experience she details in the essay "La Frontera." Her colleague, Marco, compiles fragments of others' writing, often found on the Internet, to form his poems. In a recent project, he scoured blogs, message boards, and Twitter feeds for posts from the residents of Comales, Mexico, about their daily struggles, especially those caused by the rampant drug trafficking and gang activity in the area. He then spliced the disparate phrases together into a poem. However, Jamison clarifies, "The language isn't 'poetic' because it didn't start as poetry. It started as a cry" ("La Frontera" 65). The tormented posts of the townspeople, when taken together, became a powerful work of art seen by the public. Likewise, Jamison's composition of pain is one wave of pain after another, layered on top of each other to create a desperate chorus, demanding visibility and response. Like Marco, she has composed a collage of pain—cries turned prose.

To collect this compilation, Jamison avidly sought out pain. *The New York Times* critic Olivia Laing commented on the "ethical tightrope between voyeurism and narcissism, between an unnatural interest in the woes of others and an unattractive obsession with the wounds of the self" that Jamison had to walk while exploring empathy and pain. In an interview for *The Paris Review*, Jamison remarks on her relationship with the different types of pain presented in the essays "The Morphology of the Hit" and "Devil's Bait," saying, "Going to the Morgellons conference is a choice in a way that getting hit in the street isn't. But the collection chooses to bring all of those experiences together in a certain way" (qtd. in Emre). The complex exploration of empathy Jamison has embarked on in *The Empathy Exams* requires both personal and solicited pain. She worries about this solicitation when she interviews her imprisoned friend in "Fog Count," confessing, "I'm afraid . . . that my curiosity will prove little more than useless voyeurism, a girl lifting her sunglasses to peer between the bars, stuttering *What's it like here? What part hurts the most?*" ("Count" 141).

The mentality that Jamison fears is aptly called "poverty tourism" in Heller McAlpin's NPR review of *The Empathy Exams* (McAlpin). The concept of 'poverty tourism,' alternatively called 'reality tourism,' first became prevalent in the mid-1990s in India, South Africa, and Brazil (Rolfes 421-422). International tourists would pay for guided tours of local, poverty stricken areas as part of a "*negative sightseeing*" excursion (422). The tour guides, often residents of the areas, promised the tourists an "*authentic or realistic*" excursion (Rolfes 422). Leslie Jamison embarks on an LA 'gang tour' in "Pain Tours (I): Indigenous to the Hood." The tour closely mirrors the popular poverty tours of the mid-1990s in form: Jamison and a large church group from Missouri roll through the streets of an LA neighborhood in an air-conditioned bus. They peer out the windows as two former gang members regale them with tales of their past, filling in the surrounding terrain with former girlfriends in the projects, gunfights at their junior high school, and felony statistics of the area. While this account directly parallels a 'poverty tour,' Jamison's other accounts do too—indirectly (421). Time and time again Jamison seeks out windows into others' pain. Her experience at the Morgellons   conference in Texas is an example of her hunt for pain. She extracted personal stories of loss and struggle from attendees like Dawn and Paul. She listened to speakers, perused photos of the supposed symptoms of the disease, and asked probing questions of attendees about the emotional impact of Morgellons. After the conference, she went home, free of the disease. Commenting on this experience, she writes, "I spend a day in their kingdom and then leave when I please. It feels like a betrayal to come up for air" ("Devil's" 46). Though she is aware, even ashamed, of her foray into 'pain tourism,' the awareness does not change her actions. It serves only to complicate Jamison's internal struggle regarding her relationship with pain.

Jamison's entire essay collection is a 'reality tour.' Though she details her experiences as a 'tourist' and as a sufferer, her narrative voice throughout acts as a guide. She leads the reader through trauma after trauma, drawing their attention to certain details and eliciting empathy. She, just like the poverty tour guides of LA, uses her past experiences to show her connection to the suffering that she displays. She writes that her gang affiliated tour guides were "curators and exhibits at once" (84). The same could be said of Jamison.

Leslie Jamison's ex-boyfriend called her a "wound-dweller" ("Grand" 187). He was mistaken. She is a wound-hunter. She does not passively "dwell" on past wounds; she seeks them out and interrogates them. She holds them up to the light and examines them side-by-side with other wounds.

The epigraph at the beginning of *The Empathy Exams* reads: "*Homo sum: humani nil a me alienum puto*; I am human: nothing human is alien to me." The quote first appeared in the Roman playwright Terence's play *The Tormentor*. The epigraph seems to be Jamison's declaration to the reader that no pain is foreign to her. Her very humanity grants her the right, and the ability, to relate to other people's emotions. Around the time *The Empathy Exams* was published, Jamison got this phrase, in its original Latin, tattooed on her forearm. Bold cursive letters stretch from the soft skin of her inner elbow to her wrist. Again, it appears to proclaim her natural capacity for empathy. However, Jamison confessed in an opinion piece for *The New York Times*, "my tattoo wasn't true for me, not yet. But it was what I most needed to hear, an asymptote, a horizon" ("Mark"). The tattoo serves as a reminder: a personal note that pain, a human condition, is not foreign to her. Yet this prompt, given its size and placement on her inner forearm, is visible to everyone around her. It is no wonder that the same woman who would publish *The Empathy Exams*, a raw collection of essays that is equal parts public discourse and personal discovery, would have an ink-laden needle repeatedly puncture her skin to convey such an intimate, yet public, message.

WORKS CITED

Eisenberger, Naomi. "Understanding the Moderators of Physical and Emotional Pain: A Neural Systems-Based Approach." *Psychological Inquiry*, vol. 19, no. 3/4, 2008, pp. 189–195.

"empathy, *n.*" *Oxford English Dictionary Online*, Sept. 2016, www.oed.com/view/Entry/61284?redirectedFrom=empathy.

Emre, Merve. "Nothing Is Alien: An Interview with Leslie Jamison." *The Paris Review*, 7 Apr. 2014, www.theparisreview.org/blog/2014/04/07/nothing-is-alien-an-interview-with-leslie-jamison/.

Gerdes, Karen E, et al. "Conceptualising and Measuring Empathy." *The British Journal of Social Work*, vol. 40, no. 7, 2010, pp. 2326–2343.

Jamison, Leslie. *The Empathy Exams: Essays*. Graywolf Press, 2014.
"Devil's Bait." pp. 27-56.
"Empathy Exams." pp. 1-26.
"Fog Count." pp. 133-150.
"Grand Unified Theory of Female Pain." pp. 185-218.
"La Frontera." pp. 57-68.
"Morphology of the Hit." pp. 69-78.
"Pain Tours (I)." pp. 79-90.

—. "Mark My Words. Maybe." *The New York Times*, 12 Apr. 2014, www.nytimes.com/2014/04/13/opinion/sunday/mark-my-words-maybe.html.

Laing, Olivia. "Never Hurts to Ask." *The New York Times*, 5 Apr. 2014, www.nytimes.com/2014/04/06/books/review/the-empathy-exams-by-leslie-jamison.html.

McAlpin, Heller. "'Empathy Exams' Is A Virtuosic Manifesto Of Human Pain." *NPR*, 3 Apr. 2014, www.npr.org/2014/04/03/297823566/empathy-exams-is-a-virtuosic-manifesto-of-human-pain.

Rolfes, Manfred. "Poverty Tourism: Theoretical Reflections and Empirical Findings Regarding an Extraordinary Form of Tourism." *GeoJournal*, vol. 75, no. 5, 2010, pp. 421–442.

Wrigley, Paul J., and Philip J. Siddall. "The Clinical Evaluation of Pain." *Pain Medicine: A Multidisciplinary Approach*, 2010, pp. 31–48.

Teo's analysis of Rebecca Solnit's book, The Encyclopedia of Trouble and Spaciousness, *identifies an important problem: How to write about other cultures without usurping their voices? Weaving together a range of sources, her essay responds by helping us understand the delicate relationship between representation and power. (Instructor: Gerard O'Donoghue)*

A WRITER'S OCCUPATION

Phionna Teo

Occupy, verb. The word *occupy* in the English language originates from the French word *occuper*. To occupy, in both its original and contemporary meaning, is "to take possession of, take for one's own use, seize," connoting an intrusion of space, an invasion of boundaries: in a nutshell, to take a thing or fill a place that does not belong to you ("occupy, *v.*"). But how can we clearly delineate what belongs to whom? If we consider *occuper* to belong to the French language, then the word *occupy*, ironically, becomes an example of English's occupation.

The rise of the Occupy movement, an international effort toward social and political equality, seeks to redefine its eponymous action ("About"). To occupy, as a form of protest, does not just mean to take possession of a building or a piece of land without authority; it means to take back, to repossess, to fight for a space stolen from the people by political or economic elites in the hopes of democratizing that space. Occupation originally meant conquering a territory that did not belong to the occupier. Now, as journalist Randall Amster writes, occupation aims to liberate space, to "[pry] open the inner sanctum of the dominant order" (Amster). The original Occupy Wall Street movement serves as a prime example. Founded in September 2011, Occupy Wall Street saw protesters occupy Manhattan's Financial District to fight back against "the richest 1% of people that are writing the rules of an unfair global economy" (Occupy Solidarity Network). By occupying a space that symbolized corporate financial control, protesters aimed to reclaim their rights in that space by demanding a more balanced distribution of income and a reduction in corporate influence on politics. In "The Significance of Space in Occupy Wall Street," John L. Hammond borrows and builds upon Henri Lefebvre's idea that "space is actively produced, not only in its physical disposition but its social meaning, by the activities that go on in it, or that go on in some spaces but not others" (500). Hammond draws a connection between territories and control, stating that it is "not just a matter of lines on a map; it is a cartography of power" (501). In fact, the whole world map is a cartography of power. The designation of entire countries as First World or Third World, the social and cultural influences that some countries can export to others, and the hierarchy of racial and national identities all point to the various ways in which space connotes power.

Rebecca Solnit, a contemporary writer, historian, and activist, describes her anthology of essays *The Encyclopedia of Trouble and Spaciousness* as "a book about places" ("Introduction" 1). As she explores landscapes from the Arctic to Mexico, from Japan to Detroit to Wall Street, Solnit constructs a cartography of international injustices, uprisings, disasters, and, above all, hope in humanity. Quite literally, Solnit creates a "Geographical Index," locating where each of her essays takes place on a map of the world (ii). Solnit imagines the world as a space without boundaries as she advocates a shared humanity. Yet, as she travels across boundaries, Solnit seems to reproduce, rather than subvert, the power connoted by her occupation of space.

Through her exploration of different social issues present in various societies, Solnit calls her readers—particularly her American ones—to action by urging them to reflect on their statuses as global citizens, to believe in hope and change for the better, and to be a part of that change. In "Letter to a Dead Man: On the Occupation of Hope," Solnit writes, "At this moment in history, occupation should be everyone's occupation" (220). In "We Won't Bow Down: Carnival and Resistance in New Orleans," she urges, "Don't bow down. To capital. Or to cliché or oversimplification or defeatism. Try rising up instead" (247). Sven Birkerts concurs in his review of the book, writing, "Solnit's *Encyclopedia of Trouble and Spaciousness* . . . sounds the wake-up call." Birkerts sums up what he sees as the main message of the anthology: "For us to Occupy anything we have to first Occupy Ourselves." Randall Amster, in "Occupy Ourselves," describes occu-

pying ourselves as a process in which we recognize our complicity
with the forces of our own oppression and refuse to comply with
them. However, to 'Occupy Ourselves' is not just a call for reflection
on the ways in which one is complicit in social injustices perpetuated
around the world, but also a call to find one another in a common
cause. Solnit's ideal world is one without boundaries, as the form of
humanity and hope that she celebrates in her various essays is one that
transcends the boundaries of space. It is an attempt to look past car-
tographies and borders, to focus on similarities rather than the lines
that divide us, so as to create change around the world.

To this end, Solnit breaks down the boundaries not just of
physical space, but also of time, to show that all boundaries are social
constructions. Solnit couches her experiences of a place or a phenomenon within terms of its history, exploring historical relationships and
thus giving readers a sense of living in the moment of historical rupture. In "The Google Bus: Silicon Valley Invades" and "Pale Bus, Pale
Rider: Silicon Valley Invades, Cont'd," Solnit delves deep into the
history of San Francisco as a city that has always been different from
the rest of America. It was once "a great city of refuge for dissidents,
queers and experimentalists," and the invasion of Silicon Valley has
not only displaced the poor through forced evictions—it has also
resulted in a "casual erasure" of San Francisco's historical character
("Google" 252, 255). Solnit frames the Silicon Valley tech workers as
invading occupiers, but they occupy both literal and cultural space; as
the influx of wealthy tech workers increases the cost of housing in
Silicon Valley, residents are gentrified out of their homes, with
far-reaching cultural consequences.

Solnit further relies on the etymology of key words to show that
history very much informs the present, and that to create a distinction
between the two would be to create a false dichotomy. In "In Haiti,
Words Can Kill," Solnit expounds on the origins of the word *looting*,
and how the use of this word "incites madness and obscures realities"
because of the history of its usage (128). Solnit writes, "*Loot*, the
noun and the verb, is a word of Hindi origin meaning the spoils of war
or other goods seized roughly" ("Haiti" 128). She argues that to use
the word *loot* rather than "emergency requisitioning" to describe the
actions of people who attempt to acquire necessities after a disaster is

to frame them as thieves rather than survivors or humans ("Haiti" 128). In "Letter to a Dead Man," Solnit further explores the relationship between the past, the present, and the future. Varying her verb tenses, Solnit lists disasters the world has experienced, has been experiencing, or has yet to experience, positioning the reader not exactly in the present, but in a historical moment that incorporates past, present, and future. This can be seen from her description of disasters across the globe: "Japan *was* literally shaken loose . . . by . . . the earthquake and tsunami . . . China *is* turbulent . . . Syrians *wouldn't* go home . . . Italians *have been* protesting" ("Dead Man" 214; emphasis added). A line from her essay "Arrival Gates: The Inari Shrine in Kyoto, Japan" sums up her idea that every moment is an infinitesimal transition point between past and future: "We are arriving all the time, the present is a house in which we always have one foot, an apple we are just biting, a face we are just glimpsing for the first time" (200). Solnit breaks down the boundaries between what we often call past, present, and future, forcing readers to recognize a string of continuity across time, thus advancing her vision of the world as a space without boundaries.

Because boundaries are illusory, the concept of citizenship, or a sense of belonging to a single place, becomes irrelevant to Solnit. Hence, even as Solnit discusses societies extremely foreign to her, she tries to establish authority as a sort of insider by demonstrating that she has a personal stake in them. Solnit often draws similarities between herself and victims of social injustices, attempting to give readers the impression that she can encapsulate the complexity of those victims' emotions. This tendency is evident in "The Google Bus," where she includes her personal experience of being a prospective homeowner in San Francisco, which she seems to believe enabled her to empathize with the displaced homeless in San Francisco, though this is a suspicious equivalence. In "Arrival Gates," Solnit begins with a paragraph-long sentence detailing her experience on a trip to Japan, ranging from a "speaking tour at the universities" to walking and seeing "with [her] own eyes the bombed places" and the "keloid scars from the fallout that had drifted onto the arm of a schoolboy sixty-seven years before" (196). Here, Solnit positions herself as an insider in an extremely foreign society and culture, implying that her wide-ranging experience and access to Japanese society grants her the authority to represent it. Presuming that she sees what they see, knows what they know, and feels what they feel, she presents herself as an insider in that society, breaking down boundaries created by arbitrary border lines. Even in societies or cultures where she is unable to find a personal connection, she includes experiences of her friend, her brother, or even "a young man [she] knew long ago" ("Apologies" 228), almost as a desperate attempt to find a connection to the society in order to establish a trans-border relationship with the places and people that she writes about.

This desire for 'connection' is picked up by Sven Birkerts. In his review, Birkerts argues that Solnit's work does not merely contain "news from crisis zones," but includes "a feel for the expressive image that adds a welcome affective depth" to her reports through creating a personal stake in the matter, no matter how cursory. Other journalists, such as Marcus O'Donnell, concur by arguing that this is Solnit's way of being "both personally present and attentive to her sources" (940). O'Donnell asserts that what differentiates Solnit from other journalists is her distinctively "polyphonic open journalism" (936). To O'Donnell, Solnit is able to combine journalistic practices with writerly and activist practices to produce a "distinctive open form of literary journalism," and her inclusion of many personal narratives showcases her capacity to personally engage with the subjects of her work (936). Solnit's work is "open" because it "allows for both the intentionality of argument and the meandering of associative thinking" (O'Donnell 942). Thus, O'Donnell frames Solnit as a democratizer of spaces and opinions. Yet the way Solnit struggles to pass as an insider in foreign cultures perhaps indicates that, in her attempt to take possession of a position in a society that does not belong to her, she herself is an oppressive occupier.

What emboldens Solnit to this occupation? Solnit writes that during the Bush era, "every American seemed saddled with the weight of the world" ("Introduction" 1-2). She was compelled to "become a public citizen and to think about broad issues . . . across the globe" (1-2). Although it seemed clear to Solnit that it was her 'American' burden to assume the identity of a 'global citizen,' her vision of the world centers on America. Even her "Geographical Index" places North

America squarely in the middle of the map. In alignment with the cartography of power that Hammond points out, Solnit, a Westerner and an American, is granted authoritative power to occupy spaces in societies that are not her own, much like America has occupied parts of Afghanistan and Iraq. According to geographer Zoltán Grossman, America conducted at least 148 foreign interventions from 1890 to 2014, from providing covert support to commanding entire military operations. During these interventions, the U.S. has often positioned itself as a necessary peacekeeper, yet, time and again, history has shown that interventions in foreign countries only serve to "polarize factions and further destabilize the country," not to mention the number of natives killed as collateral damage (Grossman). In both the past and the present, Western powers have often justified the expansion of empire with a vision of the world as a space without boundaries and the idea that their benevolent rule would create greater meaning and better usage of the occupied spaces. The self-righteous belief that their leadership model is necessarily the best for the world has driven both colonialism in the past and neocolonialism today. Envisioning the world as a space without boundaries is dangerous because it can be exploited to justify colonization, invasion, and the occupation of cultural spaces. If no one can claim belonging to a single place, everyone can claim any space, effectively destroying the concept of an indigenous people. The twenty-first-century trend of globalization and the call to become a 'global citizen' presents continuity between state-driven military occupation and the occupation of intangible cultural spaces that Solnit lapses into in her travels around the world.

Occupationally, Solnit is a writer, activist, and occupier. As she advances her vision of a shared humanity across a space without boundaries, she inhabits identities that do not belong to her and claims belonging to societies that she is not a part of. If Solnit sees herself as a part of Western and American society, why does she feel the need to escape from it? In an interview with Samantha Kimmey, Solnit shares that she grew up in Novato, a conservative and relatively rural part of California, where "because so many people come from elsewhere [in the country], being a local is kind of a minority culture." In a place where she considers herself a local, Solnit's family only settled down when she was five, as her family moved around a lot before that. She went to high school in Paris at the age of seventeen, knowing that the world was bigger, more interesting, and more complex than a Californian suburb. Solnit's early life was devoid of a strong sense of belonging or connection to places or communities around her. This is perhaps symptomatic of the broader American identity that Philip Fisher describes in "Democratic Social Space: Whitman, Melville, and the Promise of American Transparency" as one "without a single environment or climate, without a culture, and without, in the deep romantic sense, a language"; in sum, for Fisher, Americans are "a patchwork of peoples," and the American identity is one marked by mobility and non-belonging (61, 60). Because 'American' is such a broad identity that does not confine Solnit to a single, particular space, she chooses to occupy as a means to define her own identity.

Solnit ultimately seeks to discover what Katra Byram terms the "historicity of personal identity," to find her identity amidst boundaries of space (2). Byram proposes a new narrative strategy—the dynamic observer form—to describe a narrative situation that emerges when stories about others become an avenue to negotiate a narrator's own identity. She argues that the conception of identity is two-faceted. First, identity relies on narrative, a narrative that "emerges from individuals' history and experiences, and from their attempts to understand and explain who they are in the present by telling a story about the past" (Byram 1-2). Second, identity is relational; the story that one tells is an extremely effective way to "define who one is and has been—and who one is not" (2). Solnit is not homeless in San Francisco, she is not a Japanese person who lived through the nuclear fallout, and she has not experienced a natural disaster, yet these identities produce greater meaning for her by virtue of their differences. It is precisely because of her privilege of not belonging that she feels such a compulsion to empathize and to make a difference.

A dilemma emerges for writers as we come to realize the dangers of occupation. How can writers represent foreign subjects and cultures without occupying? Or should writers and activists be confined to representing their own communities? The very fact that a writer has the resources and permission to study another culture often implies an asymmetrical power relation, with narrative and editorial control completely in the hands of the writer. Yet in assessing such a study, it is imperative to distinguish one's sense of responsibility towards international crises and one's attempt to disguise oneself as a native. An anthropological analysis suggests the true purpose of writing about 'others' is not to attain complete understanding of them or to represent them without error; that is impossible. Instead, to write about the 'other' is to spark conversation, undermining biases that perpetuate the opposition of 'us' and 'them.' Perhaps, then, Solnit's representation of foreign societies pardons her, in part, for occupying them. At the very least, Solnit's *Encyclopedia* may attune its readers to, or liberate them from, dangerous patterns of narrativizing foreign spaces.

WORKS CITED

Amster, Randall. "Occupy Ourselves." *The Huffington Post*, 13 Dec. 2011, www.huffingtonpost.com/randall-amster/occupy-ourselves_b_1135323.html.

Birkerts, Sven. "Where Danger Is." *Los Angeles Review of Books*, 28 Oct. 2014, www.lareviewofbooks.org/article/danger/.

Byram, Katra A. *Ethics and the Dynamic Observer Narrator: Reckoning with Past and Present in German Literature*. The Ohio State UP, 2015. *Project MUSE*, muse.jhu.edu/book/38651.

Fisher, Philip. "Democratic Social Space: Whitman, Melville, and the Promise of American Transparency." *Representations*, no. 24, Autumn 1988, pp. 60-101.

Grossman, Zoltán. "From Wounded Knee To Syria: A Century Of U.S. Military Interventions." Faculty Home Page, academic.evergreen.edu/g/grossmaz/interventions.html#anchor1 469361.

Hammond, John L. "The Significance of Space in Occupy Wall Street." *Interface*, vol. 5, no. 2, Nov. 2013, pp. 499-524.

Occupy Solidarity Network. "About." *Occupy Wall Street*, www.occupywallst.org/about/.

"occupy, *v.*" *Oxford English Dictionary*, www.oed.com/view/Entry/130189?redirectedFrom=occupy#eid.

O'Donnell, Marcus. "Walking, Writing and Dreaming: Rebecca Solnit's Polyphonic Voices." *Journalism*, vol. 16, no. 7, 2015, pp. 936-52.

Solnit, Rebecca. Interview by Peter Terzian. "Room to Roam: Rebecca Solnit's Peripatetic Education." *Columbia Journalism Review*, Jul./Aug. 2007.

—. Interview by Samantha Kimmey. "Rebecca Solnit: The Self as Story." *The Point Reyes Light*, 20 June 2013, www.ptreyeslight.com/article/rebecca-solnit-self-story.

—. *The Encyclopedia of Trouble and Spaciousness*. Trinity UP, 2014.

> "Apologies to Mexico: The Drug Trade and the GNP (Gross National Pain)." pp. 224- 230.
>
> "Arrival Gates: The Inari Shrine in Kyoto, Japan." pp. 196-202.
>
> "The Google Bus: Silicon Valley Invades." pp. 248-255.
>
> "In Haiti, Words Can Kill." pp. 125-132.
>
> "Introduction: Icebergs and Laundry." pp. 1-5.
>
> "Letter to a Dead Man: On the Occupation of Hope." pp. 213-223.
>
> "Pale Bus, Pale Rider: Silicon Valley Invades, Cont'd." pp. 264-271.
>
> "We Won't Bow Down: Carnival and Resistance in New Orleans." pp. 240-247.

Discussing Teju Cole's essays on photography, Lu asks: How should we approach a medium that readily lends itself to distortion? In response, she develops an argument that urges us to reassess our identities in light of the global community with which photography can bring us into contact. (Instructor: Christina van Houten)

THE LANGUAGE SPOKEN BY ALL

Alice Lu

The camera is—and always will be—a tool, an instrument, a weapon. Whether it has a detrimental or beneficial impact is the decision the photographer must make. However, whether we let a photograph's message influence us or not is the decision we, the audience, must make. Teju Cole, a renowned writer and photographer, reckons with the positive and negative impacts of photography by relating the intricacies of the camera, the photographers, and the photographs themselves in a comprehensive ethical conversation. Cole takes his readers on a captivating journey through his collection of photo journals, using the camera as a lens to tackle cultural, technological, international, and personal issues. In doing so, he helps us rid ourselves of innocence and naivety and develop our own global perspectives. In such a diverse world, we need people with global perspectives, like Cole, to show us what we are doing wrong as brothers and sisters, as friends and strangers, and as human beings.

In his essay "Against Neutrality," Cole observes that in the eyes of many people, images "are often presumed to be unbiased." They are snapshots of the real world, but we cannot assume that they are necessarily true. We cannot say that a picture genuinely reflects the inner character of the captured subject nor that it reflects the accuracy of the situation portrayed. Hence, Cole believes that photographs can "conceal the craftiness of [their] content and selection" ("Against"). Any hidden motive would be the result of a photographer's style and intention. In support of this argument, Cole utilizes a portrait of Marion Maréchal-Le Pen, then a twenty-six-year-old French politician, photographed by Joel Saget. Photography historian John Edwin Mason notes that this professional-looking image—"reminiscent of old Hollywood headshots" ("Against")—makes the woman appear "attractive" and "desirable" (qtd. in "Against"). The way she looks away from the camera with her bare hands intertwined hints at innocence and purity. In addition, the black and white contrast and the solid background place emphasis on her earnest expression, her formality, and her uprightness. Meanwhile, the image shows nothing of Maréchal-Le Pen as a "nativist" politician with a "xenophobic vision," someone who believes that Muslims are inferior to Catholics ("Against"). Hence, this "sympathetic photograph" is the result of "manipulation" ("Against"). Mason observes that it is made "instantly recognizable as that of a celebrity profile," whose subject can be presumed to be a respectable, high-class exemplar instead of an enemy of moral principles (qtd. in "Against"). Essentially, Cole shows us how one image can make all the difference in our perception of a person, place, thing, or idea—it may even create the first impression of a subject we know nothing about.

As photo-manipulating technology weaves its way into our modern culture, Cole continues to warn that "the camera is an instrument of transformation" ("Against"). A manipulated photograph may filter its subject's ugliness and darkness while the audience remains deceived. In the essay "Memories of Things Unseen," Cole expands upon this idea, asserting that a manipulated photograph, or any photograph in general, "would be remembered by only this one angle, this single point of view, under [precise] lighting conditions" ("Memories"). Certainly, there are dangers to this single photograph, as it crops out the bigger picture. In her TED Talk "The Danger of a Single Story," Chimamanda Adichie contends that when only one perspective is considered, that perspective "show[s] a people as one thing, as only one thing, over and over again, and that is what they become." In effect, a photograph becomes a "single story," one that is worth a thousand words. Hence, it can show Maréchal-Le Pen as a sympathetic leader in a single photograph, and that would "make [that] one story become [her] only story" (Adichie). Until we introduce another perspective, her story remains incomplete. For this reason, we must reject the single story because it has the potential to create bias and inaccuracy. Accordingly, we must realize that our perception of the world cannot be based on a sole perspective "without engaging with all of the stories of that place and that person" (Adichie).

So, then, there exists a parts-to-whole relationship between one story and a collection of stories, between one photograph and a collection of photographs. Cole explores this relationship in the essay "Serious Play," in which he suggests that one photograph is like an immediate, trivial passing message, while a compilation of tens of hundreds of photographs is like "a conversation that unfolds gradually" over the course of weeks and months. Whether such conversations pertain to matters that are positive, disheartening, or serious, they all provide us with the chance to learn about the important aspects that impact a certain photographer's life. In effect, these photographic elements reckon with one's personal identity and life story. As we absorb new information from person to person, we begin to develop our own global perspective, which helps us assimilate in today's diverse media. Take, for instance, Cole's example of Instagram, a trendy social media platform designed for amateur and professional photographers alike. The more photos a user uploads onto his or her gallery, the more the work becomes a "continuity," a string of individual stories that relate to each other under various themes ("Serious"). For example, in a series of photos, photographer Dayanita Singh uses the camera as a lens to zoom into and out of just one subject of her concentration—the sunset. She captures the sunset in multiple settings, during different parts of the day, and through specific aspects such as the sky or the water. When viewed together, the photos make up a serene sunset on the shore: the orange sky of one image is followed by the shallow waves of another. Beyond that view is the intangible, for when time itself comes into play, there exists a dawn, a dusk, and a sunrise in addition to a sunset. So, when all the pictures and their hashtags are sewn together, each photographic element "illuminates and is illuminated by what came before" ("Serious"). As a result, we come to see a past, a present, and a future, all of which join together to reveal a more complete story—one that is more logical and credible with the addition of chapters.

Therefore, to avoid creating a single story in the first place, we must reckon with the limitations of media. We cannot simply assume that one depiction of a safe family in a war-torn country, or one confident smile on a soldier's face on government propaganda, is enough to characterize the subjects or the events photographed. Instead, Cole asserts that we need to see "what actually happens" in people's daily lives and "at the moment they happen" ("Against"). By doing so, we can see the world in all its brightest and darkest colors, in all its biggest and smallest moments. Especially when such news relates "to war, prejudice, hatred and violence," it "pursues a blinkered neutrality at the expense of real fairness" ("Against"). This pursuit, Cole insists, reveals that neutrality can be none other than an act of censorship. It hides the bloodshed and tears of its captured subjects when we ought to be sharing and carrying the subjects' burdens and sufferings. Regardless of who we are to one another, and regardless of race, gender, or background, we are all human beings; for that reason, we are destined to fall and rise as one collective unit.

Likewise, we should not overlook news that pertains to an insignificant person, a meaningless metro report, another car accident, or news from a distant land we will never visit in our lifetime. In his essay "Small Fates," Cole urges people to pay more attention to these seemingly trivial news stories, even if such news is not "of the kind that alter[s] a nation's course" ("Small"). No matter how local, unpopular, or unrelatable these stories may appear to us, they are nevertheless "the small fates of ordinary people" ("Small"). Hence, Cole argues that such stories are inherently powerful because they "reveal a whole world of ongoing human experience that is often ignored or oversimplified" ("Small"). And so, small news becomes what Susan Sontag describes as the "frankest representations" of any subject on the media even though such stories "seem most foreign" and "least likely to be known" (qtd. in "Against"). By immersing ourselves in these negligible stories, we will begin to understand other people, accept them for who they are, and build a community that welcomes differences, change, or just simple, ordinary individuals who are not Nobel Prize winners, politicians, or celebrities.

In a sense, "a good photograph is like a pinprick," as Cole suggests in his interview with *The Aerogram*: "It draws blood, it quickens, it's uncomfortable" (qtd. in Vikaas). In other words, the contents of "a good photograph" come as a "momentary shock to the consciousness"—an anagnorisis, an epiphany—just like the feeling of a "sudden rush of blood to the head," or a revelation (qtd. in Vikaas). In that sliver of time, we come to reckon with those in unfortunate situations, who may include those living in poverty, in underdeveloped nations, or under military rule. By doing so, we can come to see the world in a new light.

So then, how do we go about pursuing photography that is neither biased nor neutral nor exclusive? In her book of collected essays, *On Photography*, Susan Sontag argues that such a pursuit is not feasible because "photographing is essentially an act of non-intervention" (11). She implies that photographers cannot capture an action from the subject's point of view unless they risk their health or lives in doing so. Especially when it comes to photographs relating to war, prejudice, hatred, and violence, there should always be, for precautionary reasons, a distance between the photographer and the event. Take, for example, Paul Schutzer, the photographer killed on assignment in the Third Arab-Israeli War. Take, as another example, J. M. Giordano, the photographer who was beaten by Baltimore police officers during a protest of the death of Freddie Gray. These photographers did not ask to be beaten or killed. They simply wanted to capture the heart of the scene but failed to do so. They have shown us that we cannot forgo the neutrality that Cole condemns. As an alternative, we ought to prioritize safety and pursue the most candid photography possible at a reasonable distance.

And yet, when it comes to general photography, the distance between the photographer and subject still remains, perhaps because, as Sontag puts it, "the camera is a sublimation of the gun" (14). That means that to point and shoot photographs of subjects is "to violate them, by seeing them as they never see themselves" (Sontag 14). Hence, when it comes to photography, there exists a personal, private space that a photographer should not invade. Whether an image captures a victim or a perpetrator, it is immoral to capture them without their consent. After all, there are ethical and private reasons that people have for not wanting to be captured in a possibly humiliating, embarrassing, or abnormal light. This logic ties in with Cole's argument that "the photograph outlives the body," and so "our faces are becoming not only unforgettable but inescapable" ("Memories"). In contemporary society, digital photographs can never be deleted from the server, especially once they land on the Internet. As Cole suggests, this shows that photography is indistinguishable from surveillance. After all, the government may retain photographs for propaganda, and corporations or even individuals may exploit information captured on film. Soon enough, Cole warns, there will be "so much documentation of each life, each scene and event," that we could not delete or retract this digital record should we wish to remain unknown to the media ("Memories").

Now, if a camera is a "tool of power" (Sontag 8), what must we do to limit the media's power to retain our information? One solution, as Cole proposes, is to develop "a technology that simply [does] not have the ability to save the images it was transmitting" ("Memories"). The closest example of this technology today is Snapchat, a mobile app that allows users to send pictures through instant messaging. Unlike Instagram, Snapchat destroys these pictures in a matter of seconds, but users still have the capability to retain images by screenshotting. Thus, the limitations of digital media depend on the technological platforms used and their ability to retain images. The more we upload pictures online, the more we are documented in the digital world—permanently—with or without our consent. Our digital records are also affected by a platform's functionality. Because each platform has its own set of imaging tools such as filters, enhancements, and special effects, our public identity becomes vulnerable to inaccurate representations through photographic manipulation. Soon, the stories we tell may or may not cohere with the stories others think we are telling, thereby creating disharmony in our personal and public identities.

But then again, should all platforms implement software that restricts the retention of images as well as editing tools? No. In the end, regardless of how menacing the camera may be, it has just as much potential to do good as to do harm. We should not rush to constrain a camera's capabilities and functionalities when, in actuality, Cole observes that imaging technology has the power to "aid conservation, epigraphy, archeology and art history" ("Memories"). It can preserve ancient artifacts "at risk of being destroyed for military or religious reasons" ("Memories"). For instance, Vincent van Gogh's

The Painter on the Road to Tarascon is believed to have been burned during World War II, along with many of his other paintings. Fortunately, these paintings were previously captured on camera, so they have been made "visible to future generations" ("Memories"). Therefore, when a physical image or object fails to keep its form or is destroyed, modern technology may take over by preserving it so that it can still be a part of humankind's history. Hence, rather than limiting the camera's potential, we could, instead, direct our efforts towards implementing new 3D imaging technology to aid preservation.

All in all, the way that Cole thinks about the camera as a lens implies that there is more to photography than just filters or neutrality, followers or likes. What Cole strives to do with photography is not just to reckon with a controversial topic, but also to "find the language for all of what [his identity] means to [him] and to the people who look at [him]" ("Black"). This language is the universal language of all people, one that is ironically not a dialect, but a form of cognitive communication. Cole yearns to grasp this language that has the power to connect him with a person from another end of the globe. From New York City to Lagos to Switzerland, Cole has dragged himself "down into a space of narrative that [he has not] been in before," and in doing so, has "attempt[ed] to untangle the knot of who or what belongs to us," as writer Claudia Rankine notes in a 2016 review of Cole's essay collection *Known and Strange Things*. I, too, believe that his journey and search for personal identity sets an example for us. It shows that we need to step out of our comfort zones in order to become active members of the global community. We are all human beings deep down in our hearts, and we ought to reflect that humanity on the outside just as much as on the inside. Through photography, we have the means to express ourselves truly because images have become the words in the language spoken by all.

WORKS CITED

Adichie, Chimamanda Ngozi. "The Danger of a Single Story."
TED, July 2009,
www.ted.com/talks/chimamanda_adichie_the_danger_of_a_sin-
gle_story.

Cole, Teju. "Against Neutrality." *The New York Times*, 16 Jan.
2016, www.nytimes.com/2016/01/17/magazine/against-neutral-
ity.html?_r=0.

—. "Black Body: Rereading James Baldwin's 'Stranger in the
Village.'" *The New Yorker*, 19 Aug. 2014,
www.newyorker.com/books/page-turner/black-body-re-reading-
james-baldwins-stranger-village.

—. "Memories of Things Unseen." *The New York Times*, 17 Oct.
2015, www.nytimes.com/2015/10/18/magazine/memories-of-
things-unseen.html.

—. "Serious Play." *The New York Times*, 12 Dec. 2015,
www.nytimes.com/2015/12/13/magazine/serious-play.html.

—. "Small Fates." *Teju Cole*, Mar. 2011, www.tejucole.com/other-
words/small-fates.

Rankine, Claudia. "Teju Cole's Essays Build Connections Between
African and Western Art." *The New York Times*, 9 Aug. 2016,
www.nytimes.com/2016/08/14/books/review/teju-cole-known-
and-strange-things.html.

Sontag, Susan. *On Photography*. Farrar, Straus and Giroux, 1977.

Vikaas, Kishwer. "Teju Cole: 'A Good Photograph Is Like a
Pinprick.'" *The Aerogram*, 14 Apr. 2013,
www.theaerogram.com/teju-cole-on-photography.

Using a wide range of evidence, Colussi explores conflicts between individuality and community, intimacy and mundanity. Structuring the essay through this web of key terms, she develops an idea about the fragile human condition that is reflected in the objects we collect.
(Instructor: David Foley)

SEARCHING FOR SOLACE IN A LEMON PEEL

Mary Colussi

So often in fiction, people are defined by what they refuse to leave behind. If a character disappears and a police officer writes it off as them running away, it is nearly certain that someone will present a talisman and declare that their loved one never would have left home without bringing the sacred object with them. We accept this trope as truth, because we have all thought about what we would save first were our houses to burn down; we all possess and keep careful track of our own sacred objects. Though an obsession with the material is more often seen as a vice than as a virtue, the examination of the belongings we love, or even just use every day, is rich ground for discovery about both individuals and the universal qualities we share.

It is easy to criticize a modern-day fixation on objects; it seems, sometimes, as though acquiring is more essential than creating, as if owning is more important than giving. This critical point of view, however, ignores the potential that objects have in allowing us to create and imagine: what, in essence, they give us. In *Still Life with Oysters and Lemon*, Mark Doty falls in love with a painting of that same name. Through this love, this "being held within an intimacy with the things of the world," he fosters a deeper connection with the strangers who pass him on a chilly Manhattan street, enabling him to investigate the paradoxical human need to both belong to and remain separate from a larger collective (4). The painting, a still-life depiction of a glass of wine, oysters in their shells, and a partially peeled lemon, evokes this paradox in its assertion that things such as smell and taste must be set apart to be properly appreciated. Once these senses are combined, the once-disparate parts of the painting lose their individual vibrancy. The world functions best when it is a "dialogue between degrees of transparency," when we appreciate that the light that hits the subjects in the still-life hits all of us, that it illuminates us in unique ways (5). Still, it is a universal desire of human beings to be loved by others, and, in order to be loved, we must make ourselves vulnerable. Doty likens this vulnerability to "nuances of transparency and reflectivity" when discussing the peeled lemons gracing the images of many Dutch still-life painters (9). The painters used lemons as displays of technical skill, uncurling the peels in lavish manner to demonstrate artistic prowess. Doty sees a strange egotism in these elaborately painted lemons, but also admires how the artists allowed each lemon to remain intimate and ordinary, able to assert its individuality just days before its inevitable decay.

Who sees the world through the curls of a lemon peel? Doty's painting serves to reassure him: the impulse to exercise his rights as both a community member and an individual is a perfectly natural one. When we are faced with such contradictions, why would we turn to objects, rather than our values, ideals, or even our gods? Teju Cole, in his essay "Object Lesson," suggests that it is for "some kind of solace." We cannot talk with or touch our values, and it is just as difficult to book a meeting with the deity of your choice; instead, we take comfort in our domestic routines and pray to a cross or towards a city: physical reminders of the oftentimes unseen love and justice many of us believe to be inherent in the world. When we live in peaceful times, or at least in a peaceful place, we also require reminders of violence and loss to fully prove their existence to us. In his essay, Cole discusses the work of the photographer Glenna Gordon, who created an exhibition of photographs of the belongings left behind by the Nigerian schoolgirls kidnapped by the terrorist group Boko Haram. Since the actual act of violence could not be captured—and the moment of rescue has not yet occurred, nor does it seem likely to—Gordon took photos of things such as the girls' uniform blouses, an image that reminded Cole of his own education in Nigeria. The power of Gordon's photograph is two-fold: it "activated [his] own memories and emotional responses," writes Cole, and emphasized not so much the presence of the blouse, but the absence of the girl who unwillingly left it behind ("Object"). This negative space of sorts makes familiar what could be foreign. Just as Doty sees the "dark space within an embrace" in the chiaroscuro of his painting, Cole sees the violence and senselessness of the tragic fate of the Nigerian girls in the devastating emptiness of Gordon's photographs (6).

Cole's discussion of the photography of violence adds an interesting facet to Doty's claim of a universal desire for community. We find solace in images that remind us of the kidnapped girls through our recognition of ourselves in their lives: we, too, slept with school books beside our beds and wore clothing our mothers labeled with our names. We allow ourselves to tolerate an otherwise unbearable contradiction: when we see photographs of genocide and natural disaster, we ask ourselves, how can we live like this? But when we view triumphant artwork such as Doty's painting, we think, how can we not? By seeing ourselves as similar to the victims, we invite ourselves into their lives, imagining ourselves into their devastated families and community. Through this connection, we find closure. The domestic objects in Gordon's photographs bring us closer to reality, though as Doty notes in his essay, it still remains just out of our reach: we see our own reflections in the lives of these students, rather than the students themselves, thus distorting their crisis while mitigating our own.

If such lofty ideals as the ones discussed in Doty's essay are indeed universal, then it follows that they must also be mundane; a quality that all humans possess automatically may still retain a rare beauty, but its core is utility. For instance, all of us romanticize the heart, but it remains a muscle, bloody and ordinary, made to perform a singular task. Doty and Cole's essays both celebrate the personal touch of the individual: a name written on the collar of a blouse, a lemon peel twirling downwards in a show of bravado, and the marks we leave on objects we use every day. Andrea Zittel's installation *A to Z 1993 Living Unit* provides an interesting contrast to this focus. This work presents the furnishings of a room: a cot, a kitchen, and storage space. Though minimal, it presents a compelling portrait of someone's life. By filling in the surroundings, rather than the face, of an individual, Zittel creates, as Gordon did, a portrait in negative space. The installation, though furnished for a very specific, utilitarian sort of person, reminds us how little we need to live comfortably. It reminds us that the universal human habit of collecting, of making nests and safety nets for ourselves out of souvenirs and other belongings, comes not from a need to survive, but a paradoxical need to both assert ourselves as individuals, with our own unique tastes and styles, and to remind ourselves, through photographs, paintings, and other sentimental belongings, that we are a part of a larger community which we both contribute to and benefit from. Zittel's installation evokes in us both admiration and repulsion that a life could be lived so plainly, and that one would want such a life. We think we could easily live in such a place, but we could not imagine a single reason why we would want to.

When we investigate the wisdom of objects, we are attempting to navigate a world of contradiction: individualism versus community, the value of intimacy versus the value of personal sovereignty, and what we assume about others versus what we will allow them to assume about us. All of these works siphon meaning from the mundane, just as a still-life painting allows a close-up look at otherwise distant concepts. These art pieces demonstrate to us, through objects, the fragility of our human desires and needs and the value of this fragility. Though we may never see reality, we are reassured, through both our common tendency to collect what makes us comfortable and the differences in what we choose to collect, that we are real.

WORKS CITED

Cole, Teju. "Object Lesson." *The New York Times Magazine*, 17 Mar. 2015, https://www.nytimes.com/2015/03/22/magazine/object-lesson.html.

Doty, Mark. *Still Life with Oysters and Lemon: On Objects and Intimacy*. Beacon Press, 2001.

Zittel, Andrea. *A to Z 1993 Living Unit*. 1993, steel, wood, four hangers, sweater, etc., Whitney Museum of American Art, New York.

In this open letter to Vietnam's new Minister of Education, Pham warns against the failings of standardized education. He advances this argument not only with evidence from diverse sources, but also by developing an authoritative but respectful ethos. (Instructor: Benjamin Gassman)

FOR THE VIETNAMESE YOUTH

Duc Minh Pham

Minister Phùng Xuân Nhạ,

First, I would like to congratulate you on your new position as the Minister of Education of Vietnam. You have the power to shape the development of our nation for generations to come and create a bright future for Vietnam and every one of its young citizens. As a member of the Vietnamese youth, I am writing today to voice my concerns over our education system, specifically higher education, because, when it comes to providing our students with quality and equal learning opportunities, it is never not the time to act.

As a developing country still healing in the wake of two devastating wars, Vietnam realizes that education is undeniably the most valuable investment in its future. In fact, our government spends one-fifth of its budget on education and training purposes, making Vietnam one of the most education-oriented countries globally (Government, Hồng). Still, every year, 1.2 million applicants compete for only 400,000 college spaces, thus creating a need for a fair and efficient college admissions system (International Business Publications 63).

For years, the Ministry of Education and Training has tried to meet this need by radically standardizing every aspect of education. Every student in our country, from kindergarten to high school, uses the same textbooks, adheres to the same curriculum, and, when the time comes, takes the same national college exam. Public universities rank applicants by their test scores and admit the top ones without looking at any of their other strengths or weaknesses. Your predecessors have argued that such a system limits corruption, creates an equal playing field, provides educators with an inexpensive way to examine their students, and ensures that every child, regardless of their background, can be a part of the competition.

One would expect a system that ideal to function miraculously. Yet that is far from the case. Over the last three college admissions cycles alone, your ministry has repeatedly had to change the system to fix the obvious flaws. Two years ago, to address the difference in the learning conditions of students from different areas and of different ethnicities, the Ministry introduced a program that would award extra points to test-takers from rural areas or minority backgrounds. That initiative, while benefitting many, caused a national uproar. As one student puts it: "You get extra points for cycling 20km to school, but I don't get extra points for waking up at 5am, and standing for 2 hours in 3 consecutive bus routes before class" (Quyên). The following year, the Ministry got rid of that program, and there were national stories about how a test that focused on a few core subjects would not be an accurate measurement and would favor urban schools with superior instructors and facilities. Then, this year, six different school subjects were merged together to create only two—*Natural Sciences* and *Social Sciences*—forcing students to be knowledgeable in many fields. Needless to say, this arrangement is going to receive major backlash from our students, educators, and parents.

To be fair to your predecessors, it is crucial to point out that more developed countries have also tried to standardize their education. For instance, in 2002, the United States president signed into law the *No Child Left Behind Act*, which would test students from third to eighth grade annually and tie their results to their educators (U.S. Government Publishing Office). The goal of the act was to increase American youth's school performances, reduce and eradicate achievement gaps between ethnicities and regions, and give educators an incentive to deliver their best every school day. The result? Domestically, in 2015, Americans scored no higher on the SAT and ACT tests than they did before the act was passed, and the achievement gap that affected students of color and with disabilities stagnated, as it has for 50 years (Strauss, Camera). Internationally, on the PISA evaluation, a global scale to judge students' performances, the average score of an American student in Math and Reading stalled or decreased from 2000 to 2015, and the United States consistently ranked out of proportion with its economic power in the global academic ranking in that time period (National Center for Education Statistics). It seems as if all that extra pressure on students and teachers was for nothing.

Minister, perhaps you, like other lawmakers around world, are scratching your head as you try to tinker with the standardized system, hoping that one day it would accomplish its original aim. But I am here to tell you that such a system does not, and would never, work. Don't get me wrong; as a young engineer, I am a supporter of a standardized system where it is applicable. And, on the surface, such a system sounds brilliant, as it provides an unbiased, equal evaluation of all students and a platform for holding instructors accountable. "An accountability system must have a consequence," said President Bush about U.S. public education in 2001, "otherwise it's not much of an accountability system" (Bush).

But here's where that idea falls short: education is not, has never been, and will never be standard. It is an irony that we tell our children to chase their dreams, only to weigh them all on the same, basic scale. It is as if we assure our kids they can be whoever they desire, as long as they do well in Math, Science, and Reading. Standardizing, in this case, is suppressing creativity, is failing to recognize that each youngster is filled with incredible potential, each one unique. Additionally, 'accountability' forces teachers to turn each student into a problem-solving machine. Minister, I am a computer programmer. My job is to put sophisticated lines of codes into computers to solve millions of problems every second, not making a single mistake in the process. But educators are not programmers, and children cannot become cold, mass-produced machines. Standardizing our students is destroying their futures and our society's future as a whole.

And no, standardization is not a pathway to equality. From 2000 to 2014, while *No Child Left Behind* was in effect in the U.S., the number of effectively segregated schools—those in which 75% or more of the students are from the same ethnic background—more than doubled in number, and "the percentage of all schools with so-called racial or socio-economic isolation grew from 9% to 16%"

(Toppo). These schools are the result of either racial tension or economic division in the U.S., issues that standardized testing simply could not address. One can imagine why it's hard to reduce the racial achievement gap when students of different races study in different, isolated schools. In Vietnam, thanks to our evaluation systems, many Vietnamese people are led to become obsessed with money and power, which renowned professor Nguyễn Lân Dũng has called the "top 2 malformations of our culture" (Hà). Our schooling has led people to believe that there exists a scale that can measure all of us, in either money or power, and that one's self-worth and life meaning depend uniquely on that scale alone. Such a mindset narrows one's options in one's career and life. It scares individuals out of speaking their minds, and prevents us from seeing the best in one another. Education and testing standardization not only fail to solve the social problems that we have right now, but also create new ones, weakening our country's sense of community and unity.

Mr. Nha, I know it's hard to take a college freshman's words seriously. But the facts don't lie. For instance, let's look at the difference between students' dedication to Computer Science in high school and in college in our country. In the last college admissions cycle, at our top public engineering and science universities, Computer Science, as a major, had some of the strictest incoming test requirements for applicants. Furthermore, Computer Science students enjoy special programs that aren't available to other majors, such as the Advanced Program in Computer Science at the University of Science. Many universities, like the University of Technology, even invested in facilities and qualified instructors to be accredited the ABET certification in Computer Science, shared with the very top colleges in the world. Yet one would be surprised to learn that, in Ho Chi Minh City, the financial center of our nation, only three high schools offer Computer Science as a major. Of those, none of them has a Computer Science club, and one even lets applicants who marginally fail the Math or Science major join the Computer Science class. The concentration of our institutions reflect the needs of our students. And it's obvious, for high-schoolers who yearn for a career in Informatics, that their best bet is, ironically, disregarding the subject and focusing on standardized tests. This results in a considerable number of students entering college as computer scientists, despite not knowing about the subject's ideas and challenges, or whether they have the strengths or passion to commit to that career for the next forty years. And, if you don't think there is a consequence, remember that earlier this year a Chinese group hacked our largest airline and froze our air transportation for hours (Clark). A country that in theory puts its brightest minds in the Computer Science field can't even protect itself and its citizens from foreign cyber threats. At the very least, this is about preparing our young citizens for their life decisions. At the very most, this is about our national security. Minister, this needs to change.

Yes, there are challenges ahead. A thorough, personalized evaluation system for our students means training and hiring qualified personnel in all parts of the country, which costs money. But, as the only way to reach the summit is through taking little steps, we can only achieve this aim through a long-term plan. Maybe we might add the students' three years of GPA to our evaluation this year, and next year, we could add their activities, and the year after that let them speak through an essay, and so on. You could say that such changes give urban students an unfair advantage, as rural kids don't have equal extracurricular opportunities, but that, too, like all factors, should be taken into account when examining one's readiness for college. You can say that such a system invites dishonesty, in which students participate in activities simply for the sake of their college applications rather than to be involved. But doing the right thing for the wrong reason is still a right thing nonetheless. Even if the students have different motives in mind when they reach out to extracurricular activities, they would still benefit from the experience and become more confident in whichever path they choose to follow. For the ones interested in growing into computer scientists, joining a computer club would allow them to see up close what the profession is about, to practice coding and gain insights on its potential challenges, to identify their own performances, and to be absolutely sure that they want to commit to the subject for college, and for life.

If you're still not convinced, know that any reform goes beyond just education. While I would love for our government to pass laws that specifically address ethnic and income inequalities, our people must realign our views of one another based on actions, not wealth or power. All of these can eventually be achieved through education, through *you*, as the young students today will take over the country tomorrow. An evaluation system that gives students a chance to express themselves teaches them to celebrate diversity and invites constructive debates and disagreements. Through championing each individual, we can reinforce our country's sense of community, as each person will know that society protects and appreciates his or her personal endeavors. A nation of loving and energized people who feel respected in their own land—that, Minister, can be your legacy.

I know two boys my age, one who lives in the center of Ho Chi Minh City, but has to wake up every day at 5am to help set up his family's noodle store, and another from a wealthy but slightly unstable family, as his father spends six months abroad for business every year. Their profiles say they have every chance to succeed, but no standardized system can convey the hardships they go through or the beauty of their characters. Likewise, there is nothing standard about our students, because life is rarely simple enough to be contained in Math, Science, and Reading. Instead, the foundations of our strong future are to be found in the diversity of our backgrounds, passions, and beliefs. Soon, Vietnam will either have accomplished and united citizens in all fields and professions, or standardized ones, crumbling under the complicated pressures of life. The decision is entirely up to you. But whether you care about the lives of each young individual of Vietnam, or you are concerned about our country, its economy, culture, and security, please, persevere. No matter the reason, please, do the right thing. Because we, as a nation, need you to.

Sincerely,
Duc M. Pham

WORKS CITED

Bush, George W. "Press Conference with President George W. Bush and Education Secretary Rod Paige to Introduce the President's Education Program." Washington, D. C., The White House, 23 Jan. 2001, www.whitehouse.gov/news/releases/2001/01/20010123-2.html

Camera, Lauren. "Achievement Gap Between White and Black Students Still Gaping." *U.S. News*, 13 Jan. 2016, www.usnews.com/news/blogs/data-mine/2016/01/13/achievement-gap-between-white-and-black-students-still-gaping.

Clark, Helen. "The Alleged Chinese Hacking at Vietnam's Airports Shows That the South China Sea Battle Isn't Just in the Water." *Huffington Post*, 6 Aug. 2016, www.huffingtonpost.com/helen_clark/china-hack-vietnam-south-china-sea_b_11357330.html.

Government of Vietnam. "Số liệu ngân sách Nhà nước năm 2017" [State Budget Data for 2017]. Government Electronic Information Cổng Thông Tin Điện Tư Chính Phư, 15 Dec. 2016, chinhphu.vn/files/dlt/2016/12/NSNN.pdf.

Hà Nhi. "GS Nguyễn Lân Dũng: Rất nhiều người Việt ham tiền, vô cảm, hèn nhát" [Prof. Nguyen Lan Dung: Many Vietnamese people enjoy money, are insensitive, cowardly]. *Giao duc* Giáo dục, 13 May 2013, giaoduc.net.vn/Muc-cu/Vi-khat-vong-Viet/GS-Nguyen-Lan-Dung-Rat-nhieu-nguoi-Viet-ham-tien-vo-cam-hen-nhat-post117868.gd.

Hồng Hạnh. "Việt Nam thuộc nhóm nước có tỉ lệ chi cho giáo dục cao nhất thế giới" [Vietnam is among the countries with the highest education spending in the world]. *Dan Tri News* Báo Dân trí, 30 Apr. 2010, dantri.com.vn/giao-duc-khuyen-hoc/viet-nam-thuoc-nhom-nuoc-co-ty-le-chi-cho-giao-duc-cao-nhat-the-gioi-1272678374.htm.

International Business Publications. *Vietnam Export-Import, Trade and Business Directory—Strategic, Practical Information and Contacts.* IBP, Inc., 22 Jan. 2016.

National Center for Education Statistics. "Trends in Student Performance: Trends in U.S. Performance—Average Scores."

Program for International Student Assessment, 2015, nces.ed.gov/surveys/pisa/pisa2015/pisa2015highlights_6.asp#table.

Quyên Quyên. "Tranh cãi về cộng điểm ưu tiên vào ĐH" [Debate about extra points for college entrance]. *Zing*, 11 Aug. 2015, news.zing.vn/tranh-cai-ve-cong-diem-uu-tien-vao-dai-hoc-post567870.html.

Strauss, Valerie. "No Child Left Behind: What standardized test scores reveal about its legacy." *Washington Post*, 10 Mar. 2015, www.washingtonpost.com/news/answer-sheet/wp/2015/03/10/no-child-left-behind-what-standardized-test-scores-reveal-about-its-legacy/.

Toppo, Greg. "GAO study: Segregation worsening in U.S. schools." *USA Today*, 17 May 2016, www.usatoday.com/story/news/2016/05/17/gao-study-segregation-worsening-us-schools/84508438/.

U.S. Government Publishing Office. "Public Law 107-110." *GPO.gov*, 2002, www.gpo.gov/fdsys/pkg/PLAW-107publ110/html/PLAW-107publ110.htm.

Through her reading of Rebecca Solnit's A Field Guide to Getting Lost, *Wu ruminates on the idea that our words and our world are limitless. Her detailed analysis focuses on how Solnit's rhetorical style and inviting ethos guide readers into the unknown, reflecting on what it means to find connection by embracing loss. (Instructor: Jenny Xie)*

A DIGRESSIONAL GUIDE

Xiaolu Wu

From a cursory reading, Rebecca Solnit's *A Field Guide to Getting Lost* appears to be an invitation to get lost not only in the real world, but also in the world of words. Solnit's mercurial stream of thought guides readers, with no apparent motive, through personal stories, art criticism, cinematic reviews, and vivid images of landscapes. However, reading through *A Field Guide to Getting Lost* is more like going on a scavenger hunt. Pieces of evidence lead you from one foreign place to another, haunting you with the suspense and excitement of the unknown along the way. When you finally get to the last stop, you find yourself standing on an isolated island in the middle of the sea. There is no treasure to discover, just the vastness of the ocean blue, enveloping and engulfing you. You feel small. You feel invisible. You feel the power of the limitlessness. This is the prize. Solnit's purpose is never merely to disorient; rather, she guides readers out of their limited selves to discover the vastness of the world, inviting them to get lost in the unknown.

A Field Guide to Getting Lost can be divided into two parts. All the chapters with odd numbers relate Solnit's personal stories, whereas all the chapters with even numbers consist of her more objective reflections and art reviews, each of which is titled "The Blue of Distance." Solnit's essays break down generic category boundaries as they range across memoir, art criticism, philosophical writings, and even fictional stories. Though she constantly tries to pull readers out of themselves, Solnit never sounds didactic. In fact, her language is so poetic and her narration so fascinating that readers can flip through page after page without even being aware of the passage of time.

Solnit uses long melodic sentences to enchant her readers. She repeats clauses with similar grammatical structures and uses clauses of different lengths to create a sonic pleasure that mesmerizes readers. Her long repetitive clauses lay down expectations, which accumulate to a climatic burst at the end. They attract readers' attention like metal to magnets. Most of her long sentences are visually descriptive, yanking readers into the places Solnit has been and letting them experience what she went through. But sometimes they become abstract and metaphysical, pulling readers out of the physical world and pushing them into deep reflection. Readers resurface from the book only to find themselves reflecting on cultural, political, and philosophical issues. Solnit strives to immerse readers completely in the world she creates so that they can forget about themselves.

Solnit further disorients readers with her mercurial stream of thought, which jumps from one idea or scene to another. The discontinuities in Solnit's essays are not a reckless disregard for transition, but a thoughtful design that imitates the way people converse with one another. Solnit claims that she loves "the ease with which [people] can get to any point from any other point . . . [and connect] everything back up" in a conversation (qtd. in Fay 130). Solnit's nonlinear writing style serves two functions: on the one hand, targeting readers who are used to a linear narrative, Solnit tries to get them lost in her unconventional, meandering writing. On the other hand, Solnit anticipates more from her readers than merely feeling lost. She is encouraging active thought and participation from them in the hope that they will gradually find the connection between every fragment of writing and piece everything together through the course of reading. In an interview, she voices her belief that the meandering process of conversing is how "[people] think and . . . put the world together for [themselves]" (qtd. in Gritz). The way everything connects in Solnit's essays is almost like a simulation of human brain activity: the activation of one set of neurons leads to the activation of another set of overlapping neurons, leading to endless brain activity.

An example of her associative leaps appears in "Two Arrowheads," in which Solnit, with an abrupt transition, parallels a heartbreaking love story with a hermit in the desert and the film *Vertigo*, a tragic romance between a retired detective and a woman who he was asked to follow. The two stories at first seem to be separate and irrelevant to each other, but a subtle commonality links them together: both her love story and *Vertigo* are "disintegrated" ("Two" 136). Solnit's love story begins with her intriguing rendering of an intimate and carefree love in the magnificent wilderness. However, the happy story ends with heartbreak; Solnit reflects: "A disintegrated [love] lies at your feet like a shattered mirror, each shard reflecting a different story" ("Two" 136). She insists: "The stories don't fit back together, and it's the end of stories" (136). *Vertigo* could also be seen as "a disintegrated love" divided and viewed differently by the two lovers (136). In the detective's version, the story is about tracing the mysterious lover's shadow, while in the woman's version, the story is about her sacrificing herself to become another person for a man's love. Such passions are bound to lead to a dead end.

However, Solnit does not allow herself to get trapped. After the heartbreak, she creates a new story. The story is a subtle metaphor for how she herself broke through her dead love. Her new story is based on the character Midge from *Vertigo*, whom Solnit leads to the world outside the dead-end of the film. In the story, Solnit uses the temporal and spatial frame of *Vertigo* to let Midge wander through the city and engage in all kinds of adventurous activities. Abandoning the contemporary definition of 'romance'—love stories—Solnit uses instead its historical definition: an endless adventure through exciting and stimulating places (150). Through composing this story, Solnit transcends her heartbreak in a journey of infinite discoveries and possibilities. As she concludes the essay with her experience hiking on Mount Whitney, she elevates her excursion, noting that "as you get higher, the world gets bigger, and you feel smaller in proportion to it, overwhelmed and liberated by how much space is around you, how much room to wander, how much unknown" (151). Here, the 'self' is diminished before the enormity of the landscape, and there arises an awareness that there is a bigger world out there. Solnit insists that her readers experience the landscape with her, alongside her revelation: we can only gain value by breaking out of our small personal spaces and journeying into the vastness of the world. This epiphany is the ultimate prize: it is what Solnit wants readers to reach for themselves after reading her book.

Across Solnit's essays, there is always a dichotomy between being trapped in a limited space and traveling out to the limitless world. In "Abandon," Solnit reflects on the suicide of her good friend from adolescence, Marine: "Marine plunged into the unknown again and again, but she kept returning home, while I trudged on in a straight line away from where I'd started" (109). Here, suicide, like heartbreak, is a dead-end to the story, but it also represents an inability to look beyond one's personal pain. By juxtaposing Marine with herself, Solnit highlights the danger of being caged in personal space. She again implies that the right path is to push ourselves into the bigger world, in which infinite routes and opportunities are waiting to be explored and our limited selves are enlarged by the limitlessness of the world. Solnit also cautions that the process of getting lost and diving into the unknown requires the "prudent anticipation and a philosophical memory" of adulthood, things which "make you navigate more slowly and steadily" ("Abandon" 108-109). She warns readers against the dangers of the reckless act of simply "plung[ing] into the unknown," as Marine did ("Abandon" 109).

And yet despite this warning, Solnit still urges her readers to step into the unknown, to develop what the poet John Keats describes as 'negative capability,' or the ability "of being in uncertainties, mysteries, doubts" (qtd. in "Open Door" 10). The unknown represents what's outside us and our limited cognition. Solnit tries to persuade her readers to erase the boundary between their personal space and the world by being in the unknown, introducing artist Yves Klein, who makes relief maps in which everything is dark blue without distinction. Unlike conventional maps, these maps represent uncharted territory. For Solnit, the map is a forceful rejection of any boundary between individuals and the world. For example, in "Open Doors," Solnit refers to the Wintu language, in which cardinal directions are used to describe body parts. Instead of saying "left" hand, a Wintu person would say "west" hand ("Open" 17). Solnit admires with enthusiasm the "cultural imagination" behind this language, which is exactly what she is advocating: "the self only exists in reference to the rest of the world" ("Open" 17). If there is no difference between the self and the world, the fear of being lost in the unknown will become non-existent. This idea also coincides with Solnit's style of linking everything together in her writing: the self is not just immersed in the world, but interconnected with it in every single way.

By eliminating their personal boundaries, people allow themselves to come into the larger system of interconnectedness and coexistence: the unknown world. According to Solnit, the unknown not only eliminates divisions but also allows for contradictions. Referencing another Yves Klein piece, a photograph titled *A Leap into the Void*, Solnit uses "the void" as a metaphor for the unknown ("Blue" 172). She argues that the title could be read as a Buddhist phrase: the ultimate enlightenment of "embracing the emptiness" (172). In Buddhism, 'void' is defined by one sentence: "form is emptiness, and the very emptiness is form" (qtd. in Richards 251). Because "form" and "emptiness" are antonyms and therefore cannot be equal to each other, this doctrine violates "the law of contradiction" (Richards 251). Solnit's Buddhist interpretation of *A Leap into the Void* implies her belief in the power of the unknown to allow coexistence despite differences and contradictions. She argues that "embracing the emptiness"—the void—is equivalent to "embracing limitlessness," which welcomes everyone regardless of personal differences ("Blue" 172).

However, human beings are not rational machines that can always step out of the personal. The emotional effects of personal tragedies are often so strong that people cannot escape them even despite their efforts to do so. Solnit's own struggle to outgrow personal traumas can be seen in the emotional distance she strives to gain from herself. She refrains from making her essays too self-absorbed, trying to connect her deeply personal stories to bigger stories of cultural and political history. In "Abandon," Solnit seems to have an emotional outburst when recounting her memories of Marine after learning of her death (103). The whole paragraph of vivid, bittersweet memories lasts for one page, with a sense of emotional urgency that almost amounts to an explosion. However, the explosion is soon contained by a sudden jump from Solnit's memories to a deep reflection on the cultural and political atmosphere of that era: the thriving of liberals and activists, drug use, queer people, and artists, as well as Reagan's nuclear brinkmanship and the imagination of a dark future filled with nuclear ruins ("Abandon" 104). Through such a turn, Solnit elevates Marine's abandonment of her life to a generation's abandonment of hope and its subsequent fears of an apocalyptic world that would be a result of the "strange, complicated future that money, power, and technology would impose" ("Abandon" 106). In this way, Solnit distances herself from her emotions by reflecting on the cultural history of that period. A common theme across Solnit's essays seems to be that of loss: the loss of a dear friend or the loss of a lover. However, Solnit always seems to speak against indulging in the pain of personal losses, constantly striving instead to put herself in a larger context, a larger world with problems and individuals beyond herself. She urges us in an interview to "remember that other people suffer, that other things are going on in the world, that even when you're going through a huge tragedy, you can be enchanted or bewitched by some fascinating thing that comes along and forget yourself" (qtd. in Gritz).

By stressing the necessity of breaking out of our limited personal space and putting ourselves in the limitless world, Solnit is not telling us to get lost without purpose. Instead, she wants us to "[dive] into the unknown and [resurface] as someone new," someone who can reemerge from personal losses, understand the interconnectedness and the openness of the world, and see the world as infinite unknown territory to discover (qtd. in Gritz). Perhaps Solnit's motive is too idealistic for a society that creates egocentric individuals who are obsessed with personal gains and losses. However, in her battle to push herself and her readers into the bigger world, she truly raises the question: how could our limited lives be valuable in a limitless world? A feasible solution is to follow Solnit's wisdom.

WORKS CITED

Fay, Sarah. "Wide World: An Essayist and Activist Who Makes Eloquent Connections." *The American Scholar*, vol. 76, no. 3, 2007, pp. 129-131.

Gritz, Jennie Rothenberg. "Terra Incognita." *The Atlantic*, Mar. 2006, www.theatlantic.com/magazine/archive/2006/03/terra-incognita/304626/.

Richards, Glyn. "Śūnyatā: Objective Referent or via Negativa?" *Religious Studies*, vol. 14, no. 2, 1978, pp. 251-260.

Solnit, Rebecca. *A Field Guide to Getting Lost,* Penguin Books, 2006.
 "Abandon." pp. 85-109.
 "The Blue of Distance." pp. 153-176.
 "Open Door." pp. 1-25.
 "Two Arrowheads." pp. 127-152.

In this open letter, Ju seeks both to persuade Moon Jae-in, then candidate for the presidency of South Korea, to take a stand against the dog meat industry, and to convince other readers to reconsider their own positions on the topic. The piece balances respect for others' opinions with logical, focused, research-based argumentation. (Instructor: Jenny Xie)

ON DOG MEAT CONSUMPTION AND REGULATION

Jaehyoung Ju

Dear President Moon Jae-in:

Congratulations on your nomination. With recent years characterized by turmoil and instability within the Republic, I genuinely hope you can win over the people and lead us to a brighter future. You made headlines when you announced that the "First Dog" of Korea may possibly have been an abandoned stray originally scheduled to be butchered (Song). People have been generally impressed with how you've been pushing for more animal rights, but I believe it is now time for us to address the elephant in the room—the Korean dog meat industry.

In 2016, Mayor Lee Jae-myung of Seongnam City issued a decree to close down the dog meat vendors in Moran Market, the largest market for dog meat in Korea, estimated to provide a third of the total dog meat consumed in the country. All dog meat vendors and facilities are scheduled to be removed by 2017, ahead of the upcoming 2018 Pyeongchang Winter Olympics (Kim, "How Did"). Just as we proved to the world that we had risen from the ashes of war and poverty during the 1988 Summer Olympics in Seoul, I hope we can show them that we have overcome the corruption, scandal, and incompetence of our previous administration. But various interest groups are lobbying against the Olympics being held in Korea precisely because of our dog meat consumption, and I believe it is crucial to address this issue (Kim, "How Did").

According to a report from the *Hankyoreh*, a widely circulated Korean newspaper, during the 1988 Olympics in Seoul, local dog meat restaurants explicitly changed their menu items' names from *gaejangguk* (which literally means 'Dog Soup') to *boshintang* ('Soup for Helping the Body') or *yeongyangtang* ('Nutrient Soup'), in order to hide from foreign visitors the fact that they were using dog in the dishes (Kim, "80s"). I would also like to turn your attention towards a study published in the *Korean Journal of Food and Nutrition* (한국식품영양학회지, KJFN) by professor Ann Yong-geun. According to surveys conducted regarding the population's consumption of dog meat, 1,251 out of 1,502 Koreans had eaten dog meat before, with the ratio heavily skewed towards having eaten dog meat for all age groups except teens (for which the ratio was 1:1) (Ann). 50.7% had eaten dog meat because they simply ate what their family ate, as opposed to desiring it themselves (Ann). What is also notable is that, although the main reasons for not eating dog meat were that it was 'barbaric,' 'inhumane,' and 'unsanitary,' the main reasons for continuing to eat it were all related to cultural preservation and imperialism (Ann). But what does all this data even mean? It means that, as the government is slowly restricting the practice, people's thoughts are also changing. This is a good opportunity for the proposal that I have for you: regulate the dog meat trade, with the goal of slowly phasing it out entirely as the population becomes more averse to eating it. This may seem like a radical proposition, but allow me to explain.

As per the data, many Koreans believe that dog meat is brutally prepared and unsanitary. This isn't too far from the truth. In a report by SBS, a Korean news channel, a reporter went to a private dog meat farmer who operated from her own apartment. The dogs were packed together in filthy, small cages, and were riddled with diseases, while dead dogs filled up the freezer. Furthermore, the animals were killed in the open and often beaten alive to adrenalize and tenderize the meat (Han). Such barbaric practices should be reformed, and this applies to all livestock. I believe there must be as little suffering inflicted upon livestock as possible, and there should be sanitation standards to uphold. Furthermore, a large number of these dogs are strays instead of specifically being bred for food. The government does not regulate dogs the way it does other livestock, and therefore dog meat is not bound by the sanitary regulations in place for pork and poultry, leaving it susceptible to higher risks of diseases that diminish the quality of the meat. Such deplorable standards are not sufficient for any kind of meat to be prepared and consumed, much less dog meat. However, if we were to regulate the production of dog meat, the Korean government could register official dog farms and butchers who would maintain transparent breeding methods and follow strict regulations on sanitation and butchering techniques. Not only would this regulation create new jobs, but it would prevent dogs from being severely abused, while people who still wish to continue consuming dog meat would have access to a cleaner, more humane option.

I would also like to raise a few points regarding the environmental impact of dog farming. An article from *TIME Magazine* shows that around 30% of the world's land is used to raise crops that we do not eat, but instead feed to livestock. This land also represents a third of our total water consumption as a species (Walsh). Cattle can require up to 2000 kilograms of feed to produce a single kilogram of beef, and produce up to 1000 kilograms of carbon-based greenhouse gases in doing so. In 2006, the Food and Agriculture Organization issued a report stating that livestock may account for around 18% of total greenhouse gas emissions worldwide (Walsh). Korea is making efforts to promote sustainable development and renewable energy, but we haven't addressed our currently unsustainable agricultural system that uses an excessive amount of land, water, and natural resources to produce relatively miniscule amounts of meat while massively polluting the environment. Dog farming can only intensify this issue, considering that dogs themselves are carnivorous—meaning that they not only require land and water to be raised, but meat from animals that themselves require land, water, and crops to grow strong. In the current global climate crisis, we should do better to manage and gradually shrink our meat industry; farming dog meat only serves to put oil on the fire. Working towards regulation and gradual reduction is in our best interests in this regard.

To be clear, I am not advocating any moral reason to not eat dog. Often, critics of dog meat consumption are morally against it because dogs are bred as pets, and because of their high levels of intelligence and ability to 'connect' with people, as 'man's best friend.' These arguments do not hold for several reasons. For starters, dogs are not the only intelligent species of domesticated animal—according to "Thinking Pigs: A Comparative Review of Cognition, Emotion and Personality in *Sus Domesticus*," a study from Lori Marino and Christina M. Colvin for the *International Journal of Comparative Psychology*, evidence "suggests that pigs are cognitively complex and share many traits with animals whom we consider intelligent," yet they are massively farmed for meat. In addition, dog breeds such as the nureongi have frequently been specialized for food in many parts of Asia, where they are more frequently consumed (Ann). There is no distinction that separates dogs from pigs in terms of how permissible they are as food, except for the fact that most people in the West see dogs as pets and pigs as food. As *Slate* columnist Will Saletan comments in his article "Wok the Dog," the argument of these critics boils down to: "The value of an animal depends on how you treat it. If you befriend it, it's a friend. If you raise it for food, it's food." In short, the value is based on a non-fixed definition of what companion animals should be and what livestock should be. Cows are sacred in India, yet they are consumed in much of the world. Horses are often seen as work animals, yet they are commonly eaten in countries like France.

We are living in a world dominated by the West, and often we are subjected to their moral and cultural standards. It's obvious that this form of cultural imperialism is a factor in criticisms of the dog meat industry, given that almost all of the countries with a long history of dog meat consumption are in Asia, with the top three being China, Vietnam, and Korea (Ann). Critics rally supporters to take dogs from Asia destined for the market and resettle them as pets in the West. Dog eating should not be understood by the West's standards of morality. Ironically, these critics are the same people who are attempting to stop us from legalizing the industry. Instead of creating an environment that will prevent the needless abuse of dogs now, they are willing to let dogs continue suffering until Korea bans the trade outright, which is rather hypocritical for supposed animal rights activists. Since producing dog meat is neither banned nor explicitly legal, activists should be focused on how there are no standards that regulate the sanitation and wellbeing of the animals.

I support the aforementioned restrictions on the dog meat industry because I think we should pick our battles wisely—dog is not commonly eaten by a majority of the population anywhere, and if we can further improve our international image by helping to stop an already dying practice, it may be a sacrifice worth taking (Ann). Actress Brigitte Bardot (as well as Sepp Blatter, the former FIFA president) once said that dog meat is bad for Korea's "international image" (김, 학민). The fact remains that until Korea becomes influential enough to define cultural norms, our traditions will be considered barbaric to outsiders, and it may be beneficial to simply move on to bigger issues. A state's power is no longer solely defined by its military firepower, but by its cultural impact as well—and despite Korea's growing cultural exports worldwide, we will not be able to shake off this negative image of eating 'man's best friend.' I am not proposing regulations for moral reasons, but I believe my end goal is the same as the activists'.

There is nothing that dog meat offers that other meat does not and, while there are seemingly only disadvantages to eating it, there is much potential in first aiming to reduce its consumption. Even the better-known dishes that use dog meat in Korea have derivatives that are far more popular with the entire population (such as *yukgaejang*). But we are a free, democratic society, and some people will still want to eat dogs. Instead of either blindly bending to foreign demands for outright bans or tacitly approving the current abusive, unsanitary, and environmentally unfriendly methods of dog meat farming, Korea can find a middle ground that is a step towards reform. I know that you will have a lot of goals to meet in the coming five years and that this may not be something that you wish to prioritize. However, you have said before that you wish for Korea to make independent decisions for its own interests. The way I see it, this reform will not take too many resources or too much time to carry out, and has a great chance of satisfying a larger number of people. Therefore, I believe there is value in taking this proposal into consideration.

Sincerely,
Jaehyoung Ju

WORKS CITED:

Ann, Yong-geun. "Korean's Recognition on Edibility of Dog Meat." *Korean Journal of Food and Nutrition*, vol. 13, no. 4, 2000, pp. 365-371.

Han, Sehyun 한, 세현. "병든 개까지 식당으로…개고기 위생 불량 심각" ["Sickly Dogs Used At Restaurants: Dog Meat Hygiene Severely Compromised"]. *SBS News* SBS뉴스, 12 July 2013, news.sbs.co.kr/news/endPage.do?news_id=N1001880810.

Kim, Hakmin 김, 학민. "80년대, 보신탕은 울었다" ["80s, The Era of Dog Meat Prohibition"]. *The Hankyoreh* 한겨레, 418th ed., 16 July 2002, legacy.h21.hani.co.kr/section-021087000/2002/07/021087000200207160418052.html.

Kim, Kisung 김, 기성. "'이재명은'모란 개고기 시장'을 어떻게 없앴나 원문보기: a" ["How Did Lee Jaemyung Eradicate Moran Dog Meat Market?"]. *The Hankyoreh* 한겨레, 13 Dec. 2016, www.hani.co.kr/arti/society/area/774431.html.

Marino, Lori, and Christina M. Colvin. "Thinking Pigs: A Comparative Review of Cognition, Emotion, and Personality in *Sus domesticus*." *International Journal of Comparative Psychology*, vol. 28, 2015.

Saletan, William. "Wok the Dog." *Slate*, 16 Jan. 2002, www.slate.com/articles/news_and_politics/frame_game/2002/01/wok_the_dog.html.

Song, Yoonjung 송, 윤정. "문재인 반려견 '마루', 청와대 '퍼스트 도그' 된다…유기견 '토리'도 합류할까" ["Moon Jaein's Dog 'Maru' to Become the 'First Dog' of the Blue House: Will His Rescue Dog 'Tory' Join the Bunch?"]. 아시아경제. *The Asia Business Daily* 아시아경제, 13 May 2017, www.asiae.co.kr/news/view.htm?idxno=2017051314304468144.

Walsh, Bryan. "The Triple Whopper Environmental Impact of Global Meat Production." *Time*, 16 Dec. 2013, science.time.com/2013/12/16/the-triple-whopper-environmental-impact-of-global-meat-production/.

*Solomon questions what it means to empathize with someone whose expe-
rience of racial discrimination you cannot share. Weaving personal anec-
dotes and reflection into conversation with essayists Claudia Rankine,
Leslie Jamison, and Ta-Nehisi Coates, she establishes her own ethos as an
empathetic reader and thinker. (Instructor: Lorelei Ormrod)*

EMPATHY

Saianna Solomon

I shuddered at the sound of his menacing voice as he made it clear
that my presence was not welcome. "Hey boy . . . I could stick
this fork into your neck!" he bellowed. I winced. Laughter
erupted around me. He jabbed me in my back and stomped on
my feet as he continued spouting profanities and threats for me to get
out of his face and out of the store. I was terrified. I had no idea what
was going to happen next, what derogatory name he would shout at
me next, which part of my body he would seek to ravage next and with
what weapon, or if I would be strong enough to sit back and take it.

A gentle tap on my shoulder alerted me that the situation—the
simulation—was over. I opened my tightly shut eyes, peeled my hands
off the counter and placed the headphones back on the designated
rack. Petrifying, terrorizing, heart-wrenching. These words are insuf-
ficient to thoroughly depict my experience at the 'lunch counter simulator' at the Center for Human and Civil Rights, but they will have
to do. But was that experience even mine? After all, these petrifying
encounters had not actually happened to me. They were but simula-
tions of the Greensboro sit-ins, a reenactment of the encounters at
lunch counters staged by African American participants in the nonvi-
olent protests of the civil rights movements of the 1960s. Yet, even as
my eyes closed, I imagined myself at the lunch counter as a black
male, feeling the emotions that seemed appropriate in the circumstances presented. Upon opening my eyes and leaving the simulation
counter, I was brought back to the reality: I inhabit the body of an
Indo-Caribbean young adult female. How could I possibly know or
even begin to imagine what it really felt like to be an African

American male at a lunch counter sit-in decades ago? Nevertheless, shaking the gripping feelings I felt during the simulation seemed impossible. Had I been too empathetic, or was I being empathetic at all? Was I empathizing with the black male during the civil rights movement during the simulation or was I less altruistic than that? Was I simply imagining how I would feel in an experience like that? What was my relationship to the black male during the simulation? And what is the nature of empathy? Before, I had interpreted empathy as putting oneself in another's shoes to feel what that person felt. Yet I felt the same emotions of terror mixed with subtle determination even after I exited the 'body' of the black male at the lunch counter. Is empathy an ongoing experience, or is it a fleeting feeling demarcated by the beginning and end of a situation, an altercation, a confrontation, or perhaps even a simulation?

Claudia Rankine explores empathy in *Citizen: An American Lyric*, posing the question: "How difficult is it for one body to feel the injustice wheeled at another? Are the tensions, the recognitions, the disappointments, and the failures that exploded in the riots too foreign?" (116). Rankine was responding to a conversation with an English novelist in which she was asked if she would write about Mark Duggan, a black man who was shot dead on August 4, 2011, in Tottenham, London, and whose death sparked the Hackney riots. She responded to his question by asking, "Why don't you?" and was then met with "[slight irritation]" from the novelist (116). She begins to wonder how arduous it is for one's body to not just feel compassion or sorrow for the injustice hurled at another body but to actually *feel the injustice*. Rankine notes that within this English novelist's body, "grief exists for Duggan as a black man gunned down," but there is no "urgency" in his body in response to the injustices, the "compromises, deaths, and tempers" over time which she as a black American woman, a black body, is all too familiar with but which "the man made of English sky" is not and apparently cannot be familiar with (117). The very phrase "made of English sky" directly contrasts with Rankine's "black body" (117) to highlight a physical difference between Rankine and the novelist that appears to translate into the difference in the immediacy they feel regarding Duggan's murder. Because the "English sky" could never reflect "black," because he does not know what it is to move through life as a black body, the novelist unconsciously renounces any responsibility that he, as an English novelist, could be charged with in writing about the death of the English Duggan. Rankine seems to be proposing that it is truly difficult to put oneself—one's body—in another's body if, to begin with, there is hardly any commonality between the two bodies and their awarenesses, experiences, histories, and realities. But how much of the ability to empathize with another being is concerned with being able to physically imagine oneself in another's body? Do the physical differences between our bodies and thus how our "bodies [move] through the same life differently" (Rankine 117) create hurdles that prevent the journey of empathy? Is empathy, besides being an emotional journey and experience, at the same time a physical one?

To Leslie Jamison, author of *The Empathy Exams*, empathy involves getting past that hurdle. She describes empathy as moving beyond what can be seen, "acknowledging a horizon of context that extends beyond what you can see" and recognizing that the unspoken and the unseen are just as connected, if not more so, to someone's "trauma" (5). It is recognizing that the physical and the present do not comprehensively reflect a person, and that to truly empathize with that person takes genuine interest in understanding what hides behind their exterior and even deep in their past. Jamison further explores the meaning of empathy by way of its etymology, which reveals that "empathy" comes from the Greek words that mean "into" and "feeling," signifying a motion into "another person's pain as you'd enter another country . . . by way of query" (6). As physical as this imagery may seem at first, Jamison is suggesting that one has to be both mentally and emotionally invested in the journey to this foreign place. Perhaps the part where most falter, as the English novelist did, is in this initial step—being truly invested in another's pain, enough to be open to understanding it and willing to feel it as they do. Jamison seems to propose a way to launch oneself into this journey by making the conscious decision to "pay attention, to extend [oneself]" (23). In Jamison's eyes, empathy is no less genuine if the choice is made to embark upon the journey. As she analyzes her response to her brother's Bell's Palsy diagnosis she notes that "empathy isn't just something that happens to us . . . The act of choosing simply means we've committed ourselves to a set of behaviors greater than the sum of our individual inclinations" (23). Empathy involves work, the effort of "getting inside another person's state of heart or mind" (Jamison 23). It involves putting aside one's own emotions and making the decision to seek to understand rather than to be understood, to love rather than to be loved.

President Obama describes empathy as a means to "find common ground" as, in journalist John Paul Rollert's words, "we unburden ourselves of the trivial rigidities that divide us" (qtd. in Rollert; Rollert). Claudia Rankine's *Citizen: An American Lyric* and Ta-Nehisi Coates's *Between the World and Me* are both books which seem to put my empathy on trial as I consciously wrestle to "find common ground" between myself and the individuals in the books. *Between the World and Me* challenges me to journey into Coates's pain, skepticism, courage, and every emotion in between as he writes an intimate letter to his son about the realities of being black in the United States. *Citizen* gives me the opportunity to meld into the body of Rankine as she candidly details the microaggressions she experiences daily as well as striking, racist injustices against black bodies. What makes these readings especially trying are their themes of racism and prejudice, which Coates describes as a "visceral experience," something that is encountered within and thus must be felt, not merely read about on a page, to be understood (Coates 10).

Coates skillfully tackles race and what it means to be living in a black body in America in a way that leaves no room for refutation, as it is his own experience that he writes from. He writes bluntly to his son, Samori, about growing up in Baltimore: how he had to learn the codes of the streets in order to get by and "shield [his] body," and about the "myths and narratives" of the world of a black body that Samori has yet to uncover and unravel (23, 21). Through this intimate letter to his son, a reader of *Between the World and Me* becomes aware of the many overlooked injustices faced by the black body in America. Coates takes no pleasure in sugarcoating the realities of this world in this letter and, like Malcom X, whom he so admired, he "[makes] it plain, never mystical or esoteric" because, like Malcolm X, Coates's concern is rooted "in the work of the physical world" (36). While this long letter, profoundly emotional, may make readers feel uncomfortable, it is in this very way that Coates enables his readers to empathize. Through the overwhelming discomfort that engulfed me as I perused this epistolary autobiography, I was compelled to at the very least acknowledge the injustices faced by the black body in America; Coates thus brilliantly arouses in readers a longing for justice for the black body regardless of whether one is able to venture into the body mentally, emotionally, or 'physically,' like Jamison suggests.

Knowing that the pronoun 'you' was meant not for me but for Coates's son and other males inhabiting black bodies in America, it felt challenging to attempt to 'slip my skin' and see through Coates's eyes. However, upon contemplation, I came to the realization that being directly addressed was not necessary for empathy. If anything, it became easier to empathize as 'I' had already been removed from the equation. With knowledge of the biases, discrimination, plunder, and oppression of the black body, as reflected through the experiences of Coates himself, and without any reflection of my identity, my race, or my experiences, what was stopping me from truly internalizing his experiences and inhabiting his body, even for a second?

The answer I came to was that nothing was prohibiting me from 'slipping my skin' into Coates's other than the fact that I believed his book wasn't written for my demographic. Is it not a true test of empathy to make the conscious choice, as Jamison suggests, to embark upon a journey to an unknown land and be open to new findings and experiences, especially when the realities of this foreign place are so drastically different to one's own land? What better reason to choose to empathize than to experience what one cannot? By recognizing that the mind and the body are two separate things, I made the conscious decision to separate myself from my body and my experiences and was able to journey into what I thought Coates's experience would be like based on my interpretation of his written words. But did I feel what Coates felt? Perhaps I could never actually feel what Coates felt since my experience of empathy was founded in my subjective interpretation of what I had read of his experience. Perhaps this is an innate limitation of empathy itself. Perhaps empathy isn't completely void of subjectivity. Perhaps empathy in its purest form is just an ideal to which we aspire, a journey to a foreign place we long to traverse but whose final destination is inevitably influenced by our own past journeys and experiences. Perhaps each person's journey is unconsciously personalized so that no two journeys, even if they are to the same destination, are identical.

While Coates's use of the pronoun 'you' at first seemed to distance me from the intended audience, I found that Rankine's strategic utilization of the same pronoun made me feel included, like I was inside the scenes and experiences that were laid out before me in print. This is probably because *Citizen* delves into everyday encounters centered around 'you' and through the eyes of 'you.' Once again, as with Coates's *Between the World and Me*—but more so in Rankine's *Citizen*—the uncomfortable quotidian scenarios in which I found myself that were so foreign to my experiences as an Indo-Caribbean female forced me to leave my body. I confronted those uneasy, awkward, and sometimes painful encounters through the eyes of the 'you' which was sometimes Rankine and sometimes others in her book's vignettes. Yet in each uncomfortable, painful journey, I felt an ever-present comfort. It was the comfort of knowing somewhere inside of me that this body I was journeying to inhabit was not mine, will never be mine, that I probably would never face those uncomfortable confrontations in my own life. In moments like these, I was able to empathize and yet be aware at the same time that they were moments of empathy. I was aware that I was 'slipping my skin' and inhabiting a foreign place momentarily, and that no matter how painful and tearful these moments were, even if I couldn't shake these feelings afterwards, I still was not, am not, the real 'you' in the scenarios. I had the comfort of knowing that I could slip back into my own body and seek refuge there.

Even Rankine seems to recognize the limitations of empathy. She writes in the article "The Condition of Black Life Is One of Mourning" that "there really is no mode of empathy that can replicate the daily strain of knowing that as a black person you can be killed for simply being black." When asked about this statement in an interview for *The Guardian*, she clarifies that not even empathy is enough to allow one to know the burdens and plights of another body, particularly the black body. She goes on to say that "empathy is not a cure" (qtd. in Kellaway). Empathy does not heal the wounded. It provides no remedy for the ailing. Empathy itself changes nothing for the beaten and the broken. For the empathizer, the traveler, it can bring about feelings of satisfaction, pleasure, and a moment of learning, while for the person empathized with, empathy changes nothing. Regardless of whether empathy is experienced as an ongoing journey or a mere peek into another life, empathy remains the experience of the empathizer. It's even as if the person being empathized with is a mere bystander in the journey of the traveler. If empathy remains an experience for the empathizer, then what remains for the 'empathized'? What does it serve for Jamison's brother? What remains for Rankine and Coates? What is there for the black man at the lunch counter in the 1960s?

I am left asking why I or anyone else would *choose* to embark upon a journey into another's pain. Is it pleasurable for one to truly "feel the injustice wheeled at another" (Rankine 116)? Is feeling the pain of another the only way that we can truly be concerned for them? Are we so naturally self-absorbed that we need to feel another's pain to validate its existence? Do we need to first feel another's pain to recognize its importance? Or perhaps empathy is simply a mechanism we use to prove our humanity to no one other than ourselves.

WORKS CITED

Coates, Ta-Nehisi. *Between the World and Me*. Spiegel & Grau, 2015.

Jamison, Leslie. *The Empathy Exams*. Graywolf Press, 2014.

Kellaway, Kate. "Claudia Rankine: 'Blackness in the White Imagination Has Nothing to Do With Black People.'" *The Guardian*, 27 Dec. 2015, www.theguardian.com/books/2015/dec/27/claudia-rankine-poet-citizen-american-lyric-feature.

Rankine, Claudia. *Citizen: An American Lyric*. Graywolf Press, 2014.

—. "The Condition of Black Life Is One of Mourning." *The New York Times Magazine*, 22 June 2015, www.nytimes.com/2015/06/22/magazine/the-condition-of-black-life-is-one-of-mourning.html.

Rollert, John Paul. "*Between the World and Me*: Empathy Is a
    Privilege." *The Atlantic*, 28 Sept. 2015,
    www.theatlantic.com/politics/archive/2015/09/between-the-
    world-and-me-empathy-is-a-privilege/407647/.

Why did medieval mystics change their attitudes about eating over time? In this research essay, Teo challenges one-dimensional interpretations. Carefully and clearly structured, this essay argues that an understanding of fasting in medieval Christianity must consider not only changing religious doctrines but also gender ideologies. (Instructor: Melissa Vise)

THE SIGNIFICANCE OF FOOD FOR MYSTICS IN THE MIDDLE AGES

Phionna Teo

Throughout the Middle Ages, medieval mystics' conception of food and its significance changed drastically. The Benedictines saw food as a necessary source of strength for holy men, viewing extreme abstinence as a danger of spiritual pride. Yet in the thirteenth century, the founding of the Franciscan Order saw a paradigm shift in Benedictine attitudes towards food. St. Francis preached the idea of the *vita apostolica*—choosing evangelical poverty by renouncing worldly possessions. Some scholars argue that this new way of being holy resulted in the shift from moderation to extreme fasting and Eucharistic devotion. However, extreme fasting was more prominent in female sainthood than in male sainthood, which suggests that this was primarily a gendered shift. While historians are often inclined to attribute such behavioral changes to the emergence of new religious movements and beliefs, the analysis of the gendered shift in mystics' understanding of food suggests that historians must critically consider the role of both cultural and religious factors in these changing narratives. These cultures cannot, ultimately, be separated; an understanding of the interaction between them and religion is required to explain the drastic shift in the conception of food by mystics over time.

Benedictines, such as the mystics St. Bernard of Clairvaux (1090-1153), and St. Hildegard of Bingen (1098-1179), regarded food as a necessary form of nourishment for work. The Order of St. Benedict is "a monastic tradition that stems from the origins of the Christian monastic movement in the late third century"; it became "the rule of choice for European monasteries from the ninth century onwards" (Theisen). In the chapter "On the Measure of Food," the written *Rule of St. Benedict* stated that in monasteries, two cooked dishes shall suffice for dinner but to "let a third dish be added [if] any fruit or fresh vegetables are available." If the day's work was heavy, the Abbot could "add something to the fare," although frugality was to be observed, and over-indulgence was to be strictly avoided. "The sick who are very weak" were exempted from the rule that all should "abstain entirely from eating the flesh of four-footed animals." St. Benedict also permitted wine; this clause was a relaxation of the ascetic practice of the recent past, a pragmatic concession since monastics of Benedict's "time" could not be persuaded that wine was improper for them (Benedict). In a commentary on *The Rule of St. Benedict*, Paul Delatte argues that St. Benedict "[did] not propose to drive all his monks to heroic mortification and extreme severity towards the flesh," and that abbots had to sometimes persuade people to eat (293). The Benedictines "[ate] to live; [they took] what [was] needful to sustain [them] in [their] work" (Delatte 293). As monastics emphasized moderation and sustenance, there was great laxity and flexibility in their relationship with food. Twelfth-century monastics, such as Hildegard, were bolder in their reading of the dietary scriptures, suggesting that "cheese, eggs and fish might be permitted," showing that the dietary requirements of the Benedictines had become more lax over time (Clark 119).

The founding of the Franciscan order in 1209 by St. Francis of Assisi (1181-1226) heralded a new conception of food for medieval mystics. St. Francis advocated for the *vita apostolica*, or the apostolic life: an uncompromising way of following in the footsteps of the crucified Christ by returning to the gospel. Key elements of St. Francis's new mode of gospel life included absolute poverty (avoiding all contact with money), penance, devotion to the Eucharist, service to the Church, and "solidarity with the poor and outcasts" (McGinn 43-45). The apostolic life meant that St. Francis was not confined to a community as the Benedictines were, but was able to roam around in public to preach. St. Francis also had a striking rapport with animals, encouraging Pope John Paul II to proclaim him patron saint of the ecological movement (Burr). With the rise in popularity of St.

Francis's apostolic life, which urged the giving up of all worldly possessions to imitate Christ, one could expect a change in thinking about food for the mystics. Perhaps mystics would move from the moderation and laxity of the Benedictines to the extreme fasting of the Franciscans. G. J. M. Bartelink argues that extreme asceticism "makes possible the *imitatio Christi* and total devotion to God" because the "restriction of material needs" is the first step to attaining "inner abstinence" (205). In fact, "the expression 'apostolic life' had been applied to the manner of life of perfect, ascetic Christians" even before St. Francis's time (Bartelink 206). It can therefore be argued that the will to follow Christ's model in the Late Middle Ages made pious men and women lead an ascetic life, heralding a change in the conception of worldly food.

With both his emphasis on absolute poverty in imitation of Christ and his love for animals, St. Francis could be expected to advocate a stricter view of food. Yet St. Francis had a relatively liberal attitude towards eating. In his Rule of 1221, it is stated that "in obedience to the Gospel, they (the friars) may eat of any food put before them," even meat or delicacies (qtd. in Sorrell 75). Francis's opinion was a product of the return to an "evangelical standard that valued food as a part of God's creation and thus as good and worthy for humanity to eat" (Sorrell 75). Roger Sorrell argues that "this positive injunction which Francis accepted as the pattern for his revival of apostolic life harmonized well with his belief in creation's goodness and with his understanding of creation as an expression of divine largesse dispensed for humanity's needs" (75). His tolerance was considered liberal for an ascetic, and he was eager to show that following the apostolic standard in accepting a diversity of food did not necessarily mean saintly self-denial.

The leader of the revival of the *vita apostolica* did not turn to extreme fasting, but his followers—in particular his female followers—often did so in their interpretations. While the surge in popularity of the *vita apostolica* and *imitatio Christi* aimed at self-denial, men and women had different means of achieving these objectives: men generally inflicted pain on their own bodies through self-flagellation and the deprivation of all the pleasures and comforts that life could offer, while women chose to fast to imitate Jesus's suffering (Forcen

650). In fact, fasting in a religious context seemed exclusive to women. Between late antiquity and the fifteenth century, there were "at least thirty cases of women who were reputed to eat nothing at all except the Eucharist, but . . . only one or possibly two male examples of such behavior" (Bynum, "Fast" 3). Furthermore, 30 percent of female saints had "extreme austerities" as central aspects of their holiness (Bynum, "Fast" 3). Over 50 percent had "illnesses" (often brought on by fasting and other penitential practices) that were "major factors in their reputations for sanctity" (Bynum, "Fast" 3). It is thus evident that in the Middle Ages, fasting was more prominent in female than male practices of piety.

The lives of St. Catherine of Siena and St. Marie D'Oignies demonstrate the centrality of fasting to the lives of religious women. According to Raymond of Capua, St. Catherine's hagiographer, after St. Catherine received Holy Communion, "heavenly graces and consolations [so] flooded her soul" that they altered "the action of her stomach" such that she could no longer eat; to eat would cause her bodily suffering, and visions incited her not to do so (160-161). St. Catherine knew by actual experience that "to abstain from food kept her well and strong, whilst to take it made her weak and sickly" (Raymond 161). Raymond writes that "while her body fasted, her spirit fed with increasing frequency and zest on the Bread from heaven" (164). Each time St. Catherine received Communion, "the overflowing grace it brought her seemed to supersede her mere sense faculties . . . and the supernatural vitality the Holy Spirit imparted to her took possession of her . . . soul and body" (Raymond 164). Medieval ascetics considered regular food corporeal. They also saw their bodies as corporeal, and thus distinguished them from spirit. In order to go beyond the corporeal into the spiritual and supernatural, one had to feed on spiritual food—"bread from heaven"—and be nourished by it. Similarly, Jacques de Vitry writes that St. Marie D'Oignies endured such extreme fasting that "she suffered pain from a cold and constricted stomach and only a little food would cause her to bloat" (23). St. Marie fasted continuously for three years on bread and water, and at times went without any food or water for months:

> As long as her soul was so full and copiously overflowing with
> spiritual food, it did not allow her to accept any refreshment from
> corporeal food . . . when she had debilitated her body by fasting,
> by so much the more freely did she make her spirit fat. (40)

Like Raymond's description of the mystics' conception of food, de
Vitry sees in St. Marie a separation between corporeal nourishment
and spiritual nourishment. Unlike the Benedictines, who saw corporeal food as necessary nourishment for the body, women such as St.
Catherine and St. Marie sought a spiritual nourishment through
strong Eucharistic devotion and viewed corporeal nourishment as
unnecessary.

In contemporary psychiatric understanding, these medieval
female ascetics exhibited behaviors commonly associated with eating
disorders. Rudolph Bell, in *Holy Anorexia*, argues that religious
women practiced self-starvation for holy purposes because of insecu-
rity and the need to pursue a "culturally approved objective with fanat-
ical, compulsive devotion" (21). He compares the holy starvation of
religious women like St. Catherine and St. Marie to the modern-day
illness of anorexia nervosa. In both instances, self-mortification
begins as "the girl fastens onto a highly valued societal goal (bodily
health, thinness, self-control in the twentieth century/spiritual health,
fasting, and self-denial in medieval Christendom)" (Bell 20). If these
women could convince others that their fasting and self-denial were
inspired by God, they would be marked with sainthood and holiness.
Furthermore, from a psychodynamic point of view, some academics
have understood anorexia nervosa as an act of masochism: for example, as St. Catherine of Siena suffered more, the more cathartic and
holy she felt (Forcen 651). Yet to merely understand this extreme
behavior from an individual psychological approach would be incomplete, for such analysis "lacks firm grounding within the cultural context of medieval Europe" (Lester 189).

In *Holy Feast, Holy Fast*, historian Caroline Walker Bynum contends that holy fasting was in many ways distinct from anorexia nervosa, as it occurred in an entirely different sociocultural context and
for a different purpose. Then, food was important to women reli-
giously because it was important to them socially. Because of "the tra-

ditional association of women with food preparation *rather than* food consumption," food was "*the* resource that women control[led]"; hence, "women found it easier to renounce food than anything else" (Bynum, *Holy* 191). Since men controlled money and property, it was easy for St. Francis of Assisi to renounce such items in accordance with the apostolic life. However, since women controlled food exclusively, they "gave up food because [they] had nothing else to give up for Christ" (193). Yet fasting was not just a simple act of religious piety and renouncement; it was also a special way of imitating Christ. Bynum maintains that medieval ascetic women were not anorexics and bulimics only because their behaviors were expressed and experienced through a religious medium (207). She argues that food asceticism, for these female mystics, was not an act of masochism; rather, it enabled them to fuse with a Christ whose suffering saves the world (Bynum, *Holy* 218). Female fasting was not an effort to punish the flesh, but to use the flesh in an empowered way to imitate Christ: "the point was pain because the pain was Christ's" (Bynum, *Holy* 218).

However, both Bell and Bynum fail to consider the dominance of patriarchy in the Church of medieval Europe. Both of the two primary sources analyzed in this essay are written by male hagiographers, which poses a "question [about the] relationship between men's prescriptions for women and women's own self-understanding" (Hollywood 79). Raymond of Capua, in writing a hagiography of St. Catherine of Siena, may have placed greater emphasis on her "paranormal bodily experiences" in order "to prove her holiness and establish her cult as a saint" (Scott 136). Because Raymond's goal was to ultimately call for St. Catherine's canonization, his account of St. Catherine focused on her mystical experiences of the body, "first by privations and fasts, and later by supernatural experiences so strong that her weak female body could survive only by receiving more and more extraordinary graces," rather than through her theology or her public actions (Scott 142). This can be contrasted with St. Catherine's own writings, letters and treatises that demonstrate her theological understanding and show her to "have been considerably less interested and immersed in exceptional and supernatural occurrences than [Raymond] believed her to have been" (142). Raymond describes St. Catherine's condition as "at the same time filled and fasting; empty of the things of the body, filled with the things of the spirit" (164). Raymond saw St. Catherine as an empty vessel through which God worked. St. Catherine was essentially 'empty,' only filled with all things spiritual through God's will. St. Catherine herself was not wondrous; rather, her significance was that God worked wonders through her. This suggests that The Life of Catherine of Siena was ultimately a male representation of female sainthood, and that Raymond's work established the model for female sanctity—one marked by extreme fasting—which later inspired other holy women to follow suit. The question of whether or not St. Catherine did indeed exhibit extreme fasting behavior is irrelevant; what is relevant is how male portrayal of such behaviors framed the female model of sanctity.

The influence of male representations of female sanctity was so great that female saints became synonymous with fasting, despite their theological achievements and social impact. Some historians even argue that religious fasting enabled the creation of these saints' entire personas. James White argues that St. Catherine's religious fasting enabled the creation of her public and political persona. As extreme ascetic malnutrition pushed St. Catherine's body to cease menstruation, she became masculinized via her spiritual use of food. Thus, she was able to assume the (otherwise masculine) authority to intervene in political executions, exhort monarchs, and help end the Avignon papacy (White 157). These facts further point to the dominance of the patriarchy in the Church, so much so that for St. Catherine of Siena to assert authority as a religious woman, she had to first be masculinized through fasting. In St. Catherine's hagiography, Raymond describes the mental anguish that St. Catherine went through in her deliberation between following God's will to fast and her "obedience to those over her" (162). Those over her—patriarchal leaders—concluded that "she must not follow her own judgment, but rely on the guidance of her advisers" (162). This view reflects the Church's male-centric social hierarchy and the expectation of women in the Church to heed a male style of sainthood.

The drastic change in the conception of food for medieval mystics from one of moderation and laxity to one of extreme asceticism is complex. While some scholars would claim it was a result of a change in the theological conception of the corporeal world, others would note that this shift was a gendered one—only female mystics had such a unique relationship with food. Yet scholarship on the significance of food for female mystics in the Middle Ages often forms "a dichotomy between the cultural and the individual" (Lester 188). Bell and other psychologists examine the phenomenon of religious fasting through the lenses of the individual female saint and her psychodynamic concerns, omitting an analysis of her specific cultural context. Bynum, on the other hand, focuses more on the relevance of food within a specific cultural framework. She examines food as a cultural symbol, yet does not analyze the "possible psychological significance of food symbolism or ascetic practices for" female mystics (Lester 188). Furthermore, these schools of thought fail to critically examine their primary sources, omitting the role of the male hagiographer. Ultimately, to fully understand the reason behind this shift, we must consider a combination of the theological and individual psychological and sociocultural factors. Socio-culturally, women had an established relationship with food, and, with the rise in popularity of a new theological practice—the *vita apostolica*—women utilized food and fasting as a way of imitating Christ. Male hagiographers institutionalized this behavior to the extent that fasting became a model of female sanctity, which may have resulted in pressure for religious women to emulate later on. No individual factor can be extricated from the others in an attempt to completely understand this historical shift.

WORKS CITED

Bartelink, G. J. M. "Monks: The Ascetic Movement as a Return to the Aetas Apostolica." *The Apostolic Age in Patristic Thought*, edited by A. Hilhorst, Brill, 2004, pp. 204-218.
Bell, Rudolph M. *Holy Anorexia*. U of Chicago P, 1987.
Benedict. *The Rule of St. Benedict: The Abingdon Copy.* Translated by John Stephen Chambelin, Pontifical Institute of Mediaeval Studies, 1982.

Burr, David. "Selections from Thomas of Celano: First and Second Lives of St. Francis." 1996, people.bu.edu/dklepper/RN307/francis.html.

Bynum, Caroline Walker. "Fast, Feast, and Flesh: The Religious Significance of Food to Medieval Women." *Representations*, no. 11, 1985, pp. 1-25.

—. *Holy Feast and Holy Fast: The Religious Significance of Food to Medieval Women.* U of California P, 1988.

Clark, James G. *The Benedictines in the Middle Ages.* Boydell Press, 2011.

Delatte, Paul, and Justin McCann. *The Rule of St. Benedict; a Commentary.* Burns, Oates & Washbourne, 1921.

de Vitry, Jacques. *The Life of Marie D'Oignies.* Translated by Margot H. King, Peregrina Publishing Company, 1989.

Forcen, Fernando Espi, and Carlos Espi Forcen. "The Practice of Holy Fasting in the Late Middle Ages." *The Journal of Nervous and Mental Disease*, vol. 203, no. 8, 2015, pp. 650-653.

Hollywood, Amy. "Inside Out: Beatrice of Nazareth and Her Hagiographer." *Gendered Voices: Medieval Saints and Their Interpreters*, edited by Catherine M. Mooney, U of Pennsylvania P, 1999, pp. 78-98.

Lester, Rebecca J. "Embodied Voices: Women's Food Asceticism and the Negotiation of Identity." *Ethos*, vol. 23, no. 2, 1995, pp. 187-222.

McGinn, Bernard. *The Flowering of Mysticism: Men and Women in the New Mysticism: 1200-1350.* Crossroad, 1998.

Raymond of Capua. *The Life of Catherine of Siena.* Translated by Conleth Kearns, Scolar P, 1978.

Scott, Karen. "Mystical Death, Bodily Death: Catherine of Siena and Raymond of Capua on the Mystic's Encounter with God." *Gendered Voices: Medieval Saints and Their Interpreters*, edited by Catherine M. Mooney, U of Pennsylvania P, 1999, pp. 136-167.

Sorrell, Roger D. *St. Francis of Assisi and Nature: Tradition and Innovation in Western Christian Attitudes toward the Environment.* Oxford UP, 1988.

Theisen, Jerome. "The Benedictines: An Introduction." *The Order of Saint Benedict*, www.osb.org/gen/benedictines.html.

White, James. "Hungering for Maleness: Catherine of Siena and the Medieval Public Sphere." *Religious Studies and Theology*, vol. 33, no. 2, 2014, pp. 157-171.

Are journalists heroes exposing the truth for the good of their audience, or manipulators obscuring facts for their personal gain? Scott explores this problem by analyzing the film Nightcrawler *in the context of other movies about the news industry and through the history of sensational media, from yellow journalism to click-bait. (Instructor: Stephen Butler)*

A NETWORK OF LIES

Elijah Scott

Lou follows the foreman into a small, dank, and messy office to settle the price negotiation for the wire he has just stolen from a construction site. He is wearing a brown leather jacket with his hair slicked down and his hands linked behind his back. His cheekbones are sunken, yet his eyes bulge out of his head, making him look constantly alert. In a slightly robotic tone, he says, "I am willing to take less to establish a business relationship. If that's your last, best offer, then I guess I accept" (*Nightcrawler*). The foreman casually agrees, tells him to unload the material from his truck, and then gets back to work at his desk. But he is quickly interrupted by Lou again, who walks directly over to the desk. This time Lou asks for a job, giving a formal speech that almost resembles a verbal resume: "Who am I? I'm a hard worker, I set high goals, and I've been told that I'm persistent." The foreman looks back down at his work and continues to shuffle through it, listening to Lou go on. Lou tells him that he doesn't always expect consideration of his needs, despite growing up in a generational "self-esteem movement." At the end of the day, he will work his ass off, he says, because "[his] motto is: If you wanna win the lottery, you have to make the money to buy a ticket." The foreman chuckles. Thinking that he has sufficiently charmed him, Lou tries to seal the deal, even offering to start working that night. Yet the foreman quickly replies, "I'm not hiring a fucking thief." Lou's facial expressions quickly turn from angry, to sad, to slightly hysterical. The scene ends with Lou nodding his head and laughing in agreement with the foreman's decision.

This particular scene is representative of Dan Gilroy's *Nightcrawler* (2014). It establishes the attitude Lou, played by Jake

Gyllenhaal, has towards hard work, and how far he's willing to go to develop a career for himself. Yet it also establishes his lack of self-awareness, particularly of the difference between right and wrong. Before the previous scene, Lou beat up and possibly even killed a security guard to steal the wire from the construction site. Yet here he is now, already emotionally detached from his previous actions and moving on to future ambitions. It wasn't until the foreman uttered the words "I'm not hiring a fucking thief," that even I, an audience member, was reminded of Lou's sociopathic tendencies. This scene also foreshadows some of the ruthless behavior that Lou displays in the rest of the movie as he finds his calling as a stringer: a freelance video journalist who sells content to news stations. Lou blackmails Nina—KWLA 6's morning news director—into having sex with him, he adjusts the body of a dead hit-and-run victim just to "get the right shot," and he lies to the police about not being able to identify the gunman who committed a triple homicide in Grenada Hills. Lastly, after a car chase with the gunman, Lou betrays his partner Rick by telling him to go film the dead gunman, who was in fact still alive. The gunman kills Rick, and Lou stands in the background with his own camera, capturing the whole thing. As Rick takes his last breath, Lou tells him—again, without any remorse—that he didn't trust Rick enough to take the necessary actions required to work at his company. In that moment, it becomes clear that the only person Lou truly—and ironically—trusts is himself.

Nightcrawler is unlike many other well-known movies that put journalists at the center of the story. Films such as *All the President's Men* and *Good Night, and Good Luck* feature journalists as their heroes, willing to risk almost everything to expose those who are being dishonest and to provide the public with the truth. Yet in *Nightcrawler*, the journalism industry—presented through the stringer and the news station itself—is ruthless, greedy, and willing to manipulate the truth for the sake of a good story. Journalism scholar Brian McNair argues that while *Nightcrawler* might be excessive in its portrayal of the 'Fourth Estate,' it is important to expose this dishonest side to journalism. In "Rock Stars Versus Reptiles: Lou Bloom, Photojournalism and *Nightcrawler*," McNair identifies Lou Bloom as the "reptile . . . screen journalist" (615). This doesn't simply refer to Lou's reptilian features. Unlike "rock star" journalists, whom McNair describes as "glamorous, sexy, romantic rebels," the "reptile" journalist "embodies without apology or hesitation the very worst of what journalism can be in market-driven media culture" ("Rock Stars" 615; *Journalists* 139). So how culturally significant is this character in comparison to the other characterizations of journalists in film? How does *Nightcrawler* change the viewer's understanding of the news media?

Although I was somewhat disturbed by the reptilian, sociopathic behavior of Lou Bloom, I was also refreshed. I saw it as an honest way to examine how media corporations influence our news, and what we are, or are not, exposed to. Other journalism-focused movies which I had seen before, such as *All the President's Men* and *Spotlight*, depict journalists and the industry as a group of heroes, fighting to expose the truth and to seek justice. *Nightcrawler* showss, in my eyes, the industry for what it really is: a business. And as a business, news stations have an incentive to report on sensational stories that often play into people's suspicions and fears, or even manifest new ones. But is that too harsh an assessment?

In his interview with *Nightcrawler* director Dan Gilroy and producer Tony Gilroy, *Deadline*'s Mike Fleming Jr. couldn't help but wonder "what did . . . journalists, as a breed, do to offend the Gilroy clan so much that [they] could paint such a cynical picture about news gathering?" Fleming approaches this question from the context of his reflection on the life and career of *The Washington Post*'s Ben Bradlee, who had recently died. Bradlee is primarily famous for his bold decision to release the Pentagon Papers, "a secret Pentagon history of the Vietnam War" to the public (Kaiser). The Nixon administration took issue with these stories and attempted, but failed, to prevent their publication. Bradlee also oversaw reporters Bob Woodward and Carl Bernstein's investigation of the Nixon administration's involvement with the break-in at the DNC's office at the Watergate Hotel, which eventually turned into the famous Watergate scandal. Upon Bradlee's death, President Obama spoke of him in this way:

> For Benjamin Bradlee, journalism was more than a profession—it
> was a public good vital to our democracy. . . . The standard he
> set—a standard for honest, objective, meticulous reporting—
> encouraged so many others to enter the profession. (qtd. in Kaiser)

Fleming and other reporters may have been inspired by this image of
a Bradlee-esque editor. The film *All the President's Men* perpetuated
this image of Bradlee through Jason Robards's portrayal of a hard-hit-
ting editor who pushed Woodward and Bernstein to the limit. In fact,
in the movie, Bradlee tells Woodward and Bernstein: "Nothing's rid-
ing on this except the, uh, first amendment to the Constitution, freedom of the press, and maybe the future of the country. Not that any
of that matters, but if you guys fuck up again, I'm going to get mad.
Goodnight." In this film, there is a sense of responsibility, a moral
obligation to American citizens that is prioritized over anything else,
even the president himself.

Yet as the Gilroy brothers remind Fleming, such morality is no
longer the reality of the journalism industry. In his answer to
Fleming's question, Dan Gilroy (as well as many others who reviewed
and discussed *Nightcrawler*) brings up the influence of one particular
movie, 1976's *Network*: "What [*Network*] accurately grabbed was the
moment when networks decided that news divisions had to make a
profit. [It] foresaw that when that happened, news would have to
become entertainment" (Gilroy qtd. in Fleming). BBC Reporter
Nicholas Barber seems to agree with Gilroy's reflection on *Network*.
Barber notes that when the movie was first released forty years ago,
"the poster warned audiences to prepare themselves 'for a perfectly
outrageous motion picture.'" And, given the cultural climate of the
time, this movie was "outrageous." American citizens had seen the
Watergate scandal and the release of the Pentagon Papers in addition
to many political/social riots. All of this created a revolutionary fervor,
or a movement to overthrow "the system." Released a few months
prior, *All the President's Men* had pushed the idea that journalists,
not politicians, were on the side of the people. So, until *Network* was
released, journalism wasn't necessarily seen as part of "the system."

But, as *Network*'s broadcasting company chairman, Arthur
Jensen, explains to the movie's main character, Howard Beale:

You are an old man who thinks in terms of nations and peoples.
There are no nations. There are no peoples . . . There is only IBM
and ITT and AT&T, and DuPont, Dow, Union Carbide and
Exxon. Those are the nations of the world today. The world is a
college of corporations, inexorably determined by the immutable
by-laws of business. (*Network*)

Beale is a veteran anchorman who threatens to kill himself during his
final broadcast after being given two-weeks notice that his show has
been cancelled due to its low ratings. Originally, Union Broadcasting
System panics and fires Howard for his behavior. Their concern does-
n't lie in the well-being of their own newscaster, but in his stunt's
effect on their ratings. However, the network's new division president, Max Schumacher, demands that Howard be allowed to say
goodbye to his viewers with dignity. But when the time comes,
Howard rants instead, claiming on-air that "life is bullshit."
Surprisingly, this is what brings viewers back to his show. The production team, specifically Diana Christiansen, ruthlessly played by
Faye Dunaway, is then keen to rebrand Howard as "the mad prophet
of the airwaves." She understands that in the mid-1970s, "the
American people are turning sullen. They've been clobbered on all
sides by Vietnam, Watergate, the inflation, the depression. They're
turned off, shot up, and they fuck themselves limp, and nothing helps.
. . . The American people want somebody to articulate their rage for
them." In other words, Diana realizes that Beale supplies what is in
demand in the market of frustrated and distrustful American citizens.
As a result, she continues to push this new genre of news in order to
increase ratings.

Diana is a reflection of many news producers today and is
arguably the inspiration behind Rene Russo's Nina Romina in
Nightcrawler. Nina seeks to increase ratings by promoting a narrative
of urban crime creeping into the Los Angeles suburbs. This is evident
when Nina explains her goal as a news producer to Lou: "The best and
clearest way that I can phrase it to you, Lou, to capture the spirit of
what we air, is think of our newscast as a screaming woman running
down the street with her throat cut." Ultimately, *Nightcrawler*
updates the message of *Network* for viewers, confirming the once

'outrageous' theory that journalism has in fact become an industry that prioritizes its profit margins over the truth. And although these films do not necessarily depict the 'fake news' discussed so much today, characters like Diana, Lou, and Nina foreshadow the greedy and manipulative mindset that has contributed to creating this phenomenon.

However, a knowledge of nineteenth-century journalism suggests that history may simply be repeating itself, and that journalism has the potential to once again return to its moral values. In the nineteenth century and early twentieth century, "a dependence on the familiar aspects of sensationalism—crime news, scandal and gossip, divorces and sex" gave rise to the phenomenon of "yellow journalism" (Gullason qtd. in Samuel). The journalists who participated in these practices exploited "the freedom of regulation" permitted under the First Amendment, and used the industry to simply make a profit (McKerns qtd. in Samuel). Often, the result was a "deliberate suppression of certain kinds of news, distortion of news actually published, studied unfairness toward certain classes, political organizations and social movements, systematic catering to powerful groups of advertisers" (Yarros qtd. in Samuel). Yet as early as 1898, a movement to stop yellow journalism emerged. That year, an unnamed publication wrote, "the public is becoming heartily sick of fake news and fake extras" (Pomerantz qtd. in Samuel). This attitude is what allowed 'highly conservative' newspapers like *The New York Times* to thrive while more famous yellow journalist William Randolph Hearst's *New York Journal* declined in sales. Additionally, the courts began to reinforce the constitutional right to privacy, which yellow journalism often violated. Lastly, in 1910, W. E. Miller proposed the journalism industry's first code of ethics (Samuel). All of these efforts brought legitimacy back to news publications and perpetuated the narrative behind films like *All the President's Men*. As Alexandra Samuel points out in "To Fix Fake News, Look to Yellow Journalism," this doesn't mean that "sensationalistic headlines, intrusive reporting, and journalism that placed sales over accuracy" were ever completely eradicated. But over the past two decades, the financial downturn of print newspapers in the internet era has reinvigorated the industry's desire to return to sensationalistic practices. In *Nightcrawler*, the gambit is to scare viewers into believing that there is a crime epidemic in Los Angeles caused by minorities; in the 2016 U.S. election, it was to use 'click-baity' headlines that would deepen the dramatic divide between political parties. Both techniques create biases that can significantly affect the way in which news media consumers view the world.

Before the 2016 election, many seemed to think that we still lived in a world of honest, unbiased journalism. Unlike nineteenth-century media consumers, we didn't seem to question the information we were given. Yet in 2014, *Nightcrawler* attempted to teach us that our news is in fact sensational and manipulated. And looking at *Nightcrawler* and characters like *Network*'s Diana Christiansen through the lens of yellow journalism, we can see that news has been a product of supply and demand for a long time. *Nightcrawler* suggests that both the viewers and producers of news are stuck in an old cycle. The 'Fourth Estate' needs to make a profit, and so they feed us what they know we'll pay for: a confirmation of our pre-existing biases, beliefs, fears, and suspicions. And as long as we continue to pay for what we already believe—instead of demanding the truth—we will never be able to escape this cycle. Hence, as Alexandra Samuel suggests, the solution is to "read, share and support the news and commentary produced by responsible media outlets, and see click journalism wither away, just as yellow journalism did a century ago." Once we do this, we can perhaps escape the frightening world of *Nightcrawler*, returning to an age of journalism dedicated to truthfully informing the consumer and producing content that is devoid of 'alternative facts.'

WORKS CITED

All the President's Men. Directed by Alan J. Pakula, performances by Jason Robards, Robert Redford, and Dustin Hoffman, Warner Bros., 1976.
Barber, Nicholas. "The 'outrageous' 40-year-old Film That Predicted the Future." *BBC News*, 30 Nov. 2016, www.bbc.com/culture/story/20161125-network-at-40-the-film-that-predicted-the-future.

Fleming Jr., Mike. "Dan and Tony Gilroy of 'Nightcrawler' Talk Media Ugliness In The Digital Age: Q&A." *Deadline*, 2 Nov. 2014, www.deadline.com/2014/11/nightcrawler-dan-gilroy-tony-gilroy-jake-gyllenhaal-1201270981/.

Kaiser, Robert G. "Ben Bradlee, legendary Washington Post editor, dies at 93." *The Washington Post*, 21 Oct. 2014, www.washingtonpost.com/national/ben-bradlee-legendary-washington-post-editor-dies-at-93/2014/10/21/3e4cc1fc-c59c-11df-8dce-7a7dc354d1b1_story.html.

McNair, Brian. *Journalists in Film: Heroes and Villains.* Edinburgh UP, 2010.

—. "Rock Stars Versus Reptiles: Lou Bloom, Photojournalism and *Nightcrawler*." *Journalism Practice*, vol. 9, no. 4, 3 July 2015, pp. 614-616.

Nightcrawler. Directed by Dan Gilroy, performances by Jake Gyllenhaal, Rene Russo, Riz Ahmed, and Bill Paxton, Open Road Films, 2014.

Network. Directed by Sidney Lumet, performances by Peter Finch, Faye Dunaway, William Holden, and Robert Duvall, United Artists, 1976.

Samuel, Alexandra. "To Fix Fake News, Look to Yellow Journalism." *JSTOR Daily*, 29 Nov. 2016, daily.jstor.org/to-fix-fake-news-look-to-yellow-journalism/.

Serpa examines how the film Birdman *blurs the line between fact and fiction, forcing its viewers to question their certainty about what is real. Her review highlights several conventions of this genre, crafting vivid representations of pivotal scenes and drawing on outside research to inform her analysis. (Instructor: Beth Machlan)*

BIRDMAN:
REALITY TAKES FLIGHT

Gabriela Serpa

Riggan Thomson is standing on the ledge of a New York City building! His expression is unsettling, his eyes trance-like, unwavering. His body takes up the whole screen as the audience in the movie theater watches him skeptically, chewing on their popcorn a little more slowly, leaning a little farther out of their seats with curiosity. Will he jump? While street horns blare and onlookers yell in what appears to be the normal soundscape of New York City, we see a tremor begin in Riggan's jaw. We don't know what's happening. Neither the on- nor off-screen audiences of the spectacle know what to expect. A bodiless voice in the movie asks: "Hey, is this for real or are you shooting a film?" (*Birdman*). "A film!" answers Riggan, but we aren't convinced. After an hour and a half of sitting through Alejandro Iñárritu's 2014 movie *Birdman*, the question of "is this for real or are you shooting a film?" doesn't come as a shock. Instead, it vocalizes the central problem invoked by the film itself: what is real, and what is fiction?

Michael Keaton plays Riggan Thomson, a washed-out celebrity made famous by his blockbuster role as the superhero Birdman. At the time the film begins, more than ten years have passed since the climax of Riggan's career, and he is haunted by his past, unable to move on from the remnants of Birdman's fame. In a desperate attempt to reclaim his name and reputation as an actor, he stages a Broadway production of Raymond Carver's "What We Talk About When We Talk About Love," with himself in the lead role. But Riggan's road to redemption isn't easy. Mike Shiner, the gifted actor starring alongside Riggan, is constantly combative, and theater critic Tabitha is determined to foil Riggan's efforts. These prove to be only some of the problems he encounters before opening night. Perhaps his biggest challenge is letting go of his superhero alter ego. Riggan literally cannot stop being Birdman when alone; at times, he has superpowers, levitates, shatters mirrors, and moves things with the power of his mind. He is often pictured having conversations with a man in a bird costume who we can only assume to be a younger version of himself as Birdman.

To make matters worse, in the midst of the flying, the levitating, and the superpowers, Riggan is painfully unsuccessful in being happy. He isn't an attentive parent to his daughter, Sam (Emma Stone), avoids his girlfriend, and drinks himself into despicable states. Riggan Thomson is a self-destructing man, who, in a desperate attempt to nurture his own vanity, brings to light the complicated nature of the human ego. Nonetheless, this quality combined with his ability to fly—or his belief that he can—generates the feeling that nothing is real. Flying has to be fiction—at least, that's what we tell ourselves. Throughout the whole movie, time and time again, we don't know what to think and are forced to reconsider our notions of fiction and reality to figure it out.

Riggan also has a lot to figure out when, after a drunken night of self-loathing, he wakes up on the steps of a walk-up building in Manhattan, disoriented and dirty, his head resting on a garbage bag. He turns around and cringes as a bodiless voice starts to taunt him. The camera zooms and swivels around him to show us that the voice belongs to Birdman, who is close to Riggan's ear, agitatedly reminding him, "You're bigger than life. You save people from their boring, miserable lives" (*Birdman*). As this occurs, we see a day like any other in the background; that is, until Riggan snaps his fingers and Birdman flies up, a missile is launched onto a car, a SWAT team invades the scene, helicopters begin to circle the area, and Birdman fires a laser at a giant metallic bird perched on top of a building. The chaos disappears as fast as it came. What did we just see? There was no shift in the camera, no filter, no sign to indicate that what occurred was a figment of Riggan's imagination. But people can't fly, and this movie isn't about superheroes, so he must have imagined everything. Right?

Not necessarily. In this scene, our first instinct is to dismiss what we just saw as unreal, but no actual aspect of the movie depicts it as imagined. More often than not, *Birdman*'s audience takes it upon itself to decide the parameters of fiction, but there is no real logic in how we do it other than our own sense of what is conventional. In the real world, we think, people can't fly, so Riggan can't fly. But there he is, right in front of us, flying.

It seems clear to us that Riggan is losing his mind, but there are no visual indications of a break in reality—quite the opposite, actually. Throughout the movie, the use of "the mad tracking shot—a long, rapturously complicated camera move that seems to defy all spatial and temporal logic"—creates the illusion of the film happening in one single shot (Romney). *Birdman*'s director of photography, Emmanuel Lubezki, justifies this choice with the idea that "life is continuing, and maybe not having cuts was going to help immerse the audience in that kind of emotional rhythm" (qtd. in Romney). The cinematography of *Birdman*, in its unprecedented technique and nature, looks to emulate what is real; using one shot means that there is no space to edit things out, to retake or to recreate scenes, because an average day, as Iñárritu puts it, "doesn't feel like a bunch of cuts. It feels like a constant move" (qtd. in Romney).

This honesty aims to make the film emulate the nature of a play, if not of reality. According to Emma Stone, rehearsing "*Birdman* was like theater because . . . everything had to be technically perfect, but then you had to be able to completely let go and play the truth of the scene, versus a choreographed dance. It was like everyone was walking on a tightrope. . . . If anyone hit your rope, everyone fell" (qtd. in D'Alessandro). *The New Yorker*'s Richard Brody calls *Birdman* "an administrative choreography of a most delicate theatrical artifice." In channeling the medium of theater through its fluid movement and single shot, the camera enables the audience to trust it, to understand it as a living organism that cannot show anything but what is actually happening on stage. Still, when Riggan snaps his fingers and the world behind him is thrown into chaos, the whole situation seems to be a figment of his imagination. The cinematography of *Birdman* promises to show us only what is really going on, but when we pass judgment instead of believing what we see and how it is shown to us, we choose to believe what we know. What we understand as 'real' limits our ability to believe in imaginative fiction.

With films, it is harder for us to distinguish reality and fiction than it is in theater, where the coexistence of both is natural, if not a given. In an article for the International Federation for Theater Research, Professor Erika Fischer-Lichte notes that when you go to the theater, you witness real people moving around in real spaces in real time. However, "the real time, the duration of the performance, is not identical with the time represented; and the real body of each actor usually signifies the body of another, a stage figure, a character" (84). Reality imposes itself on fiction in the theater. In film, fiction tends to impose itself on reality, because, unless you're watching a documentary, movies that have fictional characters and contain imagined situations are visually set in the real world, in scenarios where fiction invades real places that we can recognize. It is no coincidence, then, that most of *Birdman* takes place either backstage or on the stage of Broadway's St. James Theatre. Adding a story within a story, and a stage within a stage, further disorients us as to what is real and what isn't. Is this fictional reality, or realistic fiction? Having a theater within the movie makes the audience forget, if not lose its grip on, the differences between what is real and what isn't. In film, particularly in *Birdman*, we are uncomfortable accepting fiction and reality as one because movies often show us a world literally identical to our own; for many, accepting reality and fiction as intertwined in the world of a film might signal an acceptance of such a relationship in our daily lives.

But why don't we want to accept the fiction in reality? Why is it that when we go to the movies, despite voluntarily signing up for a fictional experience, we don't always let ourselves get caught up in its imaginative elements? We need to know that the movie we are watching is about superheroes or some other magical thing in order to accept a break in reality. Once we settle on a film as 'being real,' we can't see it as anything but; that would imply that reality and fiction are loosely interchangeable notions, and acknowledging this can be threatening.

The threat of fiction became very real in 2013, the year that *Birdman* was filmed and produced. The movie's release followed a series of events that greatly changed how the people of the United States, if not of the world, understood their reality. The Boston Marathon bombings marked the beginning of a new era of terrorism, in which videos of men decapitating innocent people became just another segment of televised news. Meanwhile, Edward Snowden's Wikileaks release of NSA documents in response to "what he described as the systematic surveillance of innocent citizens" by the government shattered whatever illusion Americans had about Internet privacy (Gellman et al.). Terrorist bombings in the places we least expect and the realization that the government is running a technological panopticon to watch our every move are common plot points in movies, but, in 2013, those threats became real for many Americans. Dangers that had once seemed fictional to so many were now real-life worries that made some feel unsafe in their own homes.

2013 was a year that tested the boundaries of safety, and therefore threatened the constraints of reality as many knew it. Many years prior, in the aftermath of 9/11, the expression "like a movie" became a common phrase used by American television newscasters and spectators alike (Rickli). Jonathan Hensleigh, the scriptwriter of *Armageddon*, stated that he was reminded of his film while watching television on September 11. "When it actually happens and you're watching it on CNN, frankly, it gives you the creeps," he admitted (qtd. in Rickli). Steve de Souza, the director of *Die Hard*, went so far as to notice that the image of the terrorist attack looked like one of his movie posters (Rickli). The Boston Marathon Bombing and the rise of ISIS as a powerful political force have created the same kind of discomfort, revealing parallels between real world events and fictional scenarios. When the stuff of fiction becomes real, the break in reality is not only unsettling, but it also usually signifies some kind of shock to the structure of our world. Fischer-Lichte considers that the separate notions of the 'real' and the 'fictional' serve as parameters that dictate our behaviors and actions. Maybe we cling to the distinction between the two because "their destabilization, their collapse, results, on the one hand, in a destabilization of our perception of the world, ourselves and others, and, on the other, in a shattering of the norms and rules that guide our behavior" (Fischer-Lichte 95).

Birdman preys on our fear of reconciling fiction with reality by distorting how we understand both through film. It gives us a camera that appears magical in how it "ebbs and flows like water, soars and swoops like a bird," but expects us to trust it because the movie is shot in one continuous take (Dargis). It places us in the world of theater within a film to disorient us, and, in doing so, shows us that confusing fiction and reality isn't always a scary experience. *Birdman* wants to show us how to understand our world in both the contexts of fiction and reality, asking us to reconsider the relationship between the two and come to terms with the possibility that they exist as one.

But, though the movie asks us to acknowledge fiction and reality as not necessarily separate, *Birdman* knows that most of us won't want to or simply won't be able to combine both concepts. In the movie's final scene, we see the camera swerve away from an open window towards the inside of Riggan's hospital room, where he is recovering after shooting his nose off during a performance of his play. The air has a slightly gray tint to it as Sam walks into the room, looking for him. "Dad?" she murmurs repeatedly as she scrambles to find him. Her eyes lock on the open window for a moment, and her body thrusts itself towards the sill as she looks out and down in shock. There's something eerie about the drum beat playing in the background, in how it creates a noise oscillating between restrained and unhinged. The camera focuses on Sam looking out the window as her eyes, practically popping out of her head, shift down in desperation. She looks up, a defeated expression on her face, but the drums start beating a little faster, a little louder, and with a little more excitement. Her face slowly bends into a smile of awe as she looks up in surprised satisfaction. Birds call in the background, the screen goes black, and we hear her start to laugh.

Richard Brody thinks that *Birdman* "is an exercise in cinematic half-assedness: it tackles big questions and offers conventional answers," but this isn't a movie about solutions; it's a movie about questions. When Sam looks out the window, she probably sees her dead father's body below her. Most of us understand her dazed expression and laughter as a mental breakdown in the face of such a horrible scene. She is in denial. But then again, what if we are in denial? Birdman could have flown off into the air, and his daughter could be marveling at the sight of it. The dreamers and the believers could be right. With its final scene, *Birdman* makes us question whether or not our notions of reality are based on what is real or what *feels* real. It forces us to reconsider our position within reality. But, more so, it leaves us with the unsettling realization that we might be living our lives in denial of the unknown. After all, doesn't fiction only stop being real when we refuse to accept it as such?

WORKS CITED

Birdman or (The Unexpected Virtue of Ignorance). Directed by Alejandro G. Iñárritu, performances by Michael Keaton and Emma Stone, Fox Searchlight Pictures, 2014.

Brody, Richard. "'Birdman' Never Achieves Flight." *The New Yorker*, 23 Oct. 2014, www.newyorker.com/culture/richard-brody/birdman-never-achieves-flight.

D'Alessandro, Anthony. "Emma Stone on Walking the Tightrope That Was 'Birdman.'" *Deadline*, 22 Dec. 2014, www.deadline.com/2014/12/emma-stone-birdman-interview-alejandro-inarritu-1201330997/.

Dargis, Manohla. "Former Screen Star, Molting on Broadway." *The New York Times*, 16 Oct. 2014, www.nytimes.com/2014/10/17/movies/birdman-stars-michael-keaton-and-emma-stone.html.

Fischer-Lichte, Erika. "Reality and Fiction in Contemporary Theatre." *Theatre Research International*, vol. 33, no. 1, 2008, pp. 84-96.

Gellman, Barton, Aaron Blake, and Greg Miller. "Edward Snowden Comes Forward as Source of NSA Leaks." *The Washington Post*, 9 June 2013, www.washingtonpost.com/politics/intelligence-leaders-push-back-on-leakers-media/2013/06/09/fff80160-d122-11e2-a73e-826d299ff459_story.html?utm_term=.dca08a837eba.

Rickli, Christina. "An Event 'Like A Movie'? Hollywood and 9/11." *Current Objectives of Postgraduate American Studies*, vol. 10, 2009, www.copas.uni-regensburg.de/article/view/114/138.

Romney, Jonathan. "The Tracking Shot: Film-Making Magic—or Stylistic Self-Indulgence?" *The Guardian*, 4 Dec. 2014, www.theguardian.com/film/2014/dec/04/tracking-shot-film-making-magic-or-stylistic-self-indulgence-birdman.

Incorporating evidence from news reports, editorials, and Native American perspectives, Panoutsos takes on the controversy surrounding the Keystone XL pipeline. He not only constructs a compelling argument against the project but also reflects on what this debate reveals about eminent domain and our obligations to the environment. (Instructor: Lorelei Ormrod)

THIS LAND IS YOUR LAND

Nick Panoutsos

The year is 1981. The city is Detroit. Mayor Coleman Young has enthusiastically endorsed General Motors' plan to construct a new plant in the quiet neighborhood of Poletown. With the promise of six thousand jobs and a new source of tax revenue, the plant seemed a panacea for Detroit's ailing economy (Safire). But there's a catch. The plant's construction requires 465 acres to be evacuated and razed, forcing out thousands of Poletown's residents and dooming the town's local businesses (Safire). The hospital, the church, and everything in between will soon be dust. Residents have taken their concerns to the Supreme Court of Michigan, which has ruled in the city's favor, claiming that the new plant will benefit the public (Safire). As demolition day grows closer, the families and shopkeepers of Poletown pack their bags and leave with a consolatory government stipend and shattered hopes.

What stands in place of that resilient little town today is a four hundred-acre testament to the power of eminent domain. First exercised in *Kohl v. United States* (1876) to condemn a private residency for use as a post office, eminent domain allows the government to acquire private property for public use with fair compensation to the owners ("Kohl v. United States"). The final caveat is key: many residents don't feel like any amount of money could match the subjective value of their homes and way of life, no matter what the public use is. In the Kohl case, an argument for public use was clear enough. A post office is a public building, not the site of a private business. In Poletown, however, the Supreme Court's decision muddied the legal waters surrounding public use. No one could deny that the plant would have a significant public purpose: reviving Detroit's economy and retaining local jobs seemed an enticing prospect, even for those who opposed the displacement of Poletown's residents. Public use was harder to advocate. Typically reserved for government buildings or roads, public use is the legal lubricant that keeps the machine of eminent domain running smoothly. Because General Motors is a private corporation, their plant would be shut off from the public, meanwhile generating more profit for the company than the city would ever see from it (Safire). But Mayor Young and the city of Detroit were desperate. What would it really hurt for them to stretch the definition of public use?

But Young and the Supreme Court of Michigan established a dangerous precedent. Justice Ryan, the canary in the coalmine, claimed that the Poletown case "seriously jeopardized the security of all private property ownership" (qtd. in Safire). Since Poletown, there's been no shortage of prickly and emotionally fraught lawsuits involving eminent domain. An overwhelming majority of these cases rule in favor of the city, not the residents, resulting in government condemnation of homes for the price of 'fair' compensation. So what happens when the case involves a massive private infrastructure project spanning multiple states and crossing national boundaries? The construction, or prevention thereof, of the Keystone XL pipeline will set a new precedent for how the government mediates the intricate dance between corporations and the people who have made a home on the land that those corporations desire.

Proposed by multibillion dollar oil company TransCanada, the Keystone XL (KXL) Pipeline would transport crude oil from Alberta to Steele City, Nebraska, where it would then join the existing Keystone Pipeline that stretches all the way to Texas's Gulf Coast (Laughland and Mathieu-Léger). Initially vetoed by President Obama, the pipeline has recently been resuscitated by the Trump administration, which has approved its construction despite enormous backlash (Laughland and Mathieu-Léger). Supporters of the pipeline argue that it would decrease U.S. dependence on foreign oil and create domestic jobs, but its opponents criticize the pipeline's environmental and sociological impact, arguing that the pipeline would increase dependence on fossil fuels and cut through fragile ecosystems as well as Native American lands (Laughland and Mathieu-Léger). The construction of KXL has turned into a wildly polarizing debate that has been smoldering since its conception during the Obama administration. The narrative surrounding this controversy has transformed into a symbolic David and Goliath battle between the pipeline's opponents and Big Oil.

TransCanada calls KXL "safe" and "reliable" on their website ("Keystone XL Pipeline"). However, environmentalists and Native American inhabitants of the affected areas aren't sold. The pipeline passes through the Ogallala Aquifer, which comprises roughly eighty percent of drinking water for people in that area ("Native Americans"). Tribal rights attorney Tara Houska says, emphatically avoiding an 'if' scenario: "*When* the pipeline leaks, it will contaminate the water for the people in that area" (qtd. in "Native Americans"; emphasis added). She goes further to claim that the pipeline is not only a "death warrant" for native people, but for the nation at large: the United States obtains thirty percent of its irrigation water from the Ogallala Aquifer, so any leakage in the pipeline would result in a devastating blow to the nation's farming and livestock industries ("Native Americans"). For Houska and other KXL opponents, TransCanada's assurance that a spill is unlikely simply isn't enough.

The *New York Times* Editorial Board views the pipeline as a dangerous, unnecessary risk, claiming that the U.S. does not need the oil. Citing domestic oil sources in Texas and North Dakota as well as more rigorous fuel economy standards, the Times writes that the pipeline would have a minimal impact on U.S. energy security due to falling demands for importation (Editorial Board). For the cost of increasing carbon emissions that are at an "already dangerous [level]," the pipeline simply isn't worth it, especially given the damaging emissions caused by extracting and burning tar sands (Editorial Board). The Editorial Board also debunks TransCanada's lofty estimate of 9,000 jobs created overnight, citing a State Department analysis that estimates only 3,900 short-term jobs and only fifty permanent jobs would be created. On an international level, the pipeline would damage America's credibility as a leader in combating climate change: its authorization would make us complicit in destroying Canada's boreal forests and releasing more deadly emissions into the atmosphere.

Despite the debunked job myths and environmental risks, many right-wing supporters of the pipeline are still spellbound by the promise of energy independence. *NewsMax's* Jerry Shaw praises the pipeline as a reliable source of North American oil, potentially freeing us from hostile foreign suppliers. Rancher Jeff Swanson echoes Shaw's sentiments, telling *The Guardian*, "Our country needs oil. Why import it from Middle Eastern countries when we can take it right from our Canadian neighbor?" (Laughland and Mathieu-Léger). Somewhat bafflingly, Shaw also writes that the pipeline contributes more to clean energy in the long run "than any other means of energy production," citing Canada's "strong" environmental laws for drilling and TransCanada's reclamation process for drilled land. While these factors might marginally reduce the environmental impact of oil production, Shaw makes a bold claim. To state that our reliance on fossil fuels contributes to clean energy more than wind, solar, or hydroelectric power is disconcerting at best and simply false at worst (Shaw). It's worth mentioning that the NewsMax article is punctuated by advertisements which read, in red capital letters: "IS GLOBAL WARMING A HOAX?"

Forbes's John Tamny takes a slightly more refined position (no pun intended), defending the KXL pipeline as a beacon of private sector entrepreneurship that should be free of government meddling. Unlike Shaw, Tamny realizes that the pipeline won't be the magic potion for U.S. jobs and oil independence, but he still encourages its construction so that the U.S. can expend less capital on domestic oil, and more on other projects, like "[creating] the next Cisco." Tamny offers little elaboration on what this vague musing could mean. He criticizes Obama's "obnoxious" delay on the pipeline's construction, claiming that he's only "[placating] green interests." The free market demands the construction of KXL, and the government should get out of the way in the name of liberty. Right-wing KXL supporters are left with the question of whose liberty comes first: the corporation, or the landowners on the pipeline route?

Over the course of the KXL debate, the pipeline's construction has come to symbolize the future of energy infrastructure in the U.S., under both administrations. Its construction or prevention will be predictive of our future dependence on fossil fuels, specifically the "dirty oil" derived from Canada's tar sands. In one of Obama's speeches regarding the pipeline, he reminded audiences throughout the country that our reliance on fossil fuels will eventually render the earth "not only inhospitable but uninhabitable in our lifetimes" (qtd. in Editorial Board). As an advocate of energy efficiency, Obama saw the pipeline as a step in the wrong direction. His successor, however, is an outspoken supporter of the pipeline. Having tweeted that global warming is "expensive bullshit," President Trump's support of KXL is likely rooted in desire for profit, not the planet's welfare. His rhetoric surrounding eminent domain and the pipeline betrays an aggressive urge to push the project through the legal system, at whatever cost.

In a 2016 Republican primary debate, Donald Trump and Jeb Bush engaged in a clumsy squabble regarding the nature of the pipeline (Gillespie). Both candidates supported the pipeline's construction, but neither could agree on whether it was a public or private job. Bush, who seemed to possess a stronger understanding of eminent domain, fruitlessly tried to convince Trump that KXL is a public project, a necessary precondition for eminent domain (Gillespie). Trump, in response, didn't seem to care (or know) about the legal fine print. Trump told Bush, "It's a private job" (Gillespie). Trump's assertion is deeply concerning: he isn't even operating under the guise that KXL is a public project. TransCanada and oil refineries clearly stand to profit from the pipeline, yet Trump has made it clear that he will rely on eminent domain to justify the pipeline's construction on private property (Gillespie). This wouldn't be the first time the real estate mogul has used eminent domain to support endeavors of private profit. In 1994, he unsuccessfully attempted to force elderly resident Vera Coking out of her Atlantic City home to make room for a limousine parking lot for Trump Casino (Boaz). Now the stakes are higher; multiple homes and Native American lands are on the line, and the Trump administration shows no sign of curbing its abuse of eminent domain.

The pipeline has also sparked a debate about dispossession of native lands. Citing the "despicable" 2014 Apache Land Grab as a precedent, Houska says the U.S. has a "very long history" of dispossessing land from Native Americans ("Native Americans"). Continuing a tradition as old as Christopher Columbus, the KXL pipeline will infringe on Native American land without permission and with the risk of dire consequences. The pipeline would pass through the boundaries of the Ogalala Sioux and Fort Peck reservations, among others, and their inhabitants have called this passage an "act of war" ("Native Americans"). Tressa Welch, a member of the Lakota tribe, says, "Our people call it the black snake because it is evil" (Laughland and Mathieu-Léger). Why such extreme rhetoric? The pipeline crosses the Lakota's primary water source, the Missouri River, on the Fort Peck reservation, and any leakage would contaminate their water supply, disrupting their safety and way of life (Laughland and Mathieu-Léger). Welch and her group of "water protectors" have taken up the cause of fighting the pipeline's construction, inspired by earlier protests against the Dakota Access Pipeline at Standing Rock (Laughland and Mathieu-Léger).

To further examine the impact of the pipeline on surrounding communities, director Leslie Iwerks interviewed residents along the KXL's route. In Iwerks's documentary, *Pipe Dreams*, Nebraskan rancher Teri Taylor chronicles her struggle with TransCanada as she morosely traces the route of the pipeline on a map with her finger. Taylor's property has been in her family for six generations. Now she faces the prospect of having the KXL pipeline run through it, a time bomb ticking towards leakage. The David and Goliath analogy comes into full force at the mention of eminent domain, which TransCanada used to validate their construction of the pipeline. Taylor says, "We

Not everyone in Montana feels the same instinct to shield their land from KXL development. Mayor JoDee Pratt of Baker, Montana, welcomes the pipeline as a valuable asset to the preexisting oil community that will help restore her city's economy (Laughland and Mathieu-Léger). As a Trump supporter and climate change denier, Pratt feels confused by, and, in her own words, "ashamed of," the pipeline protests (Laughland and Mathieu-Léger). She has admitted that she doesn't understand the protests. This reveals a fundamental flaw in the dialogue about the KXL pipeline: those in office seem to be deaf to the grievances of their communities. If Pratt were aware of the dire implications that the pipeline has on the neighboring Lakota water supply, maybe she would think twice before calling the protests "appall[ing]" (Laughland and Mathieu-Léger).

don't have a choice" (*Pipe Dreams*). Residents face an uphill battle when competing with the power of eminent domain. As history has shown, the government typically rules in favor of the corporation, not the people.

For instance, in 2005, the city of New London, Connecticut, made plans to sell private property to outside developers, claiming that development would "create jobs and increase tax revenues" ("Kelo v. New London"). Public good, right? Susette Kelo wasn't so sure. As one of many New London residents displaced by the proposed plans, Kelo sued the city, claiming that it was violating the Fifth Amendment's takings clause, which explicitly lists "public use" as grounds to exercise eminent domain ("Kelo v. New London"). Dissenting Justice Clarence Thomas appealed to the sanctity of the home in Kelo's defense ("Kelo v. New London"). This concept holds that the home has an intrinsic or subjective value to the owner that exceeds anything the government can offer for compensation. Kelo's little pink house on the water meant more to her than any lump sum the City could offer her. More than a decade later, Nebraskan rancher Teri Taylor invokes the sanctity of the home in her battle against the Keystone XL development. She is not ready to see her family's property violated, and likely contaminated, by Big Oil. When Taylor spoke up at a TransCanada open house about her disapproval of the pipeline's construction on her property, she was told that the organization would "unfortunately have to resort to eminent domain" (*Pipe Dreams*). TransCanada has made clear that it will construct the KXL pipeline regardless of public disapproval. Like Kelo, Taylor is fighting against private development on her property. What remains to be seen is her fight's legal outcome. Nebraska is one of the last states whose legislatures haven't approved the pipeline, and Taylor's voice, among those of other local residents, can shape a new future for eminent domain policy.

What can explain the seemingly irreconcilable differences between Keystone XL's supporters and opponents? Maybe it's a fundamentally different perception of what it means to live on the land. Kiowa writer N. Scott Momaday writes that we tend to think of land in terms of ownership in Western society. This mindset causes an important and dangerous chain reaction: "ownership implies use, and use implies consumption" (Momaday 28). If we think we own the land, what can stop us from buying and selling it, exhausting all of its resources, and pushing people off it? Momaday points to the Native American perception of the land as a fascinating foil. As a Native American, Momaday acknowledges the necessity of using the land, but emphasizes his love of the land as the "first truth" that shapes his consciousness (28). In a culture that celebrates the beauty of the natural world, good stewardship is a no-brainer. Momaday writes: "Man invests himself in the landscape . . . This trust is sacred" (27). How radically different would the Keystone XL debate look if the Americans adopted a relationship of sacred trust to the land? Suddenly, eminent domain would seem irrelevant. Who are we to evict another inhabitant of the land? Transporting tar sands would lose its appeal. Why not harness the powers of the wind and sun instead of penetrating the earth and exhausting her resources? Poletown and New London would be relics of a bygone era—a time when profit dominated our commitment to the earth and to each other.

As the final inhabitants along the pipeline's route are still fighting TransCanada for rights to build on their property, America faces a troubling prospect, or, rather, an affirmation, that corporate interests can trump the sanctity of our homes and the safety of our resources. Aristotle's astute words from *Politics* come to mind: "For that which is common to the greatest number has the least care bestowed upon it" (26). The impending fate of the pipeline's construction will either perpetuate or reverse this age-old tragedy. We can only hope that the outcome alerts us to our obligation as inhabitants of the earth—to honor the land and protect it for future generations.

WORKS CITED

Aristotle. *Aristotle's Politics: Writings from the Complete Works*, edited by Jonathan Barnes, introduced by Melissa Lane, Princeton UP, 2016.
Boaz, David. "Donald Trump's Eminent Domain Love Nearly Cost A Widow Her House." *The Guardian*, 19 Aug. 2015, www.the-

guardian.com/commentisfree/2015/aug/19/donald-trumps-eminent-domain-nearly-cost-widow-house.

Editorial Board. "No to Keystone, Yes to the Planet." *The New York Times*, 6 Nov. 2015, www.nytimes.com/2015/11/07/opinion/no-to-keystone-yes-to-the-planet.html.

Gillespie, Nick. "Donald Trump, Jeb Bush, Eminent Domain, and the Keystone XL Pipeline." *Reason*, 7 Feb. 2016, www.reason.com/blog/2016/02/07/donald-trump-jeb-bush-eminent-domain-and.

"Kelo v. New London." Oyez, www.oyez.org/cases/2004/04-108.

"Keystone XL Pipeline." *TransCanada*, www.transcanada.com/en/operations/oil-and-liquids/kxl/.

"Kohl v. United States." *Justia*, supreme.justia.com/cases/federal/us/91/367/case.html.

Laughland, Oliver and Laurence Mathieu-Léger. "Life on the Keystone XL Route: Where Opponents Fear the 'Black Snake.'" *The Guardian*, 2 May 2017, www.theguardian.com/us-news/2017/may/02/keystone-xl-pipeline-route-water-native-american-reserves.

Momaday, N. Scott. "A First American Views His Land." *At Home on the Earth: Becoming Native to Our Place: A Multicultural Anthology*, edited by David Landis Barnhill, U of California P, 1999, pp. 19-29.

"Native Americans Speak Out on KXL Pipeline." *Youtube*, uploaded by The Big Picture RT, 6 Jan. 2015, www.youtube.com/watch?v=Bp8DzzsUq-g.

Pipe Dreams. Directed by Leslie Iwerks, SnagFilms, 2016.

Safire, William. "Poletown Wrecker's Ball." *The New York Times*, 29 Apr. 1981, www.nytimes.com/1981/04/30/opinion/essay-poletown-wrecker-s-ball.html.

Shaw, Jerry. "Global Warming: 5 Arguments For Building the Keystone XL Pipeline." *Newsmax*, 30 Mar. 2015, www.newsmax.com/FastFeatures/Global-Warming-Keystone-XL-Pipeline-Climate-Change-Environment/2015/03/30/id/635259/.

Tamny, John. "There Are Great Arguments For Keystone XL, But Its Supporters Don't Know Them." *Forbes*, 4 May 2014, www.forbes.com/sites/johntamny/2014/05/04/there-are-great-arguments-for-keystone-xl-but-its-supporters-dont-know-them/#2a90bd772219.

@realDonaldTrump. "This very expensive GLOBAL WARMING bullshit has got to stop. Our planet is freezing, record low temps,and our GW scientists are stuck in ice." *Twitter*, 4 Jan. 2014, 4:39 p.m., www.twitter.com/realdonaldtrump/status/418542137899491328?lang=en.

In this essay, Chen moves from the problem of how and why AI challenges our understandings of innovation to the idea that intelligence and human identity are inextricably linked. (Instructor: Courtney Chatellier)

THE DUALITY OF INTELLIGENCE

Mark Chen

A curious question of identity arises in a well-known paradox called "The Ship of Theseus," originally reported in a Greek legend. When the mythic hero Theseus returned to Athens after one of his adventures, the Athenians decided to preserve the ship that he had used. As time passed, the ship's wooden planks started to decay. When one plank began to break down, it was promptly replaced, and the Athenians agreed thereafter to replace each rotting plank with a newer, sturdier one. Not long after the first plank was replaced, a second one started to break down as well. And then a third. In due time, all of the original planks eventually rotted and were replaced. Not a single plank that had belonged to the original remained. Was it still the same ship? Or did the replacement of all of its constituent parts turn it into a different one?

It doesn't seem like this thought experiment would have anything noteworthy to offer outside of a philosophical debate, but recent innovations have given this discussion a new relevance within the field of artificial intelligence, or AI. The questions previously posed are analogous to potential questions that could also arise from the study and research of AI. Is artificial intelligence the same as human intelligence? If a human mind were replaced with a machine capable of completing the same tasks, would our definition of intelligence change? Would machines be able to process meaning in the same way that we do, or would such a process be purely syntactic? In many cases, the resolutions to these complicated questions will depend on our interpretation of what 'the same' means.

Out of all our technological innovations, AI is one of the most peculiar. In contrast to traditional processing algorithms, which use explicitly defined inputs and outputs, a computer with AI capabilities leverages machine learning, the process through which machines recognize errors and correct them in the future. Machine learning can be viewed as the main enabler of AI, allowing it to be defined as 'intelligent.' Although 'artificial intelligence' may have a futuristic connotation to it, it already plays a substantial part in our lives today. In "The Great A.I. Awakening," Gideon Lewis-Kraus describes how Jun Rekimoto, a University of Tokyo professor of human-computer interaction, heard that "Google Translate, the company's popular machine-translation service, had suddenly and almost immeasurably improved." Rekimoto decided to test these newfound capabilities. He selected an English passage from Hemingway and fed his own Japanese translation of the passage back into the service. As far as meaning went, Google's English translation was nearly identical to the original passage, only missing a single grammatical article. Lewis-Kraus attributes this improvement to the service's conversion to an AI-based system. By implementing new machine learning algorithms, the system was able to 'learn' much faster than it did previously. Lewis-Kraus also mentions that we take current AI-enhanced systems such as this one "as a push-button given—a frictionless, natural part of our digital commerce." In doing so, he suggests, we may already be relying on AI to a greater extent than we thought.

Google Translate, as a flagship case, shows the extent of AI's potential. The development of machine learning in consumer products has resulted in systems with "overnight improvements roughly equal to the total gains the old one[s] had accrued over [their] entire lifetime[s]" (Lewis-Kraus). These improvements have allowed us to tackle old problems with ease and start working on solutions to new ones. Examples include autonomous vehicles, speech recognition software, and digital assistants such as Apple's Siri or Amazon's Alexa. All of these innovations rely primarily on machine learning to 'learn' and improve their level of intelligence, yet they are nonetheless classed as 'weak AI': they are capable of focusing only within a narrow set of boundaries ("Weak"). A self-driving car would be at a loss as to what to do off the road, and a digital assistant eventually repeats or rephrases the same syntax over and over in a conversation.

A stronger artificial intelligence may be better understood by looking at how innovation has functioned historically. Steven Johnson examines such chance connections and great discoveries in "Platforms," the final chapter of his book *Where Good Ideas Come From: The Natural History of Innovation.* Johnson says that in one such discovery, two physicists were discussing the signals that were coming from Sputnik I, the first human-made satellite to orbit the Earth, and, "[a]s they listened and recorded, the two men realized that they could use the Doppler effect to calculate the speed at which the satellite was moving through space" (184). They deduced that they could use this same information to pinpoint the location of objects on the surface by tracking known satellites, thus creating the beginnings of the modern GPS system. This discovery acted like a platform, because the duo had "created an entire ecosystem of unexpected utility" (Johnson 187). Such utilities, like Lewis-Klaus's observation about Google Translate, are taken for granted today; GPS provides guidance "for everything from mobile phones to digital cameras to Airbus A380s" (Johnson 187). In another instance, Johnson reflects on how something like a coral reef, built on dormant atolls, "is a platform in a much more profound sense. The mounds and crevices of the reef create a habitat for millions of other species" (Johnson 181). Such reefs form a symbiotic relationship with many of their inhabitants, who provide it with nutrients in exchange for protection from predators. Johnson's platforms "come in stacks," in this case both figuratively and literally (189). He uses the Internet as a modern case, imagining it as "a kind of archaeological site" (189). Web sites can be made "on top of the open protocols of the Internet," a platform that has become entrenched in many people's lives. Johnson's takeaway is that "the real benefit of stacked platforms lies in the knowledge you no longer need to have," very much like the original planks of Theseus' ship that were no longer needed (210). Nobody needs to understand the physics behind GPS in order to use it. The Internet offers a similar benefit; it is home to over three billion users, all of whom can enjoy the spread of information and connectivity that it offers without necessarily understanding the mechanics behind it. When we extend this concept to AI, we see that it relies on the same principles. It's a new innovation, resting on the platform of the computer.

Johnson contends that as we move on to new platforms, the previous ones become less relevant to our experiences. We expect AI to eventually evolve into this as-of-yet hypothetical 'strong' phase, in which its intellectual capabilities and functions will "mimic" cognition in the human brain ("Strong"). However, the difference is that while the platforms leading up to weak AI can be considered an extension of our intelligence, the capabilities that strong AI will have could leave our own intelligence, and thus ourselves, behind. The intelligent capabilities of AI could render our intelligence platform—our minds—useless, like the old planks in the ship. We have always been complacent in the knowledge that we are the only bastions of "intelligence," defined by the *Oxford English Dictionary* as "the ability to acquire and apply knowledge and skills" ("intelligence, *n.*"). But the potential for AI to rival human intelligence brings up some complex existential considerations with regard to how we interact with it. Would we treat an AI with equivalent intelligence to ours the way we treat one another? Would its level of intelligence give it rights? Or would those rights only be conferred onto biological intelligence? The answers to these questions must take into account what such a capability would represent. It would be the first time a creation made in our image would be able to compete directly with us; strong AI could exhibit the potential to match or even exceed our own thinking. Despite the unpredictability that strong AI would have, our role as its creator would mean that we would have to come to terms with how to approach this new platform. It also means that we would be responsible for dictating the first move.

One potential path to strong AI lies in the research and development of brain-machine interfaces (BMIs), which allow communication "between a human or animal brain and an external technology" ("Brain-Machine"). The brain exhibits a unique feature known as cortical plasticity, allowing it to 'remap' important synapses in the event of biological damage. This feature also gives it the remarkable ability to adapt to the point of being able to handle implanted prosthetics and sensors as if they were natural components of the brain. In

"Dreaming in Code," a review of Michio Kaku's *Future of the Mind*, Adam Frank recalls the circumstances of the 2014 World Cup's ceremonial first kick, which was made by a paralyzed teenager using a BMI. Frank believes that such feats, already regular occurrences, may be our first foray "into our post-human future." Frank brings us up to speed on current progress, writing that "researchers are studying the microscopic dynamics of the brain's wiring." He explains that by tracking neural activity with an MRI, "researchers have recorded how the brain lights up when shown fragments of a video . . . they can then determine a subject's neural responses to the patterns" (Frank). The immediate applications of this research are currently being used in the medical field, allowing disabled or paralyzed individuals to regain some level of mobility. Frank's comment on how "it may even be possible for scientists to crudely identify what people hooked up to MRI machines are dreaming about" (emphasis on "crudely") shows that we have yet to grasp the full capabilities of cortical plasticity. Frank concedes that "on the ethical front . . . there are troubling issues inherent in the technologies." If prosthetics and even augmentations are no problem, it seems that it is only a matter of time before chips that could potentially enhance our intelligence or cognition will be made possible.

The exact direction that we are taking with AI and its integration into our lives is uncharted. However, at least one effort seems to lead the way through such a future. Neuralink, a company founded by Elon Musk in 2016, aims to alleviate concerns about keeping up with the potential intellectual capabilities of AI by "working to link the human brain with a machine interface by creating micron-sized devices" (Vijayaraghaven). While this doesn't seem too different from what our brains already do with artificial devices and prosthetics, Musk intends for his work to go beyond that capability. He explains that "there are a bunch of concepts in your head that your brain has to compress into this low data rate called speech or typing" (qtd. in Vijayaraghaven). All of our brains have a multitude of complex thoughts and concepts going on at the same time, and we exert effort to convey this amalgam as coherent expressions. In Musk's view, this process will be inadequate sometime in the future, because "[a]rtificial intelligence and machine learning will create computers so sophisticated and godlike that humans will need to implant 'neural laces' in their brains to keep up" (qtd. in Vijayaraghaven). The ability of the brain to incorporate prosthetic electric inputs naturally suggests that it would be receptive to more complicated electronics. A role reversal might also be possible: our brains could perhaps be controlled or augmented by these "neural laces." But we can expect that an embrace of AI should meet two developmental goals: the assurance that we will be able to keep up with it and an opportunity for a safe path towards such a coexistence.

Looking beyond these feats, we could have the same intelligence as AI yet differ from it. Even so, we might have reason to reconsider our earlier concept of 'sameness.' Siding with the interpretation that the ship discussed earlier is indeed the same one, with the same purpose and the same existence, would allow us to view the purpose of strong AI in a similar vein: as a representation of ourselves in a classical sense. Just as there are countless components and parts that make up the human body, our minds are made up of a mixture of unique thoughts and memories. It is this complex blend that gives rise to our individuality. But would AI be capable of exhibiting such individuality? If we approach this question from the other side, we can see that the ship is unoriginal, and no longer exists as the same. Can such a comparison even be made when the difference between human and machine cognition will become more philosophical than physical? Johnson's concept of stacked platforms suggests that we often take the technology around us for granted, but if an AI were to make a hypothetical demand for a right to live, what right do we have to say yes or no? We extend to individuals, almost universally, the right to a free mind, but what of AI?

Take, for example, a fictitious robot AI, physically indistinguishable from a human, interacting with someone. Said person would have little reason to treat it as anything other than human. But would the person's perception change if they found out that the conversation they were having was not with a real person, but with a collection of code and machinery? In *Reclaiming Conversation: The Power of Talk in a Digital Age*, Sherry Turkle says, "What do we forget when we talk to machines? We forget what is special about being human . . . Machines are programmed to have conversations 'as if they understood what the conversation is about. So when we talk to them, we, too, are reduced and confined to the 'as if'" (339). In her book, Turkle frames conversation as something that makes us human. We treasure genuine interaction, so does an artificial conversation devalue our nature?

We might not be ready to answer such questions, only ponder them. To call AI an innovation in the classical sense would mean taking innovation for granted, and it's becoming more and more apparent that doing so might not be the best course of action. AI seems poised to transform the way we think about innovation by putting us in the spotlight. These transformations will not resemble a Skynet-esque 'AI takeover,' but an intellectual one. The question of what we do in this scenario will most likely be worth looking into. The word 'better' is used several times to describe the general trend that innovation has taken, but nobody could have predicted AI's perpetuity. We might find ourselves going down a path of bifurcation, struggling to come to terms with this new platform, or seeing in it a potential to enhance ourselves. Every innovation thus far has been built with the perspective of our cultural and intellectual achievements. Perhaps only time will tell whether that same perspective is ready to handle AI, a radical, if not profound, departure from ourselves.

WORKS CITED

"Brain-Machine Interface (BMI)." *Techopedia*, 2017, www.techo-pedia.com/definition/27696/brain-machine-interface-bmi.

Frank, Adam. "Dreaming in Code." *The New York Times*, 7 Mar. 2014, www.nytimes.com/2014/03/09/books/review/michio-kakus-future-of-the-mind.html.

"intelligence, *n.*" *Oxford English Dictionary Online*, 2017, en.oxforddictionaries.com/definition/intelligence.

Johnson, Steven. "Platforms." *Where Good Ideas Come From: The Natural History of Innovation*. Riverhead Books, 2010, pp. 181-210.

Lewis-Kraus, Gideon. "The Great A.I. Awakening." *The New York Times Magazine*, 14 Dec. 2016, www.nytimes.com/2016/12/14/magazine/the-great-ai-awakening.html.

"Strong Artificial Intelligence (Strong AI)." *Techopedia*, 2017, www.techopedia.com/definition/31622/strong-artificial-intelligence-strong-ai.

Turkle, Sherry. *Reclaiming Conversation: The Power of Talk in a Digital Age.* Penguin Press, 2015.

Vijayaraghaven, Abinaya. "Elon Musk on Mission to Link Human Brains with Computers in Four Years: Report." *Reuters*, 21 Apr. 2017, ca.reuters.com/article/businessNews/idCAKBN17N0CU-OCABS.

"Weak Artificial Intelligence (Weak AI)." *Techopedia*, 2017, www.techopedia.com/definition/31621/weak-artificial-intelligence-weak-ai.

In this careful study of the works of Charlie Kaufman, Larson sets up the problem of the mind's relationship to reality, then explores it through a series of related concepts—how we project ourselves into reality, how we try to control it, and how this limits our ability to connect to others. (Instructor: Victoria Olsen)

PLAYING WITH PEOPLE: PROJECTION AND CONTROL IN THE WORKS OF CHARLIE KAUFMAN

Audrey Larson

John Malkovich is falling down a dark, grimy tunnel. With a crash, he finds himself in a restaurant, the camera panning up from a plate set with a perfectly starched napkin to a pair of large breasts in a red dress and a delicate wrist hanging in the air like a question mark. The camera continues panning up to the face that belongs to this body, the face of—John Malkovich. Large-breasted Malkovich looks sensually at the camera and whispers, "Malkovich, Malkovich," in a sing-song whisper. A waiter pops in, also with the face of Malkovich, and asks, "Malkovich? Malkovich, Malkovich?" The real Malkovich looks down at the menu—every item is "Malkovich." He opens his mouth, but only "Malkovich," comes out. A look of horror dawns on his face as the camera jerks around the restaurant, focusing on different groups of people, all with Malkovich's face. He gets up and starts to run, but stops in his tracks at the sight of a jazz singer with his face, lounging across a piano and tossing a high-heeled leg up in the air. A whimper escapes the real Malkovich. The buzz of "Malkovich" grows louder and the multiple Malkoviches become claustrophobic, closing in on him as he fights his way across the room, distraught.

This nightmarish scene is from *Being John Malkovich*, Charlie Kaufman's breakthrough screenplay. The film revolves around puppeteer Craig Schwartz, who discovers a portal into the mind of the actor John Malkovich. In this scene, Malkovich descends into that dark tunnel and is greeted by a bizarre reality, answering the question posed by Schwartz in the film: "What happens when a man goes through his own portal?" Or, as Kaufman seems to wonder, what would happen if we could view the workings of our own mind as an outsider? Malkovich looks out at a sea of Malkoviches, and perhaps, Kaufman suggests, we do, too. In his review of a different Kaufman film, *Synecdoche, New York*, Roger Ebert describes Kaufman's work as containing "only one subject, the mind, and only one plot, how the mind negotiates with reality, fantasy, hallucination, desire and dreams." Across his oeuvre, Kaufman struggles with this question: how much of one's life is made up of reality—and how much does one create in the mind? In the Malkovich scene, Kaufman implies that everything we observe is really a projection of ourselves. On the surface, we look out into the world and see an expanse of diverse faces. But on a deeper, subconscious level, we are reflecting our existence— the only one we truly know—onto others. Everything we observe is only understood in the context of its relationship to ourselves.

This theme of projection continually appears, in different manifestations, in Kaufman's work. His 2008 directorial debut, *Synecdoche, New York*, which he also wrote, is, in a sense, a projection, just as Malkovich had projected himself onto everyone he saw. The film is centered around a theatre director, Caden Cotard, who builds a replica of New York in a warehouse, and hires actors to play himself and the people in his life, in order to recreate his experiences and create an authentic picture of human life. But the narrative does not reflect reality. *Synecdoche, New York* is told entirely through Caden's bleak and often unreliable perspective. We experience time just as he does; it moves forward in impossible jumps or lags behind in eternity. For example, the beginning sequence of the movie, which reflects a monotonous morning routine of married life, appears to take place over the same day when it actually spans half a year (as we see subtly from news headlines, calendars, and snippets of conversation). In the beginning, the film is relatively realistic, and Caden's skewed perspective is more subtle. As the movie progresses, however, Caden's theatre experiment and the real world outside the warehouse blur as the narrative spirals into the surreal.

While our entire lived experience is essentially a projection of ourselves, there are specific moments when we externalize what we feel on the inside. In one scene in *Adaptation*, a frustrated Charlie, the screenwriter protagonist, stares at the book jacket of *The Orchid Thief*, which he is attempting to adapt for the screen. He begins to imagine the author, Susan Orlean, giving him advice to focus on "that one thing that you care passionately about and then write about that" (*Adaptation*). The film then cuts to an inspired Charlie dictating to his tape recorder, "we see Susan Orlean, delicate, haunted by loneliness, fragile, beautiful." Commenting on this scene in his essay "Still Life in a Narrative Age: Charlie Kaufman's *Adaptation*," Joshua Landy writes: "Charlie projects his own frustrated desire—in his case, for reciprocated attraction, for release from the prison of solipsism—onto the subject matter" (507-508). Charlie externalizes his feelings of loneliness and frustration in the form of Susan Orlean as a character in his screenplay. *His* Susan Orlean is not the real Susan Orlean, but a version of her generated by Charlie's mind—essentially, a projection of himself. Roger Ebert brings up the idea of projections and the reasoning behind them in his review of *Synecdoche, New York*, writing that "we place the people in our lives into compartments and define how they should behave to our advantage. Because we cannot *force* them to follow our desires, we deal with projections of them created in our minds." In *Synecdoche, New York*, Caden's reenactment puts him in control; he gets to direct the 'characters' in his life. He even goes so far as to play some of them. In the effort to attain control over the external parts of our lives—the aspects we can't manipulate, the people with their own agendas and egocentric perspectives—we create versions of these people in our minds that we can control, all based on our biased points of view.

Solipsism, or "the theory that only the self exists, or can be proved to exist," is a useful term to describe this egocentric perspective, and a word that keeps coming up in regard to Kaufman's work ("solipsism"). Characters like Charlie Kaufman in *Adaptation* and Caden Cotard in *Synecdoche, New York* can't escape their own selves—they are stuck in the bias of their points of view. We are self-centered creatures; it's how we survive. Is it even possible to escape this 'chronic egotism?' Should we strive to? Kaufman himself is a testament to this perplexing dilemma; his films have a distinct Kaufman-esque persona. He doesn't attempt to conceal his identity within these films, even going so far as to insert himself as the protagonist in one. *Adaptation*, loosely based on Susan Orlean's book *The Orchid Thief*, is about a screenwriter named Charlie Kaufman who struggles to adapt a book about orchids. Sound familiar? In an interview for *Vulture*, Kaufman discusses how he turned his struggle adapting Orlean's book into the plot of the film:

> I was stuck for a long time, and then I came upon this notion that I've used a lot since: *What am I thinking about now? What am I worried about? Where is my head at? What am I in the middle of? What am I drowning in?* And, literally, what I was thinking about was my inability to write the script, and that was a really literal translation. (qtd. in Sternbergh)

Kaufman doesn't try to escape his perspective. Instead, he embraces it. "I can't tell anyone how to write a screenplay because the truth is that anything of value you might do comes from you," Kaufman admits in a BAFTA lecture on screenwriting (qtd. in Han). "The way I work," he says, "is not the way that you work, and the whole point of any creative act is that. What I have to offer is me, what you have to offer is you, and if you offer yourself with authenticity and generosity I will be moved" (qtd. in Han). The truth is that our experience is all we have to give in the form of art. As the portrait photographer Richard Avedon once said, "Sometimes I think all my pictures are just pictures of me. My concern is . . . the human predicament; only what I consider the human predicament may simply be my own" (qtd. in Kozloff). Every film Charlie Kaufman writes is a projection of himself because anything else would be inauthentic or simply unoriginal. But at the same time, Kaufman struggles with accepting this fate. The characters in his films desperately fight to get out of their own heads, always to no avail. They often find superficial escape—for instance, Craig Schwartz taking over John Malkovich's body and life in *Being John Malkovich*. But it is only a change on the surface. Essentially, they remain prisoners to their selves and those selves' projections. Each one stands at the center of a solipsistic universe.

This solipsistic "prison" is where the desire for control originates. We strive for control of the facets of life that are the least changeable: people, events, and even the past. In Kaufman's *Eternal Sunshine of the Spotless Mind*, characters attempt to manipulate their memories of each other. Joel discovers that his ex-girlfriend Clementine has had a procedure to erase him from her memory, so he proceeds to erase her from his. However, as he is forced to relive all his memories of their time together, he begins to have regrets and wants to reverse the procedure. Joel ends up manipulating his childhood memories by 'bringing' Clementine into them in an attempt to 'hide' her from being erased. He even reverses his biggest regret—not staying with Clementine on the day they met. The film is essentially a meditation on our desire to control our experiences.

Kaufman embodies this desire through his art. "For Kaufman, creation has always been inextricably linked to control," writes David Ehrlich in an article for *IndieWire*, "control of a production, control of a body, control of space and time and memory." *Synecdoche, New York* allowed Kaufman to gain immense control in his first stint in the director's chair—a power Kaufman would like to hold on to. "I feel like the stuff that I write is personal, and I would like to be in charge of it," said Kaufman when asked about the need to direct his own scripts (qtd. in Ehrlich). This need for control is a recurring pattern in his films. In *Being John Malkovich*, Craig creates puppet versions of himself and Maxine, the woman he lusts after, which he puts into situations he wishes would play out in real life. Eventually, he even uses a real person (John Malkovich) as a human "puppet" to make Maxine like him. "It isn't just playing with dolls," Craig says to Maxine, to which she responds: "You're right, my darling, it's so much more. It's playing with people!" In *Synecdoche, New York*, Caden's replica of his life that he controls is a sort of 'puppet show.' In *Anomalisa*, which Kaufman co-directed, the characters are actual puppets that move with the use of stop-motion technology. "The fact that they're puppets being manipulated," Kaufman remarks, "becomes an existential issue as well. You know someone's manipulating them—they don't know it" (qtd. in Romney). In the final scene of *Synecdoche, New York*, the new director speaks to Caden through an earpiece as he walks through the desolate warehouse—the decaying remains of his experiment. "You have struggled into existence, and are now slipping silently out of it," the director says. "This is everyone's experience. Every single one. The specifics hardly matter. Everyone's everyone. So you are Adele, Hazel, Claire, Olive. You are Ellen." These characters are all a part of Caden because they represent his projections. They may look different on the outside, but he 'created' them all as director. Kaufman uses the creative process as a robust metaphor for how we view and control our experiences. "They say there is no fate, but there is," says the minister in *Synecdoche, New York*. "It's what you create." We are the directors of our own lives.

But the characters in Kaufman's films who 'direct' their projections are not hopeful. We don't wish to be Caden Cotard or Craig Schwartz. Kaufman himself doesn't "have any solutions and [he doesn't] like movies that do" (qtd. in Sragow). "I want to create situations that give people something to think about," says Kaufman. "I hate a movie that will end by telling you that the first thing you should do is learn to love yourself. That is so insulting and condescending, and so meaningless. My characters don't learn to love each other or themselves" (qtd. in Sragow). While Caden wastes away his life meticulously trying to control it, he loses all the people he had ever loved. Craig infiltrates John Malkovich's body so Maxine will marry him, but she soon leaves him for Craig's ex-wife. We *want* control—but will it really bring us happiness? Control is just a reinforcement of our egocentric perspectives. When the characters in Kaufman's films try to control the world around them, they are declaring that *their* experience is the most important. But what control *really* does is kill connection.

The desperate desire for connection is a major theme in Kaufman's most recent feature, *Anomalisa*, which he wrote and co-directed. *Anomalisa* is a stop-motion animation about Michael Stone, a customer service guru and author, who spends the night in a Cincinnati hotel for a business trip. To Michael, everyone has the same face and voice—from the taxi driver to his wife and son—until he meets and falls in love with Lisa, who looks and sounds different from everybody else. But Kaufman doesn't do happy endings. After a night spent together, Lisa's 'uniqueness' begins to disappear, and soon she looks and sounds exactly like everyone else. The film ends outside of Michael's perspective with Lisa and her friend driving away with their own unique faces and voices. As in *Synecdoche, New York*, Kaufman provides an unreliable narrator in Michael Stone—not in terms of narrative, but in his perceptions of others. The monotonous uniformity that Michael observes around him is really a projection of what's going on inside of him. In an article for *IndieWire*, film critic Sam Adams writes that the film makes clear "that the other characters' apparent sameness is a function of Michael's own dissatisfaction. Being the only 'real' person in a universe of clones doesn't bring him any solace; it makes him feel like he's the only one who doesn't fit." Michael feels alienated and projects those feelings of isolation and disconnect onto what he sees. Near the end of the movie, Michael makes a speech about customer service, urging the audience to view the customer as a human being: "Always remember the customer is an individual. Just like you. Each person you speak to has had a day." Yet, he can't see anyone as an individual. There's a hypocritical tension there. Kaufman seems to be posing the question: Is it even *possible* to step outside of our tunnel-vision and see people for who they are?

In an interview for *The Guardian*, Kaufman discusses how difficult it is to look at strangers and empathize with them. Yet, "when I see something that's just kind," he says, "I find it the most incredibly moving thing. . . . When someone looks at you warmly for a second as you pass them on the street—rather than just an obligatory nod— it gives you some sort of renewed faith" (qtd. in Shoard). This anecdote reveals a softer, more tender side to Kaufman. There is a deep yearning for connection, which reiterates a weaving pattern through Kaufman's films—characters that are unable to understand one another. "So much of what is wrong right now in the world is that people don't see each other," says Kaufman (qtd. in Sternbergh). Michael Stone can't see his wife, his son, his love. Caden Cotard seems to be on a different wavelength from his wife and loses all connection with his daughter. In one scene, Caden goes to visit his estranged adult daughter at a sex club, viewing her naked body through a glass partition. He desperately calls to her, shouts, pounds on the glass—but she can't hear him. This theme of disconnect is repeated over and over again. In another scene, Sammy, the stalker-turned-actor who plays Caden in the warehouse, is about to throw himself off a roof and begs Caden to see him: "I've watched you for-ever, Caden, but you've never really looked at anyone other than your-self. So watch me. Watch my heart break. Watch me jump." When everything we do is through the lens of self, how can we possibly empathize with another?

We fail to connect because we look out at a sea of Malkoviches: a sea of projections. We can't see people if all we see is ourselves. And, therefore, others can't see us, since all they see is themselves. "You spend your time in vague regret or vaguer hope that something good will come along," says the pastor in *Synecdoche, New York*. "I've been pretending I'm OK, just to get along, just for, I don't know why, maybe because no one wants to hear about my misery, because they have their own." We each live in our separate, distant worlds, inhab-ited by projections in an attempt to control the external. But living in this world of self-creation gets lonely, and we long for the day when someone will see our authentic selves instead of their own reflections. "Do you ever get lonely sometimes, Johnny?" Susan Orlean asks the orchid thief John Laroche in *Adaptation*. "Nobody liked me," answers Laroche, "but I had this idea. If I waited long enough, someone would come around and just, you know . . . understand me. Like my mom, except someone else. She'd look at me and quietly say: 'Yes.' Just like that. And I wouldn't be alone anymore." The characters in Kaufman's films rarely experience this authentic connection, and, when they do, it is both pure and fleeting. We tend to measure the worth of some-thing by how long it lasts, its continuity. A 'happy ending' to a roman-tic comedy is the couple finally coming together. But according to Kaufman, "there really is only one ending to any story. Human life ends in death . . . Everything involves loss; every relationship ends in one way or another" (qtd. in Tanz). It's the barebones truth. It's the deal we get when we enter the world. "The end is built into the begin-ning," Hazel whispers to Caden on what will be their final, and only, night together. They lie in each other's arms in a burning house—a powerful metaphor for the ephemeral nature of both life and relation-ships. There's a romantic tenderness somewhere deep in Kaufman that believes, or wishes to believe, in these moments of magic—moments when two individuals can see each other without projec-tions—when two worlds become one.

WORKS CITED

Adams, Sam. "Critics Poll Winner 'Anomalisa' Is Charlie Kaufman's Most Mundane Movie, and His Strangest." *IndieWire*, 22 Sept. 2015, www.indiewire.com/2015/09/critics-poll-winner-anomalisa-is-charlie-kaufmans-most-mundane-movie-and-his-strangest-130362/.

Adaptation. Directed by Spike Jonze, written by Charlie Kaufman, Sony Pictures, 2002.

Anomalisa. Directed and written by Charlie Kaufman, Paramount, 2015.

Being John Malkovich. Directed by Spike Jonze, written by Charlie Kaufman, Universal, 1999.

Ebert, Roger. Review of *Synecdoche, New York*. *Rogerebert.com*, 5 Nov. 2008, www.rogerebert.com/reviews/synecdoche-new-york-2008.

Ehrlich, David. "Charlie Kaufman Reflects On His Career: 'I Feel Like I F*cking Blew It.'" *IndieWire*, 12 July 2016, www.indiewire.com/2016/07/charlie-kaufman-interview-anomalisa-synecdoche-adaptation-1201702465/.

Eternal Sunshine of the Spotless Mind. Directed by Michael Gondry, written by Charlie Kaufman, Universal, 2004.

Han, Angie. "Charlie Kaufman Talks Screenwriting: 'Do You. It Isn't Easy But It's Essential.'" *SlashFilm.com*, 15 Dec. 2011, www.slashfilm.com/charlie-kaufmans-bafta-lecture-screenwriting/.

Kozloff, Max. "Richard Avedon's 'In The American West.'" *American Suburb X*, 24 Jan. 2011, www.americansuburbx.com/2011/01/richard-avedon-richard-avedons-in.html.

Landy, Joshua. "Still Life in a Narrative Age: Charlie Kaufman's *Adaptation*." *Critical Inquiry*, vol. 37, no. 3, Spring 2011, pp. 497-514. U Chicago P Journals, www.journals.uchicago.edu/doi/full/10.1086/659355.

Romney, Jonathan. "Charlie Kaufman on Weirdness, Failure, and His New Puppet Noir." *The Guardian*, 15 Sept. 2015, www.theguardian.com/film/2015/sep/15/charlie-kaufman-anomalisa-film-interview.

Shoard, Catherine. "Charlie Kaufman: 'The World is Terrifying and Destructive and Dehumanising and Tragic.'" *The Guardian*, 16 Dec. 2016, www.theguardian.com/film/2016/dec/16/charlie-kaufman-anomalisa-interview-donald-trump.

"solipsism." *Dictionary.com*, www.dictionary.com/browse/solipsism.

Sternbergh, Adam. "In Conversation: Charlie Kaufman." *Vulture*, 2015, www.vulture.com/2015/12/charlie-kaufman-anomaslisa-c-v-r.html.

Synecdoche, New York. Directed and written by Charlie Kaufman, Sony Pictures Classics, 2008.

Sragow, Michael. "Being Charlie Kaufman." *Salon*, 11 Nov. 1999, www.salon.com/1999/11/11/kaufman/.

Tanz, Jason. "The Kaufman Paradox." *Wired*, vol. 16, no. 11, 2008. *ProQuest*, search.proquest.com/central/docview/274380165/full-text/E1158928E3124761PQ/1?accountid=12768.

Through careful representation and close reading of images, Spector illuminates the role of intimacy in Nan Goldin's photographs. The essay moves reflectively from a concrete problem—how can photographs can be both real and imagined, composed and spontaneous?—to speculate about our own role as audience. (Instructor: Normandy Sherwood)

REFLECTIONS

Brennan Spector

In the photograph, she looks like a young Brooke Shields: dark permed hair, rouged cheeks, red lips. It's the kind of face that belongs on the cover of *Vogue*, or on a poster over a teen girl's bed, Cyndi Lauper blasting from the stereo. The year is 1985, if you couldn't tell.

Now zoom out to the reflection of the woman's bare shoulders, the towel wrapped around her chest. Step back further still to the borderless edge of the mirror, the dingy bathroom walls, until you see the real woman, named Sandra, standing in profile on the other side. Notice the holes in the walls, the cracks in the tiles. Notice the barren countertop, save for the used makeup wipe, single stick of lipstick, and compact of blush. And notice, too, the way in which Sandra's reflection, and not Sandra herself, seems to star in this photograph. It is as if she, the reflection, is looking for something in her real-life counterpart. Amidst her lackluster and grimy surroundings, she searches for glamor, like Alice looking backwards through a rather dilapidated looking glass.

"Sandra in the mirror, New York City" (1985) is just one image out of dozens in photographer Nan Goldin's seminal work, *The Ballad of Sexual Dependency* (24). It is a single frozen sliver of time, as all photographs are, and yet to Goldin it carries a greater significance. Each photograph in this illuminating collection, described by Goldin as her "visual diary," captures a private moment in the lives of Goldin and her friends, the sole subjects of her photography (6).

To Goldin, photography can be as intimate as sex: "People get pissed off when I won't let them photograph me. But I won't photograph anyone I don't know," she told a reporter from *The Guardian* in 1998 (qtd. in Jackson). It's "a kind of logic" with roots in Goldin's childhood that has remained central to her life's work (Jackson).

When Nan Goldin was just eleven years old, her eighteen-year-old sister Barbara committed suicide by train (Thomas). It was undeniably the most formative event of her life, something Goldin "never got over" (Thomas). In a 2001 interview with *Newsweek*, thirty-seven years after the suicide, Goldin still "reached for a napkin, weeping" when recounting the story (Thomas). She and Barbara were close as children, yet Goldin admits she has no real "tangible sense of who [her sister] was" (9). In the introduction to *The Ballad of Sexual Dependency*, she declares, "I don't ever want to be susceptible to anyone else's version of my history. I don't ever want to lose the real memory of anyone again" (9). And thus, Goldin's lifelong philosophy was born.

But Barbara Goldin didn't jump in front of a moving train, as the *Newsweek* article seems to suggest. While the article reports that she "threw herself across the railroad tracks outside Union Station in Washington and was killed by an oncoming train," Goldin tells a slightly different story (Thomas). As Goldin describes it in the introduction of *The Ballad of Sexual Dependency*, Barbara "[lay] down on the tracks," a small but important difference (8). Certainly, the former story is more sensational. How thrilling it is to imagine—the heat of the moment! The train getting closer! Is she gonna do it?!—but it is not the truth. So in this regard, perhaps Goldin has more journalistic integrity than the news magazine interviewing her. It's a testament to her unshakable desire to provide truth and "real memory" in her work (9).

To most of us viewing Goldin's work, little is known about the people in her pictures. We know they are her old lovers and friends, people who have touched her life in some way, but their lives are foreign to us save one or two frozen moments. Yet her images often feel familiar to viewers; they hold within them an innate quality of what it means to be young and wild, to feel things deeply and to love with abandon. In many ways, Goldin's photographs are like Sandra's reflection in the mirror, looking back out into the real world; they are mimetic, yet they seem to possess their own greater consciousness distinct from the real-life people they reflect.

Take a look at "Nan and Brian in bed, New York City" (1983), for example (137). See how it appears hot to the touch? The photograph's warm orange tones burn brightly in a dance of both passion and warning, perhaps suggesting something dangerous and abusive about the relationship between Goldin and her then-boyfriend Brian. Brian sits on the edge of the bed, smoking a cigarette while Nan lies curled up behind him. With Brian turned the other way, Nan can steal a look at him without him seeing the frightened longing in her eyes. Over the bed is a black and white print of another of Nan's photographs, "Brian with the Flintstones, New York City" (1981), half out of frame, so that only a shirtless Brian with a cigarette dangling from his mouth can be seen. It is almost impossible not to immediately compare the idealized, James Dean-esque Brian of 1981 to the Brian of 1983. The Brian in the poster over the bed exudes power and coolness by staring directly into the camera, but Brian of 1983 is looking away. His imposing power instead comes from camera angles; there is a considerable distance between the couple, but the camera cannot tell. What is lost in perceived depth is replaced by perceived size, so Brian, in the photo's foreground and shot from the waist up, seems to tower over Nan. All of these elements—the scene's heat, the difference in size, the reminder of what once was looming over their heads—culminate to create a Nan who appears fearful, small, and painfully nostalgic. No background information is needed to feel the emotions radiating from this photo; they come naturally when confronted with a woman shrouded in passion and danger, pushed into the background.

In both "Sandra in the mirror, New York City" and "Nan and Brian in bed, New York City" there is a mirroring of the main subject, a recurring theme in Goldin's work. The duplicated images of Sandra and Brian put real-life people and their reflections into tension with each other; they suggest that oftentimes our lives aren't quite as pretty as they appear on camera. Both tug at the idea of expectation versus reality, idealism versus realism. These themes are seen, too, in the grimy and run-down settings of each of the photographs. Goldin's photography shows "exactly what [her] world looks like, without glamorization, without glorification," but that does not necessarily mean that her subjects aren't glamorous (Goldin 6). Sandra still radiates in a world that is dirty and lackluster. It is worth noting that Goldin's photos aren't doctored—if someone looks glamorous, it is because they inherently are.

The reason I keep coming back to Sandra is because of how incongruous she feels with her surroundings. Her face is everything the eighties were; her environment is everything they weren't. It's like looking at a young Cindy Crawford held hostage in the middle of the Bowery. And just like the rest of Goldin's friends and subjects, Sandra is completely unknowable except her name. Who was she? A member of mainstream pop culture, dipping her toes in the downtown grunge scene (and thus becoming a precursor to the hipster club scene aesthetic of today)? Or perhaps I am judging based on stereotypes. Perhaps Sandra was actually the wildest, most heroin-addicted member of Goldin's clan. I don't expect to ever know the answer, and that's okay. No matter who Sandra was prior to being photographed by Nan Goldin, she still ended up in that bathroom in 1985, at the point of collision between glamor and harsh reality.

As *The Ballad of Sexual Dependency* progresses, beauty, pain, and abuse grow increasingly inseparable, culminating in one photograph, "Nan after being battered" (1984), which Goldin describes as the book's "central image" (83). Dressed in pearls and "dangly earrings," Nan's face is covered in dark bruises from a recent beating by her then-lover, Brian. The "intense red blood in the white of her swollen left eye mirrors the shade of her lipstick," and the two feel in tandem with one another (Manchester). It's a difficult image to sit with, but it demands one's attention. While the dark frame of Goldin's body seems to float shadow-like into the dim background, her brightly lit face, intense gaze, and brutal wounds push forward into sharp focus. Every detail of her abuse is made abundantly clear, and her solemn but dignified face seems to be saying, "look." But most striking to me are those bright red lips, a universal symbol of sex and vanity, unadulterated. Because the color of Nan's bloodied left eye matches so closely to the color of her lips, it is impossible not to associate the latter with blood as well. Suddenly, a kiss represents more than just sex—it represents violence and pain.

In the book's acknowledgments, Goldin attributes this photo to her friend (and oft-photographed subject) Suzanne Fletcher (147). I can't help but think of the story behind this photo—Brian beats Nan, Nan calls up Suzanne, Nan tells Suzanne to take a picture of what he did to her. It becomes clear that while Nan was very much a part of the world she photographed, there was still a planned and posed nature to her work, too.

This is the part of Goldin's work that both confuses and intrigues me the most. If the mission of her photography is to capture the true and "real memory" of her friends and loved ones, shouldn't all of her photos be completely candid? Wouldn't a posed photograph add a level of artificiality to the work? If a subject poses when being photographed, the picture is then doctored; the photo shows less of who the subject is and more of who they want to be. But the very action of making art is a conscious one (for the artist, that is), so it raises the question: to capture their true humanity, must the subjects be completely oblivious to the fact that they are being photographed?

This question is further complicated in Goldin's "Bobby masturbating, New York City" (1980), which is literally a photo of a young man masturbating (68). He is slender and hairy all over, and his head is tilted downwards, eyes closed. Bobby's right hand grips his erect penis and his left hand is right below it, too far out of frame for the viewer to see exactly what it is doing. The shot itself is very tight— from the top of his head to his mid-thighs—and the lighting is tenebristic. The dramatic lighting and tight frame place an intimate yet public and illuminating spotlight on an otherwise private activity. Bobby is not looking at the camera, and his expression is blank, as if he is in a mental state closer to meditation than ecstasy. Yet I wonder what role candor plays in capturing both Bobby's world and the worlds of Goldin's subjects. Certainly, Bobby consented to being photographed, right? And on some conscious level, he must have been aware of the presence of an audience.

But although there is something about the secluded, individual, and taboo act of masturbation that we instantly associate with privacy, maybe there is a quality to being Goldin's friend that anyone outside of her circle would never be able to understand. The woman and her camera were one and the same. She states in an interview with *Vogue*,

"If anyone took as many pictures as I do, they'd be standing up here, too" (qtd. in Bengal). Perhaps at some point, people like Bobby stopped noticing the camera in her hand. Truly, from the expression on his face, he does not look like he knows he is being photographed.

But then again, look at how tight the shot is! It's almost as if the photographer had to touch knees with Bobby to get it. And notice, too, how his right hand does not appear to be in motion; it is firmly grasping the base of his penis, so that its full length and size is purposefully in view. Could this image of Bobby really just be the lucky shot, one of the few images out of "thousands and thousands" that came out worthy of printing (qtd. in Bengal)? Are there other shots out there, lost to time, with his arm a little too blurry, or his penis out of view? Or (and the two don't have to be mutually exclusive, per se), was Bobby posing, presenting himself how he wished to be seen by all viewers to come?

This answer varies depending on who is included in the word 'viewers.' When it was first exhibited, *The Ballad of Sexual Dependency* was presented as a slideshow, screened exclusively for the "people in the pictures" (qtd. in Bengal). It was never meant to reach a greater audience, and most definitely was never expected to receive the critical and scholarly acclaim it has garnered today. So, if Bobby really was trying to look a certain way for the camera, it would have been geared towards Goldin and Bobby's friends, not some massive international audience. How could Bobby have known that he (and his genitalia) would one day be the subject of extensive academic research? In this regard, any sort of intent on his part—or on the part of the photographer—no longer matters. Was he posing? Was he not? Who cares? Time has since warped and twisted his original intentions.

So can art ever capture life—real, true, unadulterated life—without modifying it in some way? Let me leave Nan Goldin completely for a moment to look at the work of Mierle Laderman Ukeles, the Artist in Residence for the New York City Department of Sanitation. In her 1969 manifesto, *Manifesto for Maintenance Art 1969!*, Ukeles proposes the idea for an exhibition titled *CARE* that she never got to carry out. The proposal is complicated and contains many parts, but I am interested in one particular section titled "Part One: Personal." It reads as follows:

> I am an artist. I am a woman. I am a wife.
>   I am a mother. (Random order).
>
> I do a hell of a lot of washing, cleaning, cooking,
> renewing, supporting, preserving, etc. Also,
> (up to now separately I "do" Art.
>
> Now, I will simply do these maintenance everyday things,
> and flush them up to consciousness, exhibit them, as Art.
> I will live in the museum as I customarily do at home with
> my husband and my baby, for the duration of the exhibition.
> (Right? or if you don't want me around at night I would
> come in every day) and do all these things as public Art
> activities: I will sweep and wax the floors, dust everything,
> wash the walls (i.e. "floor paintings, dust works, soap-
> sculpture, wall-paintings") cook, invite people to eat,
> Make agglomerations and dispositions of all functional
> Refuse.
>
> The exhibition area might look "empty" of art, but it will be
> maintained in full public view.
>
> MY WORKING WILL BE THE WORK (Ukeles)

Her ideas are by all means intriguing. Her exhibition would be a presentation of real life itself, free of all bells and whistles, only considered art because "Everything I say is Art is Art" (Ukeles). Yet I still question whether the two—art and real life—are mutually exclusive.

Say Ukeles really did carry out her plan. Say she relocated to a museum and led her life entirely in public view. Undoubtedly, that new life would be real because she would really be there. To quote filmmaker Jean-Luc Godard, "every film is a documentary of its actors." (For example: where was Leonardo DiCaprio when Jack died in *Titanic*? He was in a wave pool in front of a bunch of cameras, that's where.) But would that new, real life inside the museum be a true reflection of the real life Ukeles led before she started living in public view? Or would that pesky label 'art' suddenly force her every-day behaviors to change in some way?

I believe it must. I believe that on some level, conscious or not, Ukeles would always be aware of her audience, and it would somehow always shape her behavior. And if this is true for Ukeles, then it is true for Bobby and Sandra and Nan Goldin as well. Goldin is sixty-three years old now, and admittedly different. In a recent 2015 interview with *Vogue*, she reflects:

> That I thought it could save the person somehow. That I thought I could keep people alive. I really believed it until recently. And I also thought I could preserve the memory of the person through a photograph. But without the voice, without the body, without the smell, without the laugh, it doesn't do much. Well, it keeps a memory, but then it becomes a memory of the picture at some point. (qtd. in Bengal)

This is true for Goldin, because the photos are her memories. But what about those of us who never knew the people in the pictures? To us, Sandra and Bobby have only ever existed as Goldin's memories, cherry-picked reflections of her past. We will never know Sandra once the makeup has been wiped away, nor Bobby, once he puts on some pants—not unless Goldin releases new photos of them, that is. Because the future of their memories is entirely in the artist's hands, we do not know what is captured and what is lost, or what is true and what is extrapolated. Like Sandra, we look back out into the real world, praying there are no smudges on the mirror.

WORKS CITED

Bengal, Rebecca. "A Conversation with Nan Goldin on the 30th Anniversary of *The Ballad of Sexual Dependency*." *Vogue*, 26 Oct. 2015, www.vogue.com/article/nan-goldin-interview-ballad-of-sexual-dependency-30th-anniversary.

Goldin, Nan. *The Ballad of Sexual Dependency*. Aperture, 1986.

Jackson, Tina. "Arts: Elegant and Wasted." *The Guardian*, 25 May 1998, www.search.proquest.com/docview/245252726/DF37441F7470 4BE7PQ/1?accountid=12768.

Manchester, Elizabeth. Summary for "Nan one month after being battered," by Nan Goldin. *Tate*, Nov. 2001, www.tate.org.uk/art/artworks/goldin-nan-one-month-after-being-battered-p78045.

Thomas, Dana. "Shooting Away the Pain." *Newsweek*, 25 Nov. 2001, www.newsweek.com/shooting-away-pain-149787.

Ukeles, Mierle L. "Manifesto for Maintenance Art 1969! Proposal for an Exhibition 'CARE.'" *Artforum*, 1971, www.feldmangallery.com/media/pdfs/Ukeles_MANIFESTO.pdf.

In this wide-ranging consideration of satire as a genre, Pagliari builds on evidence from comedy films, dystopian novels, and contemporary political parodies to make connections between art and politics. Through analysis of its history and conventions, she shows how satire can stay relevant to today's public issues. (Instructor: Michael Tyrell)

THE TRAGEDY UNDERNEATH: SATIRE AND REALITY

Martina Pagliari

At the beginning of the 1933 comedy *Duck Soup*, Rufus T. Firefly (played by Groucho Marx) is appointed leader of the fictional country of Freedonia. When asked, "How do you intend to run the nation?" he starts performing a vaudeville song illustrating "the laws of his administration": "No one's allowed to smoke or tell a dirty joke, and whistling is forbidden." The list goes on for a while, ending with the lines, "The last man nearly ruined this place, he didn't know what to do with it. If you think this country's bad off now, just wait 'till I get through with it." Later in the movie, Firefly's childish behavior leads to a diplomatic crisis and, subsequently, to a war. *Duck Soup* is widely viewed as one of the greatest political comedies of all time. Produced during the Great Depression, the film is an obvious commentary on political events around the world, "pok[ing] fun at the erratic dictators who were consolidating power in Europe at the time" (Epplin). Critic Tim Dirks emphasizes the multidirectionality of the Marx Brothers' satire by pointing out how it mocks "the pomposity of small-time governmental leaders," "the absurdity of government itself," "governmental diplomacy," "an arbitrary legal system," and "war fought over petty matters." *Duck Soup* may at first appear to be a product of its time, an artwork inseparable from the historical and social conditions that inspired its creation. However, as a comedy based on political satire, it conveys something eerily contemporary and accurate.

One could think of such a movie as pure entertainment directed at a specific, restricted public, its ultimate goal being sheer amusement. However, that thought is debatable, since the Italian dictator

Mussolini took the film as a personal insult and decided to ban it. The fascist dictator clearly saw subversive potential in the apparently innocuous humor of the Marx Brothers, which leads us to consider one question: what power does art, specifically artistic satire, bring to political critique?

The Marx Brothers' commentary on modern politics and Mussolini's reaction to it show us how satire can act as a powerful, indispensable, and inevitable instrument of democracy. As W. J. T. Mitchell explains in *Critical Terms for Literary Study*, "representation, even purely 'aesthetic' representation of fictional persons and events, can never be completely divorced from political and ideological questions" (15). Mitchell establishes a necessary relationship between these two seemingly separate realms of art and politics, exploring the supposedly "inevitable" links between artistic representations and the "political" significance inherent within these representations. The concept of "representation" as a 'transversal' medium in which art and politics are crossed is a provocative one. If fictional representations inevitably bear a connection to reality, then art in general could be summed up as an attempt to reproduce and thereby deconstruct, analyze, and interpret reality in different ways. Additionally, if we accept Mitchell's argument, political satire is inextricably linked to democracy, the form of government that is supposed to execute the will of the people through either direct or indirect representation.

Indeed, satire is a direct result of democracy, since it allows people to freely express their opinion about specific public figures and political events. In her article "The Birth of Comedy," Edith Hall reminds us that comedy was first introduced as a genre in ancient Greece after the democratic revolution overthrew the Athenian tyrants in 507 BC. She writes that comedy was "intimately tied to the democracy—the form of sovereign power (*kratos*) held by the free populace—the *demos* of Athens" (12). However, satire is never symptomatic of an *absolute*, fully developed democracy, but rather of an undeveloped democracy that is still unripe and endangered, in which freedom of expression may only be allowed within certain limits. As Brian A. Connery writes in his introduction to Matthew Hodgart's book *Satire: Origins and Principles*:

Satire . . . serves as an alternative form of power when the crimes committed escape the purview of . . . law, religion, and politics . . . this is the reason why so much satire is directed against lawyers and judges, preachers and religions, and rulers and politicians: it is . . . the corruption of the very agencies which are supposed to offer justice, order, and social and moral regulation that makes satire necessary. (2-3)

As George Austin Test points out in the book *Satire: Spirit and Art*, "it is not surprising . . . that satirists have been the most persecuted of artists—exiled, silenced, sued, physically attacked" (1). As long as the tone of the satirical sketch is kept comedic, and the frail game of allusions is steadily maintained, satire will be allowed. Consequently, if democracy were fully developed and if open criticism towards authoritative figures without fear of retribution was possible, satire wouldn't be necessary at all.

The subversive danger of satire is exemplified not only by Mussolini's decision to ban *Duck Soup* in fascist Italy, but also by the many modern nations and governments who reject and prohibit satire altogether. Hall points out that the "most recent internationally high-profile case" of censorship of political satire took place in Italy in 2002, when the government of Silvio Berlusconi obstructed a theatrical production of Aristophanes' *Frogs*, whose main protagonist was "all too intelligible to third-millennial Italian audiences" (17). Presently, Silvio Berlusconi owns Mediaset S.p.A., the largest commercial broadcaster in the country. It controls most of the nation's TV channels and several important newspapers, magazines, and publishers, as well as some other small publishers and film distribution companies. Considering his hegemonic control over the national media, it is quite remarkable that the former Italian prime minister felt threatened by a stage play. At the same time, it is not surprising that his anxiety about *Frogs* was similar to Mussolini's reaction to *Duck Soup*. Berlusconi's reaction to the play unveils the actual *power*—and, therefore, the potential *danger*—of satire, for beneath its shallow layer of parody and frivolity, satire always conceals matters of extreme seriousness and importance. Making fun of a public figure like the dictatorial Berlusconi serves a double function: it attacks his uncontested authority as a public figure, and it is cathartic. Satire converts into laughter something that is, in itself, a bleak reality, such as the fact that a ruthless dictator could be endowed with the power to control a nation. Therefore, satire is invested with the double function of attack and defense, and it is, consequently, not only a democratic art—theoretically open and accessible to all types of people and social classes—but also the artistic subgenre that most serves the ideals of democracy.

This dual nature of satire is also reflected in one of the main stylistic components of satirical language: the grotesque. The concept of the grotesque is particularly important with regard to satire, because it combines seemingly antithetical extremes: laughter and horror, amusement and disgust. Film critic James Naremore writes that, like satire, "the grotesque is structured by a dual implication . . . an 'unresolved' tension between laughter and some unpleasant emotion such as disgust and fear" (6). Satire lashes us deeply, but also relieves. In this way, it uses a unique artistic language to convert tension and stridency into balance and harmony.

One drawback of satire, however, is its 'relatable specificity,' which erodes its effectiveness. Literary scholar Stephen Greenblatt argues that genres like satire do not survive history. Instead, they age gradually and ultimately move towards a conceptual and thematic death: "Works in these genres often seem immensely important when they first appear, but their power begins quickly to fade when the individuals to whom the works refer begin to fade" (Greenblatt 226). Thus, it would appear as if satire is always and inevitably short-lived. But as Daniel Griffin writes in his review of *Duck Soup*, that "distinction must often be made between a piece of art's original purpose and how its meanings have shifted and changed when viewed through the filter of a different culture and era." He states that people cannot help inadvertently placing their own cultural backgrounds and personal observations into the text, "serendipitously giving rise to art's ability . . . to be interpreted and re-interpreted throughout the centuries." According to Griffin, art is immortal when it assumes new meanings as time goes by instead of gradually losing its initial veneer. This consideration is particularly important to satire in that its 'relatable specificity' might otherwise cause it to fade away with time. Examples like *Duck Soup* demonstrate how satire can prove to be enduring and, with hindsight, even prophetic.

Luke Epplin further emphasizes the links between *Duck Soup*'s satire and contemporary politics, arguing that "Firefly's (and, by extension, Groucho's) ludicrous personality" parallels that of U.S. President Donald Trump. Epplin points out that Firefly and Trump are both "nonpolitician[s]" lacking "solemnity and competence," who "have checkered histories of reneging on promised payments" and "pathological compulsion[s] to belittle any perceived rivals and then refuse to apologize or back down." A scenario in which an actual political figure is compared to a fictional character who is an exaggerated, grotesque, and unrealistic caricature of modern statesmen is a rather difficult reality to acknowledge. Satire operates by exaggerating and hyperbolizing actual events and public figures; it can thus skirt the need to be 'politically correct' while delivering agitating and often controversial social commentary.

Satire is usually divided into two categories based on the earliest examples of satire in the classical world: Horatian and Juvenalian. Both evolved throughout history and survive today in satirical works that encompass literature, visual art, cinema, music, and television. However, while both modes share the same basic aim, the style and provocativeness of each varies. Horatian satire, based on the writings of the Roman poet Horace, is commonly identified as the milder, less abrasive type. According to the *Encyclopedia Britannica*:

> Horace opts for mild mockery and playful wit as the means most effective for his ends. The satirist's verse . . . should be easy and unpretentious, sharp when necessary, but flexible enough to vary from grave to gay. In short, [Horace's] character . . . moved to laughter rather than rage. (Elliot)

Duck Soup could easily be classified as a modern example of Horatian satire in that its humor appears lighthearted and eschews specific attacks, instead utilizing general criticism and parody. This also accounts for *Duck Soup*'s immortality and the fact that its satire remains relevant over seventy years after its release.

In contrast to Horace, the roman poet Juvenal, in his "characteristic posture . . . of the upright man who looks with horror on the corruptions of his time," wrote verses infamous for their harsh criticism, graphic expressions, and mordant tones. In one of his poems, Juvenal declares that "satire has gone beyond the limits established by his predecessors; it has taken to itself the lofty tone of tragedy" (Elliot). Curiously enough, Juvenalian satire has thrived more in the modern age. Examples of modern Juvenalian satire include George Orwell's *Animal Farm* and *1984*, Aldous Huxley's *Brave New World*, and Anthony Burgess's *A Clockwork Orange*. But the most controversial form of Juvenalian satire, at least recently, is probably the French weekly *Charlie Hebdo*, which published a series of comic strips satirizing Islam's prophet, Muhammad, in 2006. Although the magazine's writers describe *Charlie Hebdo* as a secular, leftist, and anti-racist publication, the cartoonists' blatant and repetitive use of visually-striking images and provocative language often seems to endorse and support, rather than criticize, racism and xenophobia.

A comparable case is a cartoon that depicted Alan Kurdi, a three-year-old Syrian refugee who had drowned in the Mediterranean in 2015 while his family was trying to reach Europe. The cartoon suggested that the Syrian boy would eventually have grown up to become a sexual assailant of European women (Heer). In an article for *New Republic*, Jeet Heer interprets the cartoon as "blatantly racist," though "*Charlie Hebdo* has defenders who argue that it is an ironic commentary on racist attitudes." Heer argues that *Charlie Hebdo*'s ironic mode of satire has "diminishing returns," because in "using super-racist images to satirize racism" and "constantly publishing such racist images," the magazine's "satire of racism" conflates with actual "[expressions] of racism."

Charlie Hebdo seems like the quintessential incarnation of Juvenalian satire, which is strongly committed to provoking social change. Its advocates believe that the strongest and most violent language in satire yields the most effective results. The retaliatory terrorist attacks against *Charlie Hebdo*'s cartoons prompted social network communities around the globe to adopt the slogan '*Je suis Charlie*' to defend freedom of expression. But, as David Brooks wrote for *The New York Times* in December of 2015, such a slogan is, at the very least, "inaccurate." Brooks stresses the ambiguity of wanting to "maintain standards of civility and respect while at the same time allowing room for those creative and challenging folks who are uninhibited by good manners and taste." Brooks notes not so much the difference between 'scholars' and 'satirists,' but rather two sorts of satire: the one embodied by *Duck Soup* and the other represented by *Charlie Hebdo*. As Brooks argues, the former possesses an everlasting quality that withstands the corrosive process of time, overcoming its own 'relatable specificity' and even possibly foreseeing the future. The latter operates on the opposite principle. Its main aim is to strike and provoke its public rather than inspire critical thought. That is shown by the inconsistency of *Charlie Hebdo* in choosing its targets; for instance, their cartoonists draw satirical caricatures mocking and deriding not Muslim communities, but also Christian and Jewish ones; secondly, and perhaps most importantly, *Charlie Hebdo*'s targets are not always and not necessarily political figures (as in the case of Alan Kurdi). Horatian satire, including *Duck Soup*, is never malicious or prosecutorial. *Charlie Hebdo* is exactly that. In their cartoons, the striking visuals of the drawings surpass the limits of the grotesque, and they become more horrific than comic. This is the danger of satire: the potential misuse or misinterpretation of its language.

According to W. J. T. Mitchell, such danger arises from the nature of representation itself, which "[presents] a barrier that 'cuts across,' as it were, our lines of communication with others, presenting the possibility of misunderstanding, error, or downright falsehood" (12). Mitchell claims that in a social situation, "representation begins to play a double role, as a means of communication which is also a potential obstacle to it" (12-13). Assuming this to be true would imply that not only aesthetic and semiotic representations are potentially misleading and ambiguous, but also that specific uses of representation, such as satirical caricatures, always carry within them the potential danger of backlash. Consider, for example, the 2015 terrorist attacks on *Charlie Hebdo*.

Political satire experienced a recent 'revival' during Donald Trump's candidacy for the U.S. presidency, as television shows and newspapers mocked the tycoon's persona. Prior to the actual election, it seemed as if the writers of *Saturday Night Live* had little to invent to portray a satirical caricature of the Republican nominee. Most of Alec Baldwin's impersonations of Trump consisted of repeating him verbatim, with only the addition of histrionic gestures and attitudes. Of the satirical political sitcom *Veep*, Ben Terris writes:

> For five seasons [Veep] has deftly parodied Washington, D.C. . . . But now there's a President Trump. And he and his administration have done a bang-up job of showcasing the peccadilloes of our swampy little town . . . they've made it increasingly difficult to differentiate a Veep plot from a real-life one.

Similarly, on the latest season of *House of Cards*—a political drama centered on the Machiavellian congressman Frank Underwood—Underwood's public image is severely damaged not long before an election when a picture of his father dressed as a member of the KKK is released. This alleged connection with the KKK hurts Underwood's campaign, arousing political scandal. It is ironic that in real life, in the face of white nationalist and former KKK leader David Duke's approval of Donald Trump, and the attendance of KKK members at Trump's rallies, Trump was elected President of the United States. Both *Veep* and *House of Cards* have been outstripped by reality.

These spectacles, like satire itself, are paradoxically amusing and darkly tragic. More realistic than pessimistic, these shows seem to be a characteristic product of our time, starting from the dystopian literary tradition of the twentieth century, probably best exemplified by Orwell's *1984*. Thus, while *Duck Soup* only foresaw some of the potential 'great tragedies' of modern politics, Orwell—who participated in the 1936 Spanish Civil War and lived to experience the rise of the Third Reich in Germany and Stalin's purges in the Soviet Union—had deeper and darker insights. This disturbing entanglement of fiction and real life is particularly complex at the moment when reality merges with fantasy.

How can satire still defend certain values and attack illegitimate institutions when no room is left for exaggeration? Perhaps it is not accidental that contemporary satire has gradually shifted toward Juvenalian inspirations: when mild laughter at current events is no longer possible, the lightheartedness of the artist turns into indignation, outrage, and disgust. Consequently, comedic satire adopts what Juvenal terms "the lofty tone of tragedy" (Elliott).

It is up to the satirist's distinctive voice to offer a reflection on our times—a constructive one, it is to be hoped—thus enabling us to gain a clearer insight into our world. Edith Hall concludes that "the Athenians had discovered a timeless secret: not only is comedy a political issue but satire is a democratic duty" (17). Satire is both a duty and a necessity for a democratic society. No matter the modes in which satire operates—the mild, Horatian ones or the more abrasive, controversial Juvenalian ones—the satirist is vested with great responsibility and must be aware of the power of their instrument.

WORKS CITED

Brooks, David. "I Am Not Charlie Hebdo." *The New York Times*, 8 Jan. 2015, www.nytimes.com/2015/01/09/opinion/david-brooks-i-am-not-charlie-hebdo.html.
Dirks, Tim. "Duck Soup." *Filmsite Movie Review*, 30 Dec. 2007, www.filmsite.org/duck.html.
Duck Soup. Directed by Leo McCarey, performances by Groucho Marx and Harpo Marx, Paramount Pictures, 1933.
Elliott, Robert C. "Satire." *Encyclopedia Britannica*, 28 Mar. 2017, www.britannica.com/art/satire.
Epplin, Luke. "What the Marx Brothers' *Duck Soup* Can Teach Us About Trump." *Slate*, 31 Aug. 2016, www.slate.com/blogs/browbeat/2016/08/31/what_the_marx_brothers_duck_soup_can_teach_us_about_trump.html.
Greenblatt, Stephen. "Culture." *Critical Terms for Literary Study*, edited by Frank Lentricchia and Thomas McLaughlin, 2nd ed., U of Chicago P, 1995, pp. 225-232.
Griffin, Daniel. "Duck Soup." *Film as Art: Daniel Griffin's Guide to Cinema*, 23 Feb. 2007, www.uashome.alaska.edu/~dfgriffin/website/ducksoup.htm.
Hall, Edith. "The Birth of Comedy." *History Today*, 6 June 2015, pp. 10-17.
Heer, Jeet. "Charlie Hebdo Continues to Satirize Racism with Racist Images." *New Republic*, 13 Jan. 2016, www.newrepub-

lic.com/minutes/127583/charlie-hebdo-continues-satirize-
racism-racist-images.

Hodgart, Matthew. *Satire: Origins and Principles.* Routledge, 2009.

Mitchell, W. J. T. "Representation." *Critical Terms for Literary
Study,* edited by Frank Lentricchia and Thomas McLaughlin,
2nd ed., U of Chicago P, 1995, pp. 11-22.

Naremore, James. "Stanley Kubrick and the Aesthetics of the
Grotesque." *Film Quarterly,* vol. 60, no. 1, 2006, pp. 4-14.

Terris, Ben. "What Happens to Political Satire When the Real
World Goes Mad? 'Veep' is About to Find Out." *The
Washington Post,* 9 Apr. 2017,
www.wapo.st/2nTYSPm?tid=ss_tw&utm_term=.bf81b215e9c4.

Test, George A. *Satire: Spirit and Art.* U of South Florida P, 1991.

Thorburn uses books by Dr. Seuss to analyze the censorship of children's media and raise difficult questions about rights and responsibilities. By placing the problem in a rich historical and cultural context, she represents a variety of points of view while ultimately affirming children's right to make their own choices. (Instructor: Eric Ozawa)

DR. SEUSS,
LEADER OF THE RESISTANCE

Chloë Thorburn

I know, up on top you are seeing great sights,
but down here at the bottom we, too, should have rights.
—Dr. Seuss, *Yertle the Turtle*

It was this heroic declaration that brought the crushing weight of censorship down on Dr. Seuss's classic tale of a turtle's rebellion against dictatorship. In British Columbia in 2012, *Yertle the Turtle* was pulled from the shelves of the Prince Rupert School District for being "too political" for young readers, as demonstrated by the above apparently incendiary line (Shi). Though the picture book is indeed an allegory for Hitler's domination of Germany and much of Europe, banning the book and thereby oppressing young students' right to read freely was perhaps not the most elegant way to express objection to a book about the abuse of power. The situation is ironic in more ways than one: the contested line itself takes on a new meaning after the book's banning, suggesting perhaps that when issues of censorship arise, the rights of children to intellectual freedom are threatened.

When the children's literature industry began to take off as a separate genre in the nineteenth century, most books for young readers were written to convey strong "moral content" rather than to entertain. Authors and publishers alike tended to adhere to "an implicit code" of what material was appropriate for children (MacLeod 30-31). As the pool of early creators of children's literature was "relatively small" and like-minded, there was little cause for controversy about the content of children's books until the 1960s (33). At that point, the socio-political climate became so tumultuous that more controversial writers, now seeing children's literature as an untapped medium through which one could promote social change, began to add their voices to the mix. Books for children and teens began to "reflect the changing society that produced them," depicting sensitive but realistic issues such as drug abuse, violence, and sexuality far more openly, and, consequently, provoking an unprecedented rise in censorship controversies (37).

Parents and critics alike were uncertain how to respond to the increase in progressive, realistic, but often troubling narratives entering the children's book market, and throughout the 1960s and '70s, consumers objected to some seemingly ridiculous subjects while sometimes accepting far more explicit ones. For example, *Harriet the Spy*, which describes "an adult [telling] a child that it was sometimes necessary to lie," was banned, whereas *Steffie Can't Come Out to Play*, which features "teenage prostitution," somehow slipped by untouched (36). The panic surrounding the increase of objectionable topics in children's literature peaked when, in 1972, the landmark court case *Adler v. Board of Education* reached the Supreme Court. In *Adler*, a school board challenged Piri Thomas's *Down These Mean Streets* for containing "obscene words" (White 4). The Court voted to allow the school board to censor the book, only fueling parents' panicked convictions that they must shelter their impressionable children from such troubling narratives. This frenzied literary oppression did not seem like the wisest course of action to all involved, however; Justice William O. Douglas, one of the three Supreme Court justices to object to the school board's censorship, later wrote: "Are we sending children to school to be educated by the norms of the school board, or are we educating our youth to shed the prejudices of the past, to explore all forms of thought, and to find solutions to our world's problems?" (qtd. in White 4).

Indeed, how can children become progressive members of society if they are kept in ignorance of troubling realities such as stereotyping, violence, and racial tension? In his well-known and much-contested book *The Uses of Enchantment*, Bruno Bettelheim writes that to attempt to shelter children from the corruption of reality is unproductive; in fact, if children's "unconscious is repressed and [its] content denied entrance into awareness," their sense of "selfhood," "self-worth," and "moral obligation" may be damaged (6-7). A child is prone to make choices "not so much on right versus wrong, as on who arouses his sympathy and who his antipathy," and oftentimes the former and the latter are not the same (9). Censorship often stems from a place of genuine concern for the peace of mind and well-being of a child, as "we want our children to believe that, inherently, all men are good." Consequently, we assume that "a child must be diverted from what troubles him most: his formless, nameless anxieties, and his chaotic, angry, and even violent fantasies" (7). However, children easily recognize in themselves "that *they* are not always good; and often, even when they are, they would prefer not to be" (7). Thus, their instinctive concept of self-morality and the one-dimensional, unflinchingly good outlook on human society that is fed to them by adults are at odds with each another, and, in his confusion, "the child [becomes] a monster in his own eyes" (7).

Bettelheim proposes a solution: fairy tales. While we should not hide the shortcomings of human nature and the more distressing aspects of society from children, we also do not have to overwhelm them with complete, undiluted knowledge of these failings in order to teach them that we are flawed. Fairy tales allow a child to comprehend complex and sometimes troubling realities through the more accessible context of fantasy, a genre that more closely mirrors the imaginative nature of a child's mind. Through "spinning out daydreams—ruminating, rearranging, and fantasizing about suitable story elements in response to unconscious pressures"—a child "can achieve this understanding, and with it the ability to cope" (Bettelheim 7). Thus fairy tales may provide us with a channel through which to communicate more effectively with children about the complex realities of life.

The fact that it is less productive to engage with children about difficult topics in the same way that we would with adults suggests that while children are certainly not incapable of comprehending complex issues, they process them more effectively with a degree of removal from the issue itself. Fairy tales allow children to understand the imperfections of society and of their own characters because they present them in a more abstract, creative context. But this distancing must be approached with subtlety: while adapting the mode of communication can improve the efficacy of communication with children (reading a child *Yertle the Turtle* to introduce the distressing subject of the Nazi regime, for example), the facts of the issues being presented should not be altered. Attempting to excessively simplify or water down difficult subjects for children can unintentionally result in truly harmful misrepresentation.

On January 5th, 2016, the publisher Scholastic dropped a bombshell onto the children's literature market. *A Birthday Cake for George Washington* by Ramin Ganeshram introduces young readers to the story of George Washington's beloved enslaved black chef, Hercules, and his daughter, Delia. Almost immediately after it hit the shelves, the picture book ignited heated controversy. Objectively, the story is light and fun, telling of the quaint, wholesome troubles Hercules encounters when he discovers, while trying to bake a cake for the president, that he is out of sugar. The delightfulness of this tale is precisely the problem, however. Though Hercules and Delia are in bondage, they smile obliviously through the pages, fretting over confectionary sweeteners rather than their own human rights. Instead of longing for their freedom, they wish only to please their white master, whom they love and respect despite being enslaved by him. Upon the book's release, it became apparent what an egregiously harmful portrayal of slavery *Birthday Cake* contained, essentially showing its young audience, through jaunty illustrations and cheerfully obedient slaves, that maybe slavery wasn't so bad after all. The Internet was soon set aflame with criticism. In an online review, Kiera Parrott of the *School Library Journal* wrote that *Birthday Cake*'s "light tone . . . convey[s] a feeling of joyfulness that contrasts starkly with the reality of slave life," and warned that "young readers without sufficient background knowledge about the larger context of American slavery may come away with a dangerously rosy impression of the relationship between slaves and slave owners" (qtd. in Flood). It wasn't long before Twitter users caught wind of the questionable book, and thousands of people added their voices to the debate, starting a change.org petition to recall the book and circulating their opinions about the controversy using the hashtag #SlaveryWithASmile (Flood).

Readers rebelled, and Scholastic listened. Only two weeks after it was released, *A Birthday Cake for George Washington* was pulled from circulation, and Scholastic released the statement:

> While we have great respect for the integrity and scholarship of
> the author, illustrator and editor, we believe that, without more
> historical background on the evils of slavery than this book for
> younger children can provide, the book may give a false impres-
> sion of the reality of the lives of slaves and therefore should be
> withdrawn. (qtd. in Flood)

Responses to the banning of *Birthday Cake* were mixed. The
National Coalition Against Censorship took issue with the book's
banning, arguing that "while reasonable people can disagree about the
book's historical or literary merit, Scholastic's decision to pull it in
response to controversy is a shocking and nearly unprecedented case
of self-censorship" (qtd. in Flood). Meanwhile, author Daniel José
Older, who also publishes with Scholastic, countered that critics were
focusing on the wrong issues: "pulling a book because it's historically
inaccurate and carries on the very American tradition of whitewashing
slavery is classified as 'censorship,' while maintaining an ongoing
majority white industry that systematically excludes narratives of color
is just business as usual" (qtd. in Seltzer).

Regardless of whether Scholastic was right to censor the book,
perhaps the heated controversy itself actually gives Ganeshram and
her children's book merit despite its problems. In his essay "What Is
an Author?" Michel Foucault describes how the concept of the
"author function" allows authors to become catalysts for discourse,
and, eventually, to dissolve into the discourse they have generated
(211). Foucault claims that writing now speaks for itself: once a piece
of writing is put out into the world, the writer's individuality becomes
irrelevant. The author's work, "which once had the duty of providing
immortality, now possesses the right to kill, to be its author's murder-
er," as writing now serves simply as a launch pad for further discourse
as other authors add their commentaries to the dialogue created by
the original piece (Foucault 206).

When a writer's "author function exceeds her own work," the
author becomes what Foucault calls a "founder of discursivity," or one
who generates new discourse (217). Perhaps, then, as *Birthday Cake*

created such heated, but valuable, discussions about racial tension, whitewashing, and American slavery in books for young audiences, Ganeshram herself has been made a "founder of discursivity" through the objectionable nature of her work. Thus, the issue of censorship of children's literature is complicated. Though censorship can be viewed as an affront to free speech, when an author's controversial work is censored, it effectively turns that author into a "founder of discursivity" because their work spurs polarized reactions and creates a new, productive conversation.

It is necessary to avoid sheltering children from the troubling realities of American slavery through the whitewashing of such a history, as depicted in *Birthday Cake*. Without such knowledge, children simply become helpless pawns in the debate surrounding their own intellectual rights, at the mercy of adults who tamp down their freedom to read what they please. But in order to allow children themselves to act as "founders of discursivity" in such debates, they must be given, as Bettelheim proposes of fairy tales, an accessible medium through which to enter the conversation.

Perhaps the most effective way to both shed light on the censorship of children's literature and involve children themselves in censorship discourse is through children's media. "The Scare Your Pants Off Club," an episode in the first season of the PBS show *Arthur*, does exactly that. In the episode, Arthur and his friends are unable to put down the *Scare Your Pants Off* book series (a riff off of R. L. Stine's *Goosebumps* books), getting into trouble as they read them under their desks at school and with flashlights under the covers late at night. On the much-awaited release date of the series' most recent installment, though, the dozens of kids waiting eagerly outside the library are horrified to learn that the books, until further notice, have been pulled from library shelves after the library received complaints from the censorship-bent parental group, P.A.W.S. (Parents Against Weird Stories). Arthur and his friends leap into action, getting adults to sign a petition to bring the beloved books back. When Arthur and his group are bribed by their friend Muffy Crosswire, whose parents founded P.A.W.S., with an invitation to a party at Wonderworld for anyone who withdraws from the protests, Arthur hesitates, but is advised by his parents to keep up the fight and not "be afraid to look foolish for what you believe in" ("The Scare").

As the group most directly affected by censorship of children's literature, children should certainly not be left out of the conversation. Censorship already deprives children of complete intellectual freedom. They should not also be deprived of their awareness of this intellectual oppression. Using children's media to communicate a controversial issue like censorship creates an entrance through which children can become active participants in the debate, hopefully learning, as Arthur's parents advise, "when you add everything up, you have to do what you think is right. Even if it's a sacrifice" ("The Scare").

Though "The Scare Your Pants Off Club" makes a valuable move toward involving children in the discourse surrounding the suppression of their own intellectual rights, its impact differs from that of the conversation surrounding an actual banned book such as *Birthday Cake*. *Arthur* dramatizes the concept of censorship to make it more comfortably accessible for children. "The Scare Your Pants Off Club" itself has never been controversial, but it engagingly and informatively tells the story of a book series that was. Just as Bettelheim's fairy tales are a nonthreatening, accessible medium through which children can confront the unconscious and the uncomfortable, so too does "The Scare" create a degree of separation between children—the subjects— and the issue—censorship. *Arthur* attempts to reclaim autonomy for children by educating them about their systematic intellectual oppression, but still falls just short of giving them the reins and making them the agents of their own freedom. Rather than involving children in issues of censorship from the beginning, the episode gives them arm's-length access to the debate. "The Scare" provides a window for observation rather than a door for entrance. This begs the question: do we deny children full involvement in the discourse of their own oppression to protect them? If so, then which issues are they mature enough to confront?

Lauren, head librarian in the children's room at the Jefferson Market branch of the New York Public Library, doesn't think we should underestimate children. She says that "not only is a child capable, but they will let you know exactly what they are thinking. You typically don't have to ask them if they are enjoying something." She explains that children gravitate toward what they are familiar with, and what they are able to understand. If a child does not yet have any knowledge of a subject and cannot comprehend it, they will most likely not enjoy or be interested in the story and will not pursue it. Lauren acknowledges that the intentions of an adult who censors what books a child has access to usually "come from a place of good," a true desire to act in the best interests of the child. However, she also proposes that, much like British Columbia's inadvertently totalitarian reaction to *Yertle the Turtle*, some censors of children's literature act more reflexively out of the "impulse to control" those below them (Lauren).

In the article "Born to Choose: The Origins and Value of the Need for Control," published in *Trends in Cognitive Science*, researchers explain that "perception of control is likely adaptive for survival," because "if people did not believe they were capable of successfully producing desired results, there would be very little incentive to face even the slightest challenge" (Leotti et al.). Our need for a sense of control is hardwired into our system, as our desire for choice is "biologically motivated" and is "present in animals and even very young infants before any societal or cultural values of autonomy can be learned" (Leotti et al.). However, the biological need for control easily becomes disproportionately dominant when one feels as though they lack autonomy: "individuals who do not perceive control over their environments may seek to gain control in any way possible, potentially engaging in maladaptive behaviors" (Leotti et al.).

Our compulsive need for control has implications beyond the already catastrophic effect of motivating those who infringe upon the intellectual freedom of children. Censorship not only threatens freedom of speech and open access to knowledge, but also signifies the demise of creative freedom. As Gayle Greeno writes in "Random Notes from a Midnight Censor," censorship breeds fear and fosters creative inhibition in authors, "[forcing] them into self-censorship as they strive to second-guess what 'big buyers' want or will accept," and leading them to fear a major controversy attached to their literary reputation (19). The more writers feel they are losing control over how their work will be received, the more they will seek to regain control by anticipating potentially controversial material in their work prior to publication. Doing so "holds a chilling potential for stifling an author's creativity and ability to write honestly and honorably" (Greeno 19).

Perhaps what is most important, beyond attempting to decide what is 'appropriate' for children, is that we teach children to value autonomy above all else. Ultimately, only the individual has the right to make up their own mind and seek their own knowledge. Only the individual can choose to defend their right to creativity and free thought.

I sit cross-legged on the rug in the Jefferson Market Library Children's Room, small piles of picture books scattered around me as I conduct 'research.' I secretly just enjoy losing myself in colorful illustrations, silly plots, and rhyming phrases. From a stack by my feet, I pick up another Dr. Seuss classic, *Oh the Places You'll Go!* and lift the cover:

> You have brains in your head.
> You have feet in your shoes.
> You can steer yourself
> any direction you choose.
> You're on your own, and you know what you know.
> And YOU are the guy who'll decide where to go.

WORKS CITED

Bettelheim, Bruno. *The Uses of Enchantment: The Meaning and Importance of Fairy Tales.* Vintage, 1976.

Flood, Alison. "'Self-Censorship' of Children's Book Depicting Smiling Slave Condemned." *The Guardian*, 25 Jan. 2016, www.theguardian.com/books/2016/jan/25/censorship-childrens-book-smiling-slave-birthday-cake-washington.

Foucault, Michel. "What Is an Author?" *Aesthetics, Method, and Epistemology*, The New Press, 1999, pp. 205-222.

Ganeshram, Ramin. *A Birthday Cake for George Washington.* Scholastic Press, 2016.

Greeno, Gayle. "Random Notes from a Midnight Censor." *Virginia English Bulletin*, vol. 36, no. 1, 1986, pp. 17-23.

Lauren. Personal interview. 23 Apr. 2017.

Leotti, Lauren A., Sheena S. Iyengar, and Kevin N. Ochsner. "Born to Choose: The Origins and Value of the Need for Control." *Trends in Cognitive Sciences*, vol. 14, no. 10, 2010, pp. 457-463.

MacLeod, Anne Scott. "Censorship and Children's Literature." *The Library Quarterly: Information, Community, Policy*, vol. 53, no. 1, 1983, pp. 26-38.

Seltzer, Sarah. "How Two 'Slavery With a Smile' Controversies Are Changing the Conversation About Diverse Children's Books." *Flavorwire*, 25 Feb. 2016, www.flavorwire.com/562816/how-two-slavery-with-a-smile-controversies-are-changing-the-conversation-about-diverse-childrens-books.

Seuss, Dr. *Oh, the Places You'll Go!* Random House Books, 1990.

—. *Yertle the Turtle and Other Stories*. Random House Books, 1958.

Shi, Annie. "Seuss Won't Shush: Celebrating the 111th Birthday of the Insuppressible Dr. Seuss." *National Coalition Against Censorship*, 2 Mar. 2015, www.ncac.org/blog/Seuss-wont-shush-celebrating-the-111th-birthday-of-the-insuppressible-dr-seuss.

"The Scare Your Pants Off Club." *Arthur*, season 1, episode 28b, PBS, 13 Nov. 1996.

White, Mary Lou. "Censorship—Threat Over Children's Books." *The Elementary School Journal*, vol. 75, no. 1, 1974, pp. 2-10.

Parks's reflective essay moves from close analysis of Maggie Nelson's conjunctions in The Argonauts *to a meditation on the nature of intimacy, connection, and difference. (Instructor: Bruce Bromley)*

AND ON AND ON

Anthony Parks

Consciousness is in constant change. I do not mean by this to say that no one state
of mind has any duration—even if true, that would be hard to establish.
What I wish to lay stress on is this, that no state once gone
can recur and be identical with what it was before.
—William James, *Psychology: The Briefer Course*

Say you are a conscious anglophone. You have what they call a 'strong command' over English and its grammar, whether it be your first tongue or your second (or third). And if it's not your first, this command is something you've dutifully worked toward, learning a linguistic choreography while the rest of the room is already dancing, fluidly, fluently, around you.

I ask a friend who grew up in a bilingual household, ESL thick and through, about what it's like to reach toward the language I am writing in now, especially when much of the culture that commands this language is hostile towards those who might not, yet. And anyway, such 'command' is a farce to begin with, for how can one tame a thing as metamorphic and fickle as language?

Before she answers, I offer her my own lazy simile about learning Spanish in *un país hispanohablante*: like learning how to swim only after you've already kicked off from the dock. She recognizes my propensity for premade systems of reference; I can tell by her laugh, and her response is considerably more self-actualized in its darkness and constraint. She says that learning English—as a non-hobby, without choice—is like babysitting a child and being forced to play one of their games. A few rounds in, you start to recognize the child is making up the rules as you go along, she explains, and, though the child is quite smart, each new rule still seems to contradict the ones prior. You are always unfairly disadvantaged, and this makes you a suspect learner, but you play along because—for some reason—it's been decided the kid is boss, and his game must be played.

Alas, here we are, playing unfair games with our strong commands, our understanding of flexible syntax and dynamic diction and the imperative tense and all the different, wonderful things a colon can do. (*We are pleased to say: you've been hired; I'm so sorry: there's been an accident.*) And, probably, some of the linguistic facets of your primary mode of communication are less than named to you. You know the thing and how it works before and beyond you know what to call it. You learn when to use 'on' instead of 'over,' 'for' instead of 'with,' before you come to call these tiny words by a larger name, 'preposition.' From within, you recognize the dire importance of connecting words in both spoken word and written language, yet you may not remember your lesson on 'conjunctions' from grade school. And, admittedly, even those who cling tightly to their command might not reflect deeply about their language's grammatical nuances, prepositions and conjunctions among the many, many others.

I rarely do, at least. Well into my undergraduate studies, I find myself nose-deep in Maggie Nelson's recently published *The Argonauts*, and I'm enraptured by this singular moment in the middle of the book. A blatantly notable feature of the book is the centrality of Nelson's citational practices, which are poignant, consistent, and layered with meanings. The overhaul of referenced work and quoted prose render the work one long conversation between her, the many minds that have come before her, and the world she lives in today. Sometimes, Nelson directly engages with the cited material and the thinkers behind it; other times, scenes and quotations loom and linger among Nelson's own writing, sharp as a katana, and her thinking, clear as the Caribbean.

In this moment I find so special and particular, Nelson is citing another great mind, one from a century before herself. It's the late William James, father of modern psychology as we know it, and his words, a blend of conjunctions and prepositions and the viability of each as affect, are doing something remarkably important for Nelson:

> We ought to say a feeling of <u>and</u>, a feeling of if, a feeling of <u>but</u>, and a feeling of <u>by</u>, quite as readily as we say a feeling of <u>blue</u> or a feeling of <u>cold</u>. (54)

These words are from a chapter titled "The Stream of Consciousness" in James's 1892 collection *Psychology: The Briefer Course*, in which he describes awareness and subjectivity as linked to time and space. His prose, reflective of James as a figure, "is a rich blend of physiology, psychology, philosophy, and personal reflection" ("William James"). The deftness with which James blends these elements is one thing, among many others, that makes him an undeniably important influence on Nelson and *The Argonauts* as a whole.

Yet, before we begin to ask what 'feeling' these prepositions and conjunctions anew might allow us to do, first we might wonder why Nelson herself found it important to linger, explicitly, with James. Not all of her minds in conversation receive this treatment. As an immediate answer to James's cited prose, Nelson adds:

> We ought to, but we don't—or at least, we don't quite as readily. But the more you do, the more quickly you can recognize the feeling when it comes around again, and hopefully you won't need to stare as long. (54-55)

Though we find James's words quoted about halfway into the work, feelings of 'and's, 'if's, 'but's, and 'by's run like currents through the entirety of *The Argonauts*. And as Nelson riffs off so many brilliant, prolific, troubled, and celebrated minds—her many gendered mothers—her work is a constant 'them and.' By 'them and' I mean that her citational practices, along with the book's paratactic-paragraph form, their side-by-side arrangement, separated each by intervening white spaces, make *The Argonauts* an experiment in moments and movements. It is not only the/them/this, depending on the nature of her many references; it is always a the/them/this and more, and so, and what?

Whether Nelson describes an anecdote, cites the work of a theorist or artist, or admits an at-first unpopular opinion, stasis is never an option. There is a shark-like quality to the work, reflected in the form:

the space between one paragraph's end and a new one's beginning might lure a reader into thinking they have a moment to breathe, or dog ear the page for their next ride on the subway. But these breaths are less breaks and more brakes, and turns, accelerations, reversals, and deepenings. Between paragraphs, the reader, taking Nelson's lead, crosses vast temporal, semantic, logical, and spatial distances. Sometimes the distances are short, from a moment today to the week prior, from an artist's piece to one of their interviews, yet other times they cross centuries, disciplines, artistic mediums, and distinct emotions. Like a shark: if the work was to stop, it would die.

To think alongside James and Nelson, of prepositions and conjunctions and the powers within each, I head to the web. A simple search yields an "English 101" grammar exercise by CU Denver, documented in a faculty-distributed white sheet titled "Prepositions Versus Conjunctions (a few examples with potential pitfalls)." With this, the obvious is put into words: "a preposition 'glues' a noun or pronoun into a sentence," while "a conjunction can connect any two like elements together in a sentence," meaning "conjunctions can connect two sentences together" ("Prepositions"). Put simply, a preposition is indeed a vital grammatical feature for spoken and written language, yet conjunctions are even more vital if one's command is to move from the simple to the complex. Even more simply put, the life and liberty of complex sentences depend on conjunctions. We weaponize conjunctions against simplicity. We might conclude, then, that complex ideas and arguments are built on our ability to feel with these conjunctions, but this isn't enough. Considering the paper's forewarning of "potential pitfalls," we remember that to use, command, learn, or love a language is a risky affair, and the stakes are never the same for two different individuals. Within the realm that Nelson is conjuring through the prose of William James, I'd argue that we mustn't conflate all conjunctions as equals, or position the feelings they might spark within us as sending us across the same distances, and especially not to the same places.

This travel is at the *The Argonauts'* core. And how does Nelson sustain such momentous motion for 143 pages? One intellectual propellant that moves Nelson (and us in her wake) is that she refuses to satiate our unfortunate human appetite for 'either/or' polemics. Sure:

'or' deserves the same conjunctive rights as 'and' and 'but.' 'Or,' objectively, will allow a speaker to build a complex sentence or two. But, in my opinion—and I like to think Nelson's as well—holding on to 'or' as a primary mode of thinking rarely allows us to build complex arguments. Instead, Nelson's work shouts a 'yes, and' into our binaric void, along with a 'yes, but.' This is primarily why I find James's prose—and his work at large—so integral to Nelson's conceptual and writerly labors.

While written theory might feel abstract to many, detached from our lived realities and miles above the ground we walk around on, Nelson's "autotheory"—a word found on the book's back cover—is an effort to close the gap, rectify this rupture. *The Argonauts* uses Nelson's "own experience as an engine for thinking that spins out into the world and backwards and forwards in time" (Lorentzen). Instead of a theoretical route akin to her forebears in critical theory and queer theory (the kind that can read as totalizing and alienating for anyone not already in the know), Nelson's web of theories and arguments and burning questions flow from the self, first, so they rarely claim to know the truth of another. (In part, we might take a moment to buck against the possibility of one's 'truth,' a whole or absolute truth, ever even existing.)

That hunt for the one truth can get the better of any of us. The moment directly before William James's prose is cited, Nelson describes how twentieth-century composer John Cage was asked by a (rather simple) journalist to "summarize himself in a nutshell" (54). Cage responded, "Get yourself out of whatever cage you find yourself in" (qtd. in Nelson 54). Though Nelson never uses Cage's words as analogous or representative of her own work, Nelson's autotheory represents, among many other things, one of a million ways to pick the lock of one's own cage. Of course, we must first be able to see the shape of the bars, the space of the cell. We look to the gaps between the bars, sun spilling through them, to remind us of our own trapping. The syntax of Cage's answer here is interesting; Cage places the imperative to "get" oneself out before the clause "whatever cage you find yourself in," and a listener may find an emphasis on either verb in their reading, "get" or "find." As I consider myself a reader more interested in endings than beginnings, I find that "find[ing]" to be the core of Cage's answer, the "get[ting] oneself out" a mere entrance. To think of his answer syntactically reversed—"Find whatever cage you are in and get yourself out"—Cage is read with a considerably distinct effect. (The finding part, for me, indeed sounds more difficult.)

Thinking of locks and cages, bars and spaces, I'm reminded again of why I so often find that little word 'or' to be so dirty, in all its tininess. Such a small word's capacity to limit, such a tiny idea—this, or that—can be its own intellectual and ideological cage. Considering the crushing, totalizing constraints of our many binaries (gender's and sexuality's among the many), the centrality of 'or'-ness in our cultural ideology enacts violence galore. (For instance, it is not only queer folks, women, and those outside normative gender identities who feel binary-based violence. Feeling with James here helps: it is them and them and them and them; the space opened by an 'or' is more claustrophobic than we like to believe, and even those in the dominant, those on the 'right' side of whatever 'or,' understand the riskiness of divide, too.)

One of the most compelling 'yes, and' moments (movements) in *The Argonauts* revolves around Nelson's very complicated relationship with pregnancy and motherhood. As an intellectual descendant of so many radical thinkers of the twentieth century (Eve Sedgwick, Judith Butler, Walter Benjamin, and more)—and a queer theorist in her own right—Nelson's relationship with family as a whole is one of the most fruitful tensions driving *The Argonauts*. Nelson offers her peculiar, potentially never before admitted position: "Never in my life have I felt more prochoice than when I was pregnant," and she posits an unfathomable (feminist) bumper sticker: "IT'S A CHOICE *AND* A CHILD" (94). This is radical, and different, and beautiful; it is also an impossible intellectual leap within our belovedly human (unproductive, futile, lazy) either/or polemic. It's this type of movement that makes Nelson such a remarkable speaker; the fact that someone could write something that feels so radically new within such a tired, repetitive, yet still vital discourse around abortion is precisely due to Nelson's ability to hold onto 'and' as an affective, artistic, and writerly mode. And, if we were to think of Nelson's having read William James in this moment's explicit context, we might look to his own writing on parenthood and childbearing. On parenting's perils in his *The Principles of Psychology*, James writes:

> Our father and mother, our wife and babes, are bone of our bone and flesh of our flesh. When they die, a part of our very selves is gone. If they do anything wrong, it is our shame. If they are insulted, our anger flashes forth as readily as if we stood in their place. (292)

Writing from decades before, walking through the earth in a different body, a differently gendered body, than Nelson, we might not value James's words in the context of our modern abortion debate. Yet I think we can hold onto James's notion of what one loses upon the death of a child, along with Nelson's words of "a choice *and* a child." We might even consider the empathic potential of centralizing this in our abortion discourse, and its potential to make us feel more complexly about this impossibly difficult decision to begin with. Such a difficult decision (and a direly important one to have the capacity to make) deserves a more complex discourse than 'child or choice.'

And, because she refuses the either/or, Nelson also knows how to write 'but.' Of the debate surrounding whether sexuality is biological and genetic or fluid and self-determined, Nelson cites Mary Lambert and Macklemore's "Same Love," a song adored by the masses. Mary Lambert's chorus, in part, speaks to a conception of rigidity in popular renderings of queerness, the absence of choice and (at times, if we're lucky) the absence of a desire to change. Thus, someone steeped in queer theory may not find it to be the all-too-powerful, reifying deterministic discourse and assimilative plea for acceptance into the dominant. Nelson writes gently:

> But while *I can't change, even if I tried*, may be a true and moving anthem for some, it's a piss-poor one for others. At a certain point, the tent may need to give way to field. (74)

That 'but' is critical, here. These discursive distinctions Nelson identifies around sexuality and identity politics are held at equal value, in each of their own rights. One might conclude that Nelson sides more with the latter, but those who wish to sing along to Lambert with pride and passion still find themselves on Nelson's pages. Her writerly capacity to do so speaks to the "feeling of *but*" she found compelling in James in the first place, and in feeling this 'but,' Nelson holds onto 'and' as well. The two feelings are mutually nourishing; feeling of, feeling with, and feeling through these conjunctions open rather than close, extend rather than stunt. And thinking of growth, of this quality of being in bloom that prose like Nelson's makes one feel, I can't help but notice the love (familial, romantic, sexual) that charges *The Argonauts.*

I remember that paper from CU Denver once more, how prepositions "glue" and conjunctions "connect." I remember the type of loves I want to feel, and how adhesion sounds frightening, whereas contact, connection, feels enlightening. "To connect" rather than "to glue": I'd say that conjunctions are considerably sexier than prepositions. In a linguistic sense, the former do in fact carry in them a usage from outside our English grammar, regarding a type of meeting, of synchrony or simultaneity. This noun's etymology is steeped in sex: "from Old French *conjonction* 'union, joining, sexual intercourse'" ("conjunction, *n.*"). Again: without them, how could we get the groups of letters we call words, and the groups of words we call clauses, to flirt, buck, and fuck?

And the fruits and pleasure and residues of those tensions are never the same, were never and will never be. "Consciousness is in constant change," notes James ("Stream" 154). But? And? "*Even identical genital acts mean very different things to different people,*" Nelson quotes Sedgwick, then adds: "This is a crucial point to remember, and also a difficult one. It reminds us that there is difference right where we may be looking for, and expecting, communion" (93). Maybe all we are is bottled difference. Trials, feelings, and echoes: at times, the glass is known to shatter. We cling to the recycle, an effort to return, and contain, but the clutch is futile. Spillage is vital, that mess of effort, in practice and performance. In her deep recognition of (awe for) that difference, Nelson affirms our welling over. The tent gives way to the field; the bottle to the sea.

But? And?

WORKS CITED

"conjunction (n.)." *Etymonline,*
    www.etymonline.com/index.php?term=conjunction.
James, William. *The Principles of Psychology, Vol 1.* Cosimo, 2007.
—. "The Stream of Consciousness." *Psychology: The Briefer
    Course.* Dover, 2001.
Lorentzen, Christian. "Is Radical Queerness Possible Anymore?
    Poet Maggie Nelson's New Memoir." *Vulture,* 4 May 2015,
    www.vulture.com/2015/05/poet-maggie-nelsons-queer-new-
    memoir.html.
Nelson, Maggie. *The Argonauts.* Graywolf, 2015.
"Prepositions versus Conjunctions." *UCDenver,* clasfaculty.ucden-
    ver.edu/tphillips/grammar/prep_vs_conj-intro.pdf.
"William James." *Stanford Encyclopedia of Philosophy,* 29 Oct.
    2013, plato.stanford.edu/entries/james/.

Structured around the task of investigating and unpacking binary opposi-
tions, Whitehead's essay uses Maggie Nelson's The Argonauts *as an occa-*
sion for a larger reflection on the binary logic of patriarchy. The essay
concludes with a call for inclusive listening. (Instructor: Bruce Bromley)

BOYS WHO CRY SAINT

Taylor Whitehead

In his farewell speech to the White House, with tears glistening in his eyes, Richard Nixon canonized his mother: "I think of her, two boys dying of tuberculosis, nursing four others in order that she could take care of my older brother for three years in Arizona, and seeing each of them die. . . . Yes, she will have no books written about her. But she was a saint." It is clear that Nixon speaks out of veneration and affection. But the term "saint" is inextricable from the experience of suffering and, ultimately, death. The *Oxford English Dictionary* defines "saint" as "one of the blessed dead in Heaven," and even colloquially, "saint" is understood to mean "an extremely good or long-suffering person" ("saint, *adj.* and *n.*"). By aligning his mother with sainthood, Nixon praises her pain.

Female pain existed long before Nixon's speech in 1974. Despite the social and political movement toward the liberation of women, it has endured to the present day. Maggie Nelson addresses the question of female pain as it relates to identity in her memoir *The Argonauts*— how can we become ourselves in a culture that has a strained relationship with certain identities? What does it mean to be a mother when motherhood is both venerated and denigrated? What does it mean to be a woman when womanhood is treated in much the same way? What does it mean to be married? What does it mean to love?

Love is central to Nelson's questions. *The Argonauts* posits the idea of a love that is constantly recreated until it contains nothing of its original self, yet still goes by the same name (Nelson 5). Nelson represents this idea via Roland Barthes's metaphor of the mythological ship *Argo*: "Just as the *Argo*'s parts may be replaced over time but the boat is still called the *Argo*, whenever the lover utters the phrase 'I love you,' its meaning must be renewed by each use, as 'the very task of love and of language is to give to one and the same phrase inflections which will be forever new'" (5; qtd. in Nelson 5). This idea of an evolving love is the vessel that carries the experiences encompassed within *The Argonauts*. Nelson sets apart the experiences of womanhood, motherhood, and family-making from the norms of contemporary American culture. Her experiences of 'family,' for example, contain almost no conventional notions of the average family unit—Nelson's partner Harry is genderfluid, their first son comes from Harry's previous relationship, and their second son is conceived via a sperm donor.

Yet it can still be called 'family,' because it is a family. Many of Nelson's experiences coincide with queerness, yet she also grapples with the ways in which her experiences can be interpreted as 'hetero.' For instance, a friend refers to Nelson's family portrait emblazoned on a mug as "heteronormative" (Nelson 13). The family portrait depicts Nelson, pregnant, wearing a dress, and Harry and his son, both in suits—there is nothing in the image that explicitly expresses queerness. Yet queerness plays an essential role in their family unit. Through this tension, Nelson asks us to reconsider what the term 'queer' means to us—whether queerness must remain entirely separate from procreation and domesticity, or whether there is a place for family-making within it.

Within the tension that Nelson underlines between the terms 'queer' and 'straight' is the idea that 'straightness' is somehow undesirable for her; she feels uncomfortable being aligned with the term 'hetero.' Nelson's discomfort reveals to us that narratives of heterosexual marriage are, for her, almost inextricable from narratives of female pain. How did this happen? How did womanhood and motherhood become so closely aligned with suffering?

In a 2005 study, researchers Susan E. Stiritz and Britt-Marie Schiller observed:

> [During the Victorian period,] images of saints helped articulate the new expectations for women. Newly resurrected images and stories about saints called on women to be the nurturing and

available objects men were able to demand, given the asymmetrical power arrangements that existed between the sexes. (Stiritz and Schiller, 1145-46)

Although women have since gained more political and social leverage in Western culture—as evidenced in the implementation of the 19th Amendment, *Roe v. Wade*, and Title IX—a 2016 study found that in terms of gender roles, people still perceive men and women as very different from one another. According to this study, "comparisons between [the 1980s and 2014] show stability of gender stereotypes across all components except female gender roles, which showed a significant increase in gender stereotyping" (Haines et al. 353). In other words, despite formal recognitions of women's equality in American culture—the right to vote, to play sports, to claim bodily autonomy—ideas about gender roles may remain too similar to old, outdated ones.

In light of this information, we must confront the fact that there is still something very broken in the way straight men and straight women interact with one another. In fact, there are certain factions of feminists who believe that women today cannot be truly liberated unless they remove men from their personal lives. Regarding the early history of this movement, known as lesbian separatism, Robert Kulpa notes that:

> [Lesbian separatist Charlotte Bunch] even insisted that heterosexual women could not fully understand and become feminists, because they remained within the male-oriented spectrum of heterosexual patriarchy. Only by . . . complete detachment from men could women fully develop their potential. (491)

Lesbian separatism can be considered a political stance, and a fringe one at that. However, the existence of such discourse among feminists leads us to the idea that by participating in 'straightness,' women are hurting themselves.

Many statistics support the idea that heterosexual marriage benefits men and harms women. *Harvard Men's Health Watch* states that "a major survey of 127,545 American adults found that married men are healthier than men who were never married or whose marriages ended in divorce or widowhood" ("Marriage and Men's Health"). The article goes on to note that there are not enough data on gay and lesbian marriages to draw the same conclusions as in the case of heterosexual marriages. Another study found gender differences in the association of mental disorders and substance abuse between men and women, and that "these differences may be related to gender differences in the experience of multiple role demands within marriage, especially those concerning parenting" (Scott et al.). At its core, the Western cultural norm of marriage between men and women is closely associated with female suffering, leading to the veneration of female sainthood. It is worth noting that in the Catholic tradition, the practice of canonizing saints stemmed from "[promotion of] the veneration of the martyrs" (Beccari). To be formally recognized as a saint by the Catholic Church, one must first die.

Despite the morbid associations of sainthood, the celebration of women as saints continues to saturate Western attitudes towards women. It is perhaps the result of centuries of political discourse on gender that I found myself in a situation where a man whom I was dating, in a casual conversation about spinach (of all things!), called me a bitch. When I responded with anger and hurt, he insisted that it was a joke, just a part of his vocabulary that had always been there and that slipped out sometimes. And, he insisted, it didn't really mean anything. I found it incredibly strange. As Nelson says, *"How can the words not be good enough?"* (7). It meant something to me. I asked him if he would ever call his mother a bitch. He responded with indignation—"My mother was a saint," he told me.

Here, we find ourselves in a binary; if you are not a bitch, you must be a saint, and vice versa. Part of this binary manifests in Sigmund Freud's 'Madonna-whore complex.' Like much of Freudian psychology, this term has made its way into conventional Western ideas about female sexuality. But what this term originally referred to is a sexual disorder in which one experiences "an inability to maintain arousal within an intimate and committed relationship" (Kaplan 4). Freud attributed this to "a splitting of the tender and the sensual dimension of sexuality" (Hartmann). In other words, Freud found that his patients were experiencing dysfunction as they were not able to view committed partners with both respect and desire, because of Victorian ideals of sexuality that aligned respectability with sainthood, purity, and suffering. To them, a woman could not possibly be both respected and desired.

Where does that leave us with this strange nexus of political, social, and sexual realities—a series of binaries inside which no person, regardless of gender, could be expected to fit seamlessly? How, as Nelson rightly asks, are we supposed to navigate this great journey of life in a culture where the very existence of womanhood is under attack? Can love between men and women occur peacefully in a world where men glorify the suffering of women instead of respecting them?

The answer can be found within the pages of *The Argonauts.* Nelson's work demonstrates that we can write about our suffering; we can write about love; we can write about the process of making a family; we can write and write and write. We can write our realities as they exist for us, despite a culture that will deny us those realities. Storytelling is radical because it denies those in power the ability to claim that our realities do not exist.

The Argonauts functions primarily through storytelling. Though it is, at heart, Nelson's memoir, it also exists, beautifully, in the liminal space between memoir and criticism. Nelson's writing is not strictly personal, or strictly political; instead, for her, the personal is political. This integration begins in the formatting of *The Argonauts.* Nelson does not demarcate chapters, sections, or subsections. Instead, there is merely plain text, a format that is more familiar in, for example, an epic poem. No single idea that Nelson posits can truly be categorized. Instead, her words simply exist adjacent to one another—not in a binary, but perhaps on the collective plane of Nelson's experience.

Nelson also weaves many voices into her story by citing the authors of italicized quotes in the margin. Often, marginal citation is the only citation offered; in the body of the text, Nelson's thoughts flow seamlessly with those of other writers. This is first seen when she quotes Ludwig Wittgenstein: "[she] stopped smugly repeating 'Everything that can be thought at all can be thought clearly' and wondered anew, can everything be thought" (4). Here, Nelson brings to light the first of many binaries that she will interrogate: the question of what is thinkable and unthinkable, what is nameable and "unnameable," "things whose essence is flicker, flow" (4). The essence of *The Argonauts* itself seems almost to be that of "flicker" and "flow." Nelson's writing incorporates many different perspectives and ranges across many different topics, but it all seems to return to one word: *Argo*. *Argo* is love, family, experience; it is the fragile thing that she is building with her partner and her sons and her mother and her partner's mother and the very project of existence itself. The title of her book, *The Argonauts*, implies seamanship—that is, she and her family, her Argonauts, are embarking upon a journey with love as their vessel.

Throughout that journey, myriad complications arise, many of them centered around the binary of "queer" and "straight." In the instance of marriage that Nelson discusses in *The Argonauts*, there is a certain type of cognitive dissonance that she experiences—the friction in our minds that occurs when our idea of love is met with strangers, "with YES ON PROP 8 signs hammered into their lawns, stick figures indefatigably rejoicing" (Nelson 23). But Nelson's experience of marriage holds nothing of the conventional straight experience of marriage. Rather than casting herself, her partner, and her children on one side of a binary—either as straight or queer, sinner or saint—Nelson allows us to see that it is possible to embody both sides of the binary. As a result, we see that the binary has multiple dimensions; it is not just one or the other, but an entire spectrum of places in which one can exist as oneself.

Nelson recognizes that there is more care taken in this, in understanding that each person exists on their own terms, than in anything else. She comes to this understanding through her evolving relationship with Harry. Harry's position within certain binaries is already complicated by the culture that he lives in: he is a genderfluid person who identifies as male and uses masculine pronouns. Nelson describes a trip to a pumpkin patch where Harry pays for the pumpkins with his card, which has the name 'Harriet' on it, and the cashier assumes the card belonged to Nelson: "We just froze in the way we freeze, until Harry said, 'It's my card.' Long pause, sidelong stare. A shadow of violence usually drifts over the scene. 'It's complicated,' Harry finally said" (89). These moments are complicated and unsettling for Nelson and her partner; there is a sinister presence in them, what Nelson calls the "shadow of violence." This particular form of suffering that manifests in Harry and Nelson's relationship with the world is not the same one that we see echoed in straight marriages. Straight marriages' relationship to suffering is tied to harmful gender roles for both men and women. But the suffering that Nelson and Harry experience is specifically tied to their place within the spectrum of things a marriage could be: not just between a straight man and a straight woman, but between "two human animals, one of whom is blessedly neither male nor female, the other of whom is female (more or less)" (142). Their suffering rejects the binaries of straight or queer, good or bad; it merely is. In *The Argonauts*, Nelson describes moments where she did not yet understand the way that Harry merely is. She finds tension in the ways in which Harry's values, his very being, rub up against hers. She asserts that "words are good enough," but "before long [she learns] that [Harry] had spent a lifetime equally devoted to the conviction that words are not good enough" (3-4). Nelson seems to conclude that perhaps the answer lies on that boundary; neither of them is right, but each of them is not wrong to believe in being right, because each reality is true. They exist, and their beliefs exist, on their own terms.

Through this tension, Nelson explains that no one binary is as simple as we often make it out to be. Nelson's thoughts on abortion, for example, are at once startlingly complex and simple: she imagines a bumper sticker that reads "IT'S A CHOICE AND A CHILD" (94). On the American political spectrum, Democrats typically believe in the choice, and Republicans typically believe in the child, but neither of those beliefs encompass the truth, which is that this dichotomy is a false one. In contrast, Nelson's take on this issue is extraordinarily feminist and full of care.

No human being, complex and simple animals that we are, can truly be encompassed by any binary. This is why marriage has become so treacherous for straight women, because Western culture too often places the intrinsic value of women within a binary. You can be Nixon's mother, the saint, tending to little boys dying of tuberculosis, or you can be the sinner—or the bitch, or the whore, or whatever name is chosen for you. Each label has an ascribed value: the saintly mother is venerated, but the woman called 'bitch' or 'whore' is denigrated. The common thread between these two labels is the overwhelming silence that surrounds them, evidenced by the absence of books in their honor. Or perhaps absence is not the right word, because we have before us *The Argonauts*, a work full of honor and care. Perhaps what we are facing is an absence of honor for the books themselves. Although *The Argonauts* has received glowing reviews from many accredited publications and was a *New York Times* bestseller, some remain unconvinced as to its value. In a book review for *The Ark Review*, Giovanna Barbara Alesandro writes that "[she] want[s] to shake the book for the opinions to rearrange themselves and for something that is just a tiny bit braver and a little less self-congratulatory than what it is now: A Carrie-Bradshaw-gone-queer-memoir in the style of something straight out of a women's magazine." Alesandro's main criticism here is that *The Argonauts* is somehow less valuable for containing Nelson's thoughts about herself, her family, and her experiences. In other words, *The Argonauts* does not fit into Alesandro's definition of what 'good' books by women should look like, or what books about pregnancy should look like, or any number of impossible binaries into which we attempt to cast one another. Instead, Alesandro rejects Nelson's work, along with other media considered pointless because its target audience is women. But by denying Nelson the intrinsic value of her narrative, Alesandro is denying Nelson her reality.

More than anything else, Nelson is asking us to stop and *listen* for a while. The proliferation of theory that is so tightly woven into the text of *The Argonauts* reveals that this is not just a project in ego. It is the result of many voices coming together to speak important truths; it is about centuries and centuries of discourse on the binaries of gender, sexuality, and love that have led us to where we are now— the very same discussions that led Nelson to her marriage and her sons. It is about how we can continue to go forward from here. The end that Nelson eventually arrives at is not so grand; she wonders, "is there really such a thing as nothing, as nothingness? I don't know. I know we're still here, who knows for how long, ablaze with our care, its ongoing song" (143). But this ending does not need to be grand; it only needs to be a point where we are left, a point from which we can leave one story and begin the next.

Where does the next story begin? In the name of ongoing love, I believe that the troubling gender politics found in straight marriage can be combated with something of the energy that runs throughout *The Argonauts*—love, perhaps, but also something more concrete than that: a refusal to place any one human being in a binary where they do not belong. No more women who are saints, no more women who are bitches, no more women who suffer silently in the roles given to them, only women who are. Women who exist, somewhere, on their own terms.

However, the world is large and unforgiving. To simply erase thousands of years of tradition and stereotypes would be an impossible task. But I offer one endeavor, a journey one can take: listen. To Nelson, and to the voices she has curated inside *The Argonauts*. To voices both supporting and opposing. To the world, as it buzzes around you. To human beings existing on their own terms. Then think about Nixon, that perpetrator of binaries, who called his mother a saint and then lamented all the books that would never be written about her. You, too, reader, listener, can write. You, too, can be an Argonaut. And the ship you make may just carry you, along with others.

WORKS CITED

Alesandro, Giovanna Barbara. "Maggie Nelson's 'The Argonauts': A Somehow Disappointed Review." *Ark Books*, 11 Oct. 2016, www.arkbooks.dk/the-argonauts-by-maggie-nelson/.

Beccari, Camillo. "Beatification and Canonization." *The Catholic Encyclopedia*, vol. 2, 1907, www.newadvent.org/cathen/02364b.htm.

Haines, Elizabeth L., Kay Deaux, and Nicole Lofaro. "The Times They Are a-Changing . . . or Are They Not? A Comparison of Gender Stereotypes, 1983-2014." *Psychology of Women Quarterly*, vol. 40, no. 3, 2016, pp. 353-363.

Hartmann, Uwe. "Sigmund Freud and His Impact on Our Understanding of Male Sexual Dysfunction." *The Journal of Sexual Medicine*, vol. 6, no. 8, 2009, pp. 2332-39.

Kaplan, Helen Singer. "Intimacy Disorders and Sexual Panic States." *Journal of Sex & Marital Therapy*, vol. 14, no. 1, 1988, pp. 3-12.

Kulpa, Robert. "Lesbian Separatism." *Encyclopedia of Gender and Society*, edited by Jodi O'Brien, SAGE Publications, 2009, p. 491.

"Marriage and Men's Health." *Harvard Men's Health Watch*, July 2010, www.health.harvard.edu/newsletter_article/marriage-and-mens-health.

Nelson, Maggie. *The Argonauts*. Graywolf Press, 2015.

Nixon, Richard. "White House Farewell." 9 August 1974, The White House, Washington, DC.

"saint, *adj*. and *n*." *Oxford English Dictionary Online*, March 2017, www.oed.com/view/Entry/169847?rskey=YBbTnp&result=1&is Advanced=false#eid.

Scott, Kate M., et al. "Gender and the Relationship Between Marital Status and First Onset of Mood, Anxiety and Substance Use Disorders." *Psychological Medicine*, vol. 40, no. 9, 2010, pp. 1495-505.

Stiritz, Susan E., and Britt-Marie Schiller. "Transforming Feminine Categories: Genealogies of Virginity and Sainthood." *Journal of the American Psychoanalytic Association*, vol. 53, no. 4, 2005, pp. 1133-59.

In this persuasive essay, Stanley-Coughlan reveals how attitudes in the social work field punish rather than empower sex workers. Using evidence from personal narratives, academic research, and historical accounts, she exposes how New York social services have failed sex workers and argues for a more sex-positive view of their profession.
(Instructor: Laura Weinert-Kendt)

SEX WORK AND SOCIAL WELFARE: ANTI-OPPRESSIVE SOCIAL WORK PRACTICE

Aidan Stanley-Coughlan

Jenna Torres started selling sex at the age of fifteen to pay for books and school supplies. In August 2013, on the same day she was supposed to pick up her college schedule, she was arrested for prostitution (Torres). Torres's case was heard in New York's newly-created Human Trafficking Intervention Courts (HTICs), which were instituted to offer "vital services instead of punishment to these defendants" (Crabapple). After taking a guilty plea, however, she found herself in a much worse position than she had previously been in. She was mandated to attend ten therapy sessions at a "prostitution diversion program," missing registration day for her classes and putting her only true shot at upward mobility in serious jeopardy (Torres). Like so many of our clients in social work, Torres had difficulties attempting to balance all the social service involvement in her life. Rushing to Child Services aftercare meetings in Brooklyn, or the prostitution diversion program in Harlem, all the while caring for three young children and trying to get her education at the College of Staten Island quickly became overwhelming and unsustainable (Torres). Eventually, she was forced to drop out of school, and, instead of going to classes, she had to face the same fate that so many of our clients do—to spend every day bouncing back and forth between court-mandated appointments, seeing no progress in her situation, and feeling completely and utterly powerless.

Jenna Torres represents a significant and divisive controversy in the field of social welfare. And while her situation seems like a complete failure of New York social service agencies, the majority of social workers have embraced the school of thought that produced HTICs (Torres). New York state law designates social work clients who are involved in the sex industry as 'prostituted peoples'—people who have been manipulated, pimped out, or trafficked into performing sex for money. This mindset has been advocated extensively by feminist groups who are pushing for a shift towards the client-criminalization . model, and continues to be the most influential in shaping New York City services (Torres). Since the seventies, however, significant opposition to this long-held belief has grown quickly. A new stream of sex-positive feminists advocate full legalization of prostitution and rebranding prostitution as legitimate and potentially empowering "sex work" (Torres). As the times have progressed and prostitution courts have become increasingly more service-oriented, social workers have become increasingly more involved in the lives of women and LGBTQ people involved in the sex industry, mainly as facilitators in government-mandated anti-prostitution programs and 'rescue' agencies. The growing presence of social workers within agencies that work with sex workers necessitates a deeper consideration of how this cultural debate influences the services we provide to our clients.

The way New York social services approach their work with sex workers has changed slightly throughout history but, at its core, has remained rather stagnant in its determination that all women involved in sex work are victims. It is clear in its assumption that Jenna Torres, and all other women and LGBTQ people like her, are not capable of deciding for themselves to enter sex work, completely overlooking Jenna's thought-out plan to use prostitution as a way to economically further her educational goals. To them, Jenna Torres is a slave to her circumstances and to the clients who solicit sex from her. Speaking to the origins of this ideology, historian Erin Gallagher-Cohoon describes how "during the Progressive Era in the United States of America, there were fears that not only was prostitution a growing industry of sin, but that women were being coerced into becoming prostitutes" (36). The media at the time dubbed the growing prevalence of prostitutes in cities "white slavery" (36). In this understanding, prostitutes had no agency in their position. The women, specifically white women, for whom the public expressed concern were said to be completely helpless, caught up in the deviant hypersexuality of the urban, ill-intentioned man. The "white slavery" model, problematic as it may be, has continued to shape the discourse around prostitution in the social welfare and legal communities, as well as in the public lexicon.

Prominent sex-positive organizations and sex worker advocacy unions have taken a radically different approach, casting off the white slavery model, itself, as a form of oppression. They argue that when groups like the National Organization of Women express concern over the exploitation and subjugation of women in the sex industry, they actually end up disempowering the workers themselves. Often anti-prostitution feminists and 'advocates' even go as far to say that there is no such thing as voluntary sex work. While this assertion seems radical, it has had a powerful impact. In New York state, there is no legal distinction made between human trafficking and voluntary sex work. In her *VICE* article, "Special Prostitution Courts and the Myth of 'Rescuing' Sex Workers," Molly Crabapple discusses how the advent of New York State's HTICs have blurred this line even further. She describes how the 2013 creation of "these courts [legally] redefined prostitutes as trafficking victims rather than criminals" (Crabapple). Operating under the assumption "that the vast majority of individuals charged with prostitution offenses are commercially exploited or at risk of exploitation," they completely overlook the conscious, consenting, and entirely voluntary participation of the overwhelming majority of sex workers (Crabapple).

Crabapple, in one of her visits to one of the largest HTICs in Queens, asked the presiding judge about how these cases are handled differently than *actual* international sex trafficking. She responded, "no little girl dreams of being a sex worker," and, loud enough for the defendants in the courtroom to overhear, she presumed the majority of sex workers had been molested (Crabapple). Even though these courts supposedly handle 'trafficking' cases more compassionately and are centered around *helping* sex workers, Crabapple argues that they assume that "anyone who's been arrested for sex work is raw material, incapable of making his or her own choices." For Jenna Torres, and all of our clients who made conscientious, albeit economically-driven, choices to participate in the sex industry, this assumption is deeply degrading, disempowering, and oppressive.

Too often, social workers have engineered, or at least participated in, the disempowerment of voluntary commercial sex workers, acting as a cog in the machine that systematically removes agency from our clients. This participation, however, is well-intentioned. As the people on the front lines, social workers are very familiar with the senseless acts of violence and traumatic experiences that are indelibly associated with the industry of prostitution. In a New York City-based study, it was found that "80% of street-based sex workers reported experiencing violence or threats in the course of their work," and "60% reported being violently forced into doing something they didn't want to do" (Thukral and Ditmore 10). Seeing this data, it makes sense that social workers have a hard time recognizing the assertions of sex worker advocacy organizations like the Red Umbrella Project—that sex work is nearly always voluntary, and empowering. In fact, opposition to this mindset is very common among social workers, who, unlike policy-makers, have uniquely intimate experiences working with women and LGBTQ people in the sex industry. In the prominent *Journal of Trauma Practice*, for instance, psychologist Melissa Farley and her colleagues were very clear in their assertion that:

> prostitution dehumanizes, commodifies and fetishizes women, in contrast to non-commercial casual sex where both people act on the basis of sexual desire and both people are free to retract without economic consequence. In prostitution, there is always a power imbalance, where the john has the social and economic power to hire her/him to act like a sexualized puppet. Prostitution excludes any mutuality of privilege or pleasure: its goal is to ensure that one person does not use her personal desire to determine which sexual acts do and do not occur—while the other person acts on the basis of his personal desire. (Farley et al. 34)

Conceptualizing prostitution in this way, especially in a publication that informs our practice with traumatized clients, is impactful, but it frames the way we deliver services incorrectly. It primes us to immediately step into a place of judgment, succumbing to stigmas around sex work; not to respect the choices our clients make; or even to think that our clients are unable to make decisions about their own lives. Following this mindset, social workers who work with sex workers are not supportive facilitators, but 'saviors.'

Unfortunately these 'saviors' are all too common within our profession. Even though social work is perhaps one of the most introspective and self-evaluating professions, many come into social work without recognizing power imbalances in their relationships with clients. Project ROSE, a famous diversion program engineered by a group of social workers, is a good example of this 'savior' ideology making its way into the services we provide sex workers. Dr. Dominique Roe-Sepowitz, a professor at the Arizona State University School of Social Work and distinguished social worker, worked with the Phoenix Police Department to create the program, which aims to rescue women, especially transwomen, from their dangerous and illegal lifestyle ("Free Monica Jones"). Over the course of two days, police, to accommodate the "social service program," ramped up prostitution raids, bringing in over 100 women and LGBTQ people and giving them a choice between participating in the program and gaining access to services aimed at removing them from the sex industry or going to jail ("Free Monica Jones"). Roe-Sepowitz believes her service "provides a life-saving choice for her clients," but in the end what she is doing is rounding up prostitutes and making them choose between therapy and a cold cell. That is not a choice; that is a social worker dictating the clients' lives with no respect for their situation or feelings ("Free Monica Jones"). Roe-Sepowitz, like her many contemporaries in the social welfare community, is not the savior she imagines herself to be—she is an extortionist with a Master of Social Work.

The way social workers talk about and provide services to sex workers must change. We, more so than any other profession, must employ critical consciousness to reflect on how we affect our clients. While the social welfare community has made a lot of progress advancing beyond the savior mentality in racial justice work and in international development, there is a long way to go in advancing our theories of practice with sex workers. The goal can no longer be 'diversion' or exit from the sex industry, as it has been in New York City; it has to be empowerment and actualization. In her entry in

Social Work with Groups, Margot Breton describes the rather newly introduced empowerment-driven model of social work practice. She writes "for those in the 'helping professions' following the principle of collegiality," meeting the client where they're at, and abandoning the position of savior, "may involve significant shifts in . . . perception" (28-29). This problem runs deeper than a few rogue social workers with inflated egos: it is cemented deep in the ideological roots of our profession. Breton points out that the majority of "social work models are imbued with medical thought and language, creating the iatrogenic effect whereby we disqualify people's ability to handle their problems-in-living in the absence of expert advice" (29). In this way, social workers have asserted power over their clients, especially those involved in commercial sex work, replicating the very systems of hierarchical oppression that our profession was born to dismantle.

In a press release on the matter, the National Association of Social Workers, the governing organization of American social work, affirmed that "social workers must hear and validate the voices of adult women and men who work, or have worked, as commercial sex workers" (3). They insisted, "we must acknowledge that there is a continuum of experiences within the commercial sex trade industry, and by doing so we validate the reality of all people engaged in this work rather than circumscribe their experiences within a specific moral code" (National Association of Social Workers 3). The sentiment is good, but it does not mention the lack of action accompanying this assertion; it is conservative about the scope of the work that must be done to transform the landscape of services in New York and throughout the country.

Social work, at least when done well, is radical. We, upon taking our oath, commit to acknowledge the lives and experiences of the many people who have been beaten, bruised, and left to starve by a vicious and perpetually unequal socioeconomic structure. Sex workers lie at the dangerous intersection of capitalism and the cisheteropatriarchy, making them particularly vulnerable. Through our empowerment-based work, we cannot stick our heads in the sand as many sex-positive groups have done and claim that sex work, in itself, is empowering. It may be for a privileged few, but the majority of commercial sex workers, like Jenna Torres, use their bodies to make money. Besides the socially-constructed patriarchal and heteronormative rules which form the 'whore stigma' that isolates sex workers, their experience is by no means a foreign one. When sex worker advocacy organizations insist that 'sex work is work,' they don't even realize how accurate their assertion is. Indeed, there must be a recognition of prostitution as a form of legitimate labor, but in the Marxist sense. Under capitalism, people's bodies are used to accrue profit for those at the top of the economic food chain. Work is inherently exploitative. While some people manage to sneak into a job they actually enjoy, the majority do not feel empowered in their day to day lives, but they continue on because that is how they survive.

Sex workers are no different, and they deserve all the protections we grant to those laboring in more traditional industries. While capitalism and the patriarchy are big systems for social workers to grapple with, our job is to address their ills. The services that are available for sex workers, especially those that sex workers are mandated to attend, are unacceptable. While we may disagree on the symbolic political implications, or even the legality of sex work, we cannot in good conscience allow these services to continue to fail women and LGBTQ people like they failed Jenna Torres. The only way we can address this problem, as service providers, is to change the way we gear services for clients involved in the sex industry. The code of ethics mandates us to treat sex workers, and all our clients, with dignity and respect, and to fight for their economic advancement and health equity. But we need to accept that the most impactful way to do this is to involve our clients themselves—empowering and giving them the tools to take control of their own lives and positions within society.

WORKS CITED

Breton, Margot. "On the Meaning of Empowerment and Empowerment-Oriented Social Work Practice." *Social Work with Groups*, vol. 17, no. 3, 1994, pp. 23-27.
Crabapple, Molly. "Special Prostitution Courts and the Myth of 'Rescuing' Sex Workers." *VICE*, 5 Jan. 2015,

www.vice.com/en_us/article/sex-workers-and-the-city-0000550-v22n1.

Farley, Melissa, et al. "Prostitution and Trafficking in Nine Countries: An Update on Violence and Posttraumatic Stress Disorder." *Journal of Trauma Practice*, vol. 2, no. 3-4, 2004, pp. 33-74.

"Free Monica Jones: Sex Workers in Phoenix Organize." *Al Jazeera*, 2014. *Vimeo*, 9 May 2017, www.vimeo.com/85804433.

Gallagher-Cohoon, Erin. "The Dirt on 'White Slavery': The Construction of Prostitution Narratives in Early Twentieth-Century American Newspapers." *Constellations*, vol. 5, no. 1, 2013, pp. 36-49.

National Association of Social Workers. *Commercial Sex Workers and Social Work Practice*. NASW, 2008, www.naswdc.org/assets/secured/documents/da/da2008/reffered Commercial%20Sex%20Work-SW%20Speaks %20Version.pdf.

Thukral, Juhu, and Melissa Ditmore. *Revolving Door: An Analysis of Street-Based Prostitution in New York City*. Sex Workers Project at the Urban Justice Center, 2003, www.sexworkersproject.org/downloads/RevolvingDoor.pdf.

Torres, Jenna. "How New York City's Treatment of Sex Workers Continues to Harm Us." *Rewire*, 22 Sept. 2015. www.rewire.news/article/2015/09/22/new-york-citys-treatment-sex-workers-continues-harm-us/.

Galanter's consideration of the relationship of beauty, community, and interpretation draws not only on a detailed analysis of Mark Doty's "Souls on Ice" but also on representations of experiences at Madame Tussauds and the Whitney Museum of American Art. (Instructor: Victoria Olsen)

HUMANS AND DOGS AND FISHES! OH MY!

Andrew Galanter

My dad is not made out of wax. This did not stop a woman from once thinking otherwise. September 2010's hottest party was my thirteenth birthday at Madame Tussauds, the perfect medley of my two favorite things: celebrities and wax. The invitation was exclusive, extending to an elite group of one friend, my dad, and my grandmother. Seeing so many dead celebrities can take on the air of a funeral home, but you can't spell 'funeral' without 'fun.' And if a day of idly looking at the ideal idyll of your idols doesn't sound fun, then you may as well be dead yourself.

We had paused to regain our sense of direction when it happened. My dad, immobile, stared at a floor map. A woman zeroed in on him. She extended a wary hand toward him. My dad jumped. She jumped. He blinked. She scurried away. I'd pay double the entrance fee to find out her thoughts. Just which famous person did she think my dad was? Surely her mental plaque didn't read 'Suburban New York Dad. Father of Two. Accountant.' If the alive could pass for the unalive, it took one trip to the Whitney Museum of American Art to show me the reverse was just as possible.

It's a living room on pause. A woman sits on a chair, surrounded by art buffs and modest "Writing the Essay" students alike who are held rapt in a communal experience equal parts mundane and beautiful. The mundane refers to the woman's activity, or perhaps more accurately, lack thereof; her posture is casual if not slumped as she contemplates the day's mail strewn haphazardly on her lap. She sports a blue floral print dress—Phidian drapery in the temple of the every-day. Onlookers aside, she is not alone: a dog lies curled at her feet (meticulously flip-flopped), nonchalantly demonstrating hallmark canine torpor. Beautiful is the scene's uncanny aliveness; each of my steps toward her felt like the dot of a question mark as I shamelessly hummed Bon Jovi's "Dead or Alive." This balance between the inanimate and animate is Duane Hanson's *Woman with Dog*, on view in the Whitney's Human Interest exhibit (Hanson). The exhibit explores the very notion of portraiture, and Hanson's creation is no exception as it masterfully presents a microcosm of our quotidian experience. At the piece's core is a stunning representation of life from various inherently non-lifelike substances. It's a math equation with a surprising sum. To say that polymer plus oil added to vinyl cast could look so much like life would shock even the Einsteins among us. This 'aliveness puzzle' suggests that living and breathing might not be central to what we call aliveness. There is some external force that allows us us to experience this beautiful stillness as the unplaceable condition we call humanity.

This sensation of beautiful stillness is no stranger to poet Mark Doty. It's the underpinning force of this stillness, and the desire to uncover its origin, that drives him in his essay "Souls on Ice." The essay documents the sprawling creative process of his poem "A Display of Mackerel," a work inspired by the titular image as seen at his local Stop & Shop. It was love at first sight. He writes: "They were rowed and stacked, brilliant against the white of the crushed ice. I loved how black and glistening the bands of dark scales were, and the prismed sheen of the patches between, and their shining flat eyes" ("Souls"). This image would become the base for the poem's lexicon, an artistic vocabulary that seems to hinge on three words: "splendor, and splendor" ("Display"). For Doty, splendor is interpreted in exceedingly visual and beautiful ways. No longer are the fish merely "black and glistening" ("Souls"); instead, they are "the wildly rain-bowed / mirror of a soapbubble sphere" ("Display"). Gone are the "shining flat eyes" ("Souls"), replaced with the vivid image of "sun on gasoline" ("Display"). This sense of beauty is not tangential to the splendor Doty experienced, but, rather, its prerequisite. Had the fish seemed dull or nondescript, Doty's eye would never have been drawn to them; beauty serves as a distinguishing characteristic that hints at animate substrata where none would have previously existed. If such beauty was the first half of our aliveness puzzle, it was up to Doty to solve the second: how do the fish retain beauty even after death?

Fish are animals distinctly known for their aliveness. Indeed, the very word conjures up associations of brilliant groups of brightly colored schools flitting between reefs. But behind the display case of Stop & Shop, the fish are anything but that. At least, at first glance. Doty breaks ground by seeing past the fishes' physical form and clarifying their emotional context. It isn't their individual colors or patterns that make them beautiful, but rather their grouped dynamism. If their collective identity is the source of our awe, then it shouldn't necessarily preclude dead fish too; as long as the fish remain grouped, whether they are living or not is wholly incidental. This is what Doty realized when he looked upon the display case of fish. For him, the dead fish behind their clear case coffin were still evocative as "the vehicle . . . to help [him] think about human identity" ("Souls"). Despite being sold at Stop & Shop, they were still together, albeit in a markedly different state. Their power came not from a temporary state, but from the permanence of their group identity. This realization—that "the one of the kind, the singular, like [his] dear lover, cannot last. And yet the collective life, which is also us, shimmers on"— helped comfort Doty after the death of his lover from AIDS ("Souls"). Viewed in isolation, Doty's loss would seem singular and harrowing. And while a metaphor may not have erased his grief, he could have begun to understand its context. In a very real sense, Doty's loss was part of the larger AIDS epidemic. The power of his lover's life belonged to and lived on in the larger gay community. Just as the dead fishes' remarkability remained undiminished, so should the human life Doty lost. Metaphor taught Doty that dying does not exclude "splendor." Beauty is a constant protected by group identity.

Given Doty's understanding of what forms aliveness—the intricate intersection of and interplay between beauty and community— we are better equipped to understand the disarming vivacity of *Woman with Dog*. Where the woman's soul lies suddenly comes into focus. It is in her aesthetic appeal. The potential of finding collectivity within her identity keeps it sustained. At first, this 'collective' seems

at odds with Hanson's apparent intention of capturing a single human
being. However, such community lies not in her form but in her context. The woman is checking her mail, a daily ritual with universal
connotations. We see past her specific action to the times when we
have done it ourselves—the excited beeline to the mailbox, with opening letters taking on the revelry of unwrapping presents—so that she
becomes "a container for emotion and idea, a vessel that can hold
what's too slippery or charged or difficult to touch" ("Souls"). Not
only have we all excitedly opened mail, but we have sat lazily in a
chair. We have had our beloved pets nearby. If not reminding us of
ourselves, the piece evokes other people we know. Maybe the woman
is our mother, our grandmother, our aunt. Indeed, the very fact that
she is titled 'Woman' provides a blank space over which we can all
overlay our own emotional frames, showing us that "our glory is not
our individuality . . . but our commonness" ("Souls"). We have seen
Doty's beautifying force breathe life back into dead mackerels.
Hanson underscores this force's power by capturing life where none
had ever existed. It is not the woman's individual clothes, actions, or
appearance that make her lively, for she was never alive in the first
place. It is the larger ideal of domestic serenity that they evoke, a community that extends to onlooking art buffs and occasional "Writing
the Essay" students. Doty allows us to see the unnamed woman's
humanity just as he saw his own poetry—as "a *made* version of an
experience" ("Souls").

If humanity is made, what does it say about its makers? Perhaps
it suggests humans are hardwired to seek humanity in the distinctly
inhuman, playing a game where the realistic representation of life is
the objective. The very existence of an institution such as Madame
Tussauds—a museum dedicated to recreating the likeness and image
of famous humans—seems to affirm this. A sense of humanity can be
created from the inanimate. But nowhere is it written that the union
of beauty and group identity is the rule and not the exception. These
exceptions are evident at Madame Tussauds. Walking through the
museum is like being a human pinball, perpetually bouncing off
celebrity bumpers. There is no denying the aesthetic composition of
wax Elton John's sparkling suit. And yet, the fact that I remember not
his form itself is revealing. While the aesthetic composition is present,

it lacks the second part of community. No longer can we fill in the blank spaces with our own experiential references, as we did with Hanson's piece; the spaces are already filled, the product of a media culture where we can see a celebrity on stage just as easily as we can see her eating lunch. Beauty and community work together, and removing one lessens the effect of the other. There's a reason wax Elton is at Madame Tussauds and not the Whitney.

The intertwining of beauty and community is richly paradoxical. Community may be a powerful force, but it seems most potent when bolstered by our individual experiences. Hanson's work remains evocative because we get to mentally build the community ourselves. Take that freedom away, as Madame Tussauds does, and you're left with the air of a funeral home. Doty's mackerels are not strangers to this paradox. Doty was struck by the fishes' collective identity, but ultimately stayed invested because he could overlay the individual death of his lover on top of them. We did not have the same experience, and thus may not have been as spellbound had we been in Doty's place. We bring our individuality to established group identities, creating unique experiences that can be interpreted according to the values of the viewer. Doty looks at fish and sees a poem. I look at fish and see dinner.

WORKS CITED

Doty, Mark. "A Display of Mackerel." *Atlantis: Poems*, HarperCollins, 1995.

—. "Souls on Ice." *Academy of American Poets*, 18 Jul. 2000, www.poets.org/poetsorg/text/souls-ice.

Hanson, Duane. *Woman with Dog*. 1977, acrylic and oil on cast polyvinyl with clothing, hair, eyeglasses, etc. Whitney Museum of American Art, New York.

Structured to move from a particular controversy—Kim Kardashian's nude selfie—to the larger questions it raises, Milne's essay stages a conversation between critics about the relationship of photography to gender and self-presentation in the twenty-first century. (Instructor: Lane Anderson)

NO LONGER A PASSIVE SUBJECT: THE REVOLUTIONARY POTENTIAL OF THE NUDE SELFIE

Amelia Milne

> To be on display is to have the surface of one's own skin, the hairs of one's own body, turned into a disguise which, in that situation, can never be discarded. The nude is condemned to never being naked. Nudity is a form of dress.
> — John Berger, *Ways of Seeing* (54)

In the televised *Ways of Seeing*, visual arts theorist and critic John Berger speaks about fine art, focusing on depictions of female nudity. Although photography is arguably the primary visual medium through which we now communicate, many of Berger's theories about the interaction of art, subject, and audience are still applicable. Berger begins *Ways of Seeing* by explaining that women were the principal and enduring subject of nude paintings. He delineates between simply being naked and being nude in the context of aesthetic art. Whereas being naked allows a woman to be wholly herself, being nude renders her as a sight to be seen by another who is dressed. According to Berger, "a nude has to be seen as an object in order to be a nude" ("Episode 2"). Most nudes have been lined up for the pleasure and judgment of a male proprietor; those who are judged beautiful become owned and available. The nude becomes a sign of submission to the proprietor's demands. In today's image- and media-saturated world, the female nude remains a popular subject. However, the increased accessibility of art means that it is often ordinary people—women, the 'subjects'—who hold the power and drive the creative direction of such work, even producing it themselves. Arguably, photography and its position within social media have democratized the female nude to the point where Berger's analyses are no longer indiscriminately applicable. Can women transcend his definition as merely 'passive' subjects in depictions of nudity? Can they instead use their own photographs to reclaim their own narrative and sexuality?

To explore these statements and thus perhaps problematize Berger's work, I will examine the nude photograph Kim Kardashian posted to her personal Instagram and Twitter account on March 7, 2016. The photograph depicts Kardashian posed nude in front of a mirror and focuses almost entirely on her famous and well-documented curves. The image is not pornographic in nature—the composition, Kardashian's expression, and her humorous caption, "When you're like I have nothing to wear LOL" (Kardashian)—places it more in the realm of an intimate artistic nude. Kardashian is a social media star whose career depends in part on her ability to create controversial and conversation-provoking content, so posting this nude selfie may have been a concerted effort to rise above a constant stream of digitized content and generate attention. As such, Kardashian's performance was successful. The response was enormous and immediate: commentary, controversy, attention from individuals and media platforms alike. The image was lauded and decried in turn, and the discourse moved to a consideration of female sexuality and the representation of women in media. Harriet Harman, former deputy leader of the U.K.'s Labour party, commented, "there's a kind of bravery and pioneering spirit" in Kardashian's image (Burnett). However, not everyone has shared this view—Kardashian faced backlash for behaving inappropriately, revealing too much, and acting in a way that was unsophisticated and unbefitting of a mother. Fellow celebrity Chloë Grace Moretz tweeted at Kardashian, "I hope you realize how important setting goals are for young women, teaching them we have so much more to offer than our bodies" (qtd. in Moon). Similarly negative sentiments echoed across the Internet.

Given that the nude female body has been appearing in media since the advent of art, what is it about Kardashian's selfie that provokes such disparagement? What does that response say about the way modern women can or cannot use photography as a tool for empowerment? John Berger's theories on the painted nude seem applicable in this circumstance: "You painted a naked woman because you enjoyed looking at her, put a mirror in her hand and you called the painting 'vanity,' thus morally condemning the woman whose nakedness you had depicted for your own pleasure" (*Ways of Seeing* 51). Viewers of Kardashian's photograph condemn her for her enjoyment and celebration of her own naked body. Historically, in the periods Berger discusses, women had no agency over the way they were depicted and represented. Contemporaneously, however, women can exercise some such agency, but this is still subject to the demands of the patriarchal gaze Berger describes. Arguably, it is the fact that Kardashian exercises agency outside of the space society has designated for her, thus controlling the depiction of her sexuality, that acts against dominant historical norms and causes such controversy. Kardashian is a celebrity who has made her living by performing for a public fascinated and excited by her body and its propensity to be seen as a sexual object.

However, many members of that same audience consider it impermissible for her to reclaim and repurpose this sexuality in an exaggerated and playful way. In her essay "In Plato's Cave," Susan Sontag describes the act of photography as one with the capacity to "presume, intrude, trespass, distort, exploit" (9). She links this quality with that of the camera as a tool for perversion, for acting out fantasies that are both "plausible and inappropriate" (9). To illustrate this correlation, she references movies including *Peeping Tom* (1960) and *Blowup* (1966), both of which utilize cameras to execute literal or metaphorical violence against female protagonists. These images graphically and intentionally illustrate Berger's propositions about the subjugation of female bodies by men through art. A more salient point is that movies like *Peeping Tom* and *Blowup* receive respect and critical acclaim, whilst the image of Kardashian is critiqued.

An apt contemporary illustration of this kind of violence is the public reaction to leaked naked photos of female celebrities. Vanessa Hudgens and Jennifer Lawrence, women of similar public standing to Kardashian, have privately taken nude selfies, which were released publicly without their consent. As with Kardashian, these images created an Internet firestorm, but one of a different tone: these images were forwarded, circulated, crowed over by the (male) public. A cursory Google search will reveal entire websites—vanessahudgens-

nude.org, celebsunmasked.com—with headlines such as "YES!
Vanessa Hudgens NUDE Pictures Leaked!" These outlets position
the images as titillating, sexy, exciting, and focus far more on their
potential as masturbation aids than on the morals of their subjects. It
could be argued that when a woman is in control of these sorts of
images—consenting to or even enjoying her own sexualized representation in the public forum, like Kardashian and unlike Hudgens and
Lawrence—then that representation suddenly becomes unacceptable.
This follows Berger's theories about the patriarchal understanding of
the nude, and how one must satisfy the male gaze in order to obtain
validity and legitimacy. These public reactions demonstrate that it is
the context as well as the content itself that make up this satisfaction.
Kardashian is criticized for having the "mirror in her hand," or, as it
may be, having a mirror in front of her (Berger, "Episode 2").

Sontag refers to this phenomenon as the "camera as phallus" (10).
When the metaphorical instrument of male desire becomes repur-
posed by a female subject, when the sexualized image ceases to
covertly titillate its audience first and foremost, and instead works as
a transparent, intentional addition to discourse on the female body,
the audience decries it.

Can Kardashian's photograph—which operates in a space of self-
awareness and self-reference—transcend Sontag's theory of
exploitation, as well as Berger's ideas of the female nude? Is she really
showing how the power of photography, by virtue of its position in
social media, can be used by women to subvert and counter dominant,
oppressive norms related to their representation? In both Sontag and
Berger's works, the idea circles around the artist's ability to exert a
measure of force. The artist may utilize their subject(s) to showcase
their own artistic vision, to promote their own agenda, or perhaps to
participate in the economic circulation of images, motivated by
personal gain of a more material kind. However, the fact that
Kardashian created this image—that it is still wildly popular, and thus
successful personal marketing—indicates that perhaps by seizing back
control with enough conviction, women are able to reject this dominant paradigm.

Kim Kardashian rose to fame and notoriety on the back of a
leaked sex tape and has since maintained her position in the public eye

in some part due to her famous curves, which she showcases in a way that plays directly into what her audience wants. The photograph in question is self-referential in the extreme. From her caption to the focus on her famous figure, it fits with the image of herself Kardashian has created, capitalized on, and has a vested interest in perpetuating. One could say that this selfie is in fact a complete distillation of her personal brand and message. It's a reductive encapsulation, perhaps, but an encapsulation nonetheless. The photo is Kim Kardashian's assertion of what she purports is the very essence of Kim Kardashian. She is the one who will ultimately profit from the attention and excitement it generates. When this image inevitably generates clicks, sells magazines, and encourages viewers, she will gain both capital and, more importantly, recognition.

Sontag claims: "To photograph is to appropriate the thing photographed. It means putting oneself into a certain relation to the world that feels like knowledge—and therefore, like power" (2). But in Kardashian's case the 'subject'—the other, the alterity, the objectified—becomes complicit in her own objectification. As exemplified by her selfie, the subject's intention is to commodify her physical form and fully realize this commodification in the final work of art. Kardashian's selfie would appear to subvert the traditional hierarchy of artist-over-model. More specifically, contrary to both Sontag's and Berger's assumptions, it subverts the tradition of male-artist-over-female-model. Thus, Kardashian's presentation of her own narrative through her selfie suggests that photography can, in fact, be used by women as a means of relaying their narratives and aims, a much more hopeful and modern assessment than that of Berger or Sontag.

What about this selfie allows it to transcend our understanding of the photographed as passive or exploited? Obviously, there is the fact that Kardashian took the image herself, with no other photographer holding power over her. However, there is arguably a particular aspect of this photograph that makes it perfectly representative of the way social media can be utilized to redirect and repurpose the portrayal of marginalized social bodies (in this case, female bodies). It involves the way the image combines public and private photography.

In her essay "In Our Glory: Photography and Black Life," critic bell hooks describes the ability of black people to take private pictures of themselves as a way to "transcend the limits of the colonizing eye," calling these images "counter-hegemonic" (60-61). Although the narratives of women and black people are not equivalent, a parallel can be drawn. For both these types of social bodies, private photos display a side of the subject that counters public, oppressive discourse. However, social media has allowed the nude selfie, a conventionally private photo, to transcend its boundaries and let women make these 'representative' discourses public.

Similarly, in his later work "The Uses of Photography," John Berger remains hopeful about the revolutionary potential of photography, if only it can be harnessed correctly: "It is just possible that photography is the prophecy of a human memory yet to be socially and politically achieved" (57). The vital distinction between private and public photography is particularly important to Berger. He argues that private photographs—"the portrait of a mother, the picture of a daughter, a group photo of one's team"—retain meaning because they have a context and thus "contribute to living memory" ("Uses" 51-52). By contrast, public photographs present strangeness. Thus, what is problematic, and needs to be challenged, is the public use of photographs. Kim Kardashian's photograph can be considered a 'public' photograph and thus, according to Berger, cannot create meaningful social change. He says that it can only reinforce established views because of its lack of context. Berger asserts: "The contemporary public photograph usually presents an event, a seized set of appearances, which has nothing to do with its readers or with the original meaning of the event" (52). Arguably, Kardashian's portrait stands in contrast to Berger's ideas about the public photograph being 'ripped' from original meaning. Whilst it is clearly meant for public consumption— it is not an intimate personal photograph of the kind he would define as 'private'—it nevertheless contributes to a living memory and is surrounded by, and carries its own, meaning. Kardashian's photograph does freeze an individual event and appearance, thus supporting Berger's critique of photography as appealing closely to our form of visual perception, that a photograph becomes the preferred means of isolating and fixing an event in memory. However, it seems inescapable that it directly references the surrounding context of

Kardashian's life. The context of her role as a celebrity figure cannot be ignored.

I would propose that Kardashian's selfie illustrates the idea that the wholly private image is rapidly becoming antiquated with the availability of social media, thus eroding Berger's binary understanding of public and private photography. Images that previously would have been understood as public can be part of an extenuating narrative, due to the public's ability to witness and participate in the lives of others via social media. These 'public' images can thus resonate and generate meaning just as 'private' ones do. This erosion, when occurring in images like Kardashian's selfie, can be utilized to further women's ability to claim control over their public portrayals.

The increasing public availability of private images is making it easier than ever for women to control representations of their bodies and sexuality in highly visible and effective ways. However, it must be conceded that this may be a privilege afforded only to images of (recognizable) westerners, or, to be more precise, celebrities. Given that these subjects already have a discernible public identity prior to being photographed, images of them are a reinforcement for or a supplement to their pre-existing public personas. Kim Kardashian is still considered an autonomous being irrespective of this photo, illustrative as it may be. Berger describes a private photograph's power as being "read in a context which is continuous with that from which the camera removed it," and Kardashian's decidedly public photograph also fulfills this function (51). Her images are read in the context of her reality show, her Instagram feed, and her published book of selfies. However, for unrecognizable or unremarkable faces, a portrait can be seen to reduce, rather than supplement, identity. To an observer, there is no extenuating personhood or narrative, merely what is captured in a still image. Without the contextual information that we automatically call up when looking at a celebrity, a photograph becomes a summation of its subject's entire existence. To the viewer, that person is not a person because "photographs in themselves do not narrate. Photographs preserve instant appearances" (51). Therefore, whilst it is perhaps admirable for Kardashian to reinforce and simultaneously repurpose her public identity, it is worth recognizing that other people operate within limitations that prevent them from doing the same.

Kim Kardashian's selfie exemplifies the ways in which modern media, and social media in particular, democratize photography and blur the boundaries between its private and public uses. As Sontag says: "Photography is not practiced by most people as an art. It is mainly a social rite, a defense against anxiety, and a tool" (5). I believe the importance of this shift lies in its redistribution of power to the subjects, allowing them the immediate ability to craft and cultivate their own image and to control how their narrative is presented to the world. As such, women are, more than ever, capable of reclaiming their own identities, whether they are performed or not, thus rejecting the previous passiveness and exploitation that both Berger and Sontag present. Although this power is still unavailable to those most marginalized, who do not have access to the visibility and resources that people like Kardashian command, public photographs are starting to act in the same way that Berger claims only private ones do: as a "memento from a life being lived" ("Uses" 52).

WORKS CITED

Berger, John. "Episode 2." *Ways of Seeing*. British Broadcasting Corporation, London, 8 Jan. 1972.

—. *Ways of Seeing*. British Broadcasting Corporation and Penguin Books, 1972.

—. "The Uses of Photography." *About Looking*, Pantheon, 1980.

Burnett, Rachel. "Kim Kardashian's Nude Selfies are Pioneering, says Harriet Harman." *The Independent*, 24 May 2016, www.independent.co.uk/news/people/kim-kardashians-naked-selfies-are-pioneering-says-harriet-harman-a7044396.html.

hooks, bell. "In Our Glory: Photography and Black Life." *Art on My Mind: Visual Politics*, The New Press, 1995.

@KimKardashian. "When you're like I have nothing to wear LOL." *Twitter*, 7 Mar. 2016, 4:11 p.m., www.twitter.com/KimKardashian/status/706754164047667200/photo/1.

Moon, Rachel. "Chloe Moretz vs. the Kardashians: A Look at Their Feud as Khloe Declares War with X-rated Snap." *The Mirror*, 18 July 2016, www.mirror.co.uk/3am/celebrity-news/chloe-moretz-vs-kardashians-look-8442998

Sontag, Susan. "In Plato's Cave." *On Photography*, Picador, 1977.

In this essay, Wang investigates the problem—and importance—of paying attention to other people. The essay's structure enacts that asymptotic goal, illuminating the question with surprisingly different examples in order to give readers the experience of trying to see beyond their own perspective. (Instructor: Laren McClung)

WRESTLING BLIND: GROPING AN ELEPHANT IN THREE ACTS

Benjamin Wang

1.

The elephant stands like a big, bloated blob amongst a gaggle of blind men. You can tell they're blind because their cartoonishly expressive eyes hang pupil-less above their gaping mouths in a look of absolute dumbfoundedness. There are a dozen of them, at least, with maybe more hidden behind the towering elephant. They are groping the trunk, hugging the leg, hanging from the tusks—some men have even managed to make their way on top of the beast by way of an absurdly tall ladder. What makes this painted scene even more amusing is the very serious Edo Period watercolor style renowned nineteenth-century artist Ohara Donshu used to render this otherwise ridiculous work entitled *Blind Men Appraising an Elephant*.

I know it's wrong to laugh at the blind, but these men approach their elephant examination with such dedication and absolute conviction. Donshu even painted in a few sighted passersby, pointing and sniggering, as if to say "it's *okay* to laugh." Even the elephant has an air of ridiculing amusement about his squinted eyes and toothy, upturned mouth.

The tale of the sightless men and the elephant is a traditional folk story well-circulated in India and East Asia. In fact, I can distinctly remember this story being a staple of my own mother's pre-bedtime moral enhancement suite. As the story goes, some blind men had learned there would be an elephant passing through town with a circus. These men, unfamiliar with the animal, set off to figure out just what exactly this whole elephant business was about. Upon reaching the beast, each of them stumble upon a different appendage and declare that they alone understand exactly what an elephant is. One hugs a leg and proclaims that the elephant is like a tree. Another fondles the trunk and says something along the lines of: "What are you on about, you faff, the elephant is like a snake!" Another grabs an ear and says: "You're both idiots, the elephant is like a fan." And so on and so forth until the whole scene ends in a big blind fight, complete with light obscenities and silly sound effects. At least, that's the way my mother told it. This story, in one incarnation or another, has circulated everywhere from Donshu's homeland of Japan to the folktale compendiums of Western Europe. Its immense geographic reach is, no doubt, at least partially due to its resonant moral value. Each blind man only 'sees' a small portion of the elephant, yet stubbornly believes he has the whole story and dismisses any counterargument as wholly false. It is in their inability to understand the complexity of the whole, through the views of others, that these men are truly blind.

It's easy to laugh when the elephant is literal—we know what an elephant is, so we know these men are wrong. Viewing the scene as an omniscient outsider allows for a disconnect between art and spectator. It's a lot harder to see the blind men's fallacies when we ourselves are the blind ones and the elephant represents something far more complex and ungraspable than a big grey mammal with pointy tusks. I'm reminded of David Foster Wallace's 2005 Kenyon College commencement address "This is Water," in which Wallace condemns the mentality that allows individuals to "[operate] on the automatic, unconscious belief that [they are] the center of the world" (5). He lays out a binary for being: you are either "aware enough to choose what you pay attention to and . . . how you construct meaning from experience," or you are "unconscious, a slave to your head and to your natural default-setting of being uniquely, completely, imperially alone, day in and day out" (3). Wallace would see the blind men as unconscious, unaware men living shallowly in the fallacy provoked by the fact that "everything in [their] own immediate experience supports

[the] deep belief that [they are] the absolute center of the universe, the realest, most vivid and important person in existence" (2).

There is an unofficial word for the moment of cathartic change, the moment when a mind shifts from unconsciousness to awareness. The Dictionary of Obscure Sorrows is a compendium created by writer John Koenig in an attempt to give names to as yet undefined neologisms. The project coined this term:

> Sonder
> n. the realization that each random passerby is living a life as vivid and complex as your own—populated with their own ambitions, friends, routines, worries and inherited craziness—an epic story that continues invisibly around you like an anthill sprawling deep underground, with elaborate passageways to thousands of other lives that you'll never know existed, in which you might appear only once, as an extra sipping coffee in the background, as a blur of traffic passing on the highway, as a lighted window at dusk.
> (Koenig)

Sonder is the moment when I think about the guy who cut me off in traffic. He might have fallen in love, lost friends, changed careers, taken up writing. Yet, in that singular moment when he cut me off, he was just a "stupid and cow-like and dead-eyed and nonhuman" being who, it seemed, existed solely for the purpose of getting "in my way" (Wallace 5). Without sonder, we see the 'others' of our lives, the strangers that exist beyond our immediate acquaintance, as extras in our movie—one dimensional and expendable. Sonder is the switch that turns on between unconsciousness and awareness. So then, how can sonder be encouraged to grow in the modern world? How do we solve the epidemic of unconsciousness?

Wallace proposes that it is possible to "[learn] how to exercise some control over how and what you think" through education and self-reflection (3). Of course, Wallace's entire argument for living with awareness was that "it [was] about making it to . . . 50 without wanting to shoot yourself in the head" (8). He gave up on that endgame when he hung himself from a patio two years after giving the speech—he was 46 years old. Perhaps the danger of Wallace's mantra was the strict binary nature of consciousness and unconsciousness. To him, there were two distinct states of being, and one was right, while the other was wrong. Maybe the key to understanding lies not within the binary of being aware or unconscious that switches on in a single moment of sonder, but rather a gradual transition into understanding and seeing humanity in the 'other.'

2.

In late summer of 2013, when American xenophobia and debates on race relations were reinvigorated by the Boston Marathon bombings and the Zimmerman trial, a little known indie game developer named Lucas Pope released a video game that dared to challenge the tribalistic rhetoric of a divided nation. A black screen greets you, accompanied by the low rumblings of a single tuba. It blasts a low, two-note alternation, a stern and impassive march which is soon accompanied by a shrewd crooning balalaika. The title crawls slowly up the screen to the rhythm of the march: *Papers, Please.*

Papers, Please is a document inspection simulator game. The player assumes the role of an inspection agent at an immigration checkpoint for the fictional communist-era Eastern-Bloc-style country of Arstotzka. At the beginning of each day, the player reports to the inspection booth where instructions are given for who to admit into the country. Entrants must produce all the necessary paperwork, and every document is to be inspected for errors indicating possible forgery. At first the rules are simple—entry is granted to anyone with a valid passport. But as immigrants carry out terrorist attacks and international relations become strained, the Arstotzkan Ministry of Admissions becomes more immoderate in their document requirements and more draconian in their punishment for failure of compliance. This goes so far as to confront the player with moral dilemmas. A woman pleads for her expired passport to be approved—returning home means certain death at the hands of her government. In these moments, the player has the agency to decide whether to comply with the rules set by the game's world, and, indeed, the rules set by the game itself, denying the woman entry, or doing the morally consequential act of admitting her against those rules. The decision is made harder by the government's deducting a considerable chunk of your daily salary for every wrongly admitted entrant—money that would have gone towards the rent of your apartment, food for your family, and medicine for your sick son. A lack of sufficient funds means sacrificing household amenities, which may lead to the deterioration and death of your family. The game is over when your entire family is dead. Because of the unique system of incentives set up by the game's world and rules, the player, although given full agency to admit or decline anyone he'd like, is forced to make difficult decisions regarding how to prioritize his morality and his duty.

Dr. Terry Schenold of the University of Washington's Critical Gaming Project observes that, in contrast to most games which occupy a homogeneously "'action-based medium,' [*Papers, Please*] is primarily about human judgment." The game subverts the pervasive single-minded and unconscious trope of the "male power [fantasy]" within the medium (Schenold). When "[p]laying as Mario (or most 'heroes' in games, for that matter) one only has to think about the problem in front of you, the explicit task at hand," but in *Papers, Please*, the player is forced to grapple with the ambiguous agency of "judgment *enacted*, as form of player action, [and] also judgment *perceived*" (Schenold).

What's most profound about the game is its intentional decision to cast the player not only as a layman with a day job, but also as a representation of the 'other.' To the non-playable characters in the world of the game, the player is just a man in a glass box who stands in the way of immigrants seeking their personal goals. When they get denied, they call you names, and some ask how you could be so cruel. These characters are focused on the dilemmas of their personal narratives and thus reject any notion of a narrative for the player. They are 'unconscious' to the complexities of the man in the booth.

In this way, the game allows the player to see the other side—what happens when the man in the booth goes home and has to worry about having enough money to afford medicine for his sick son. So often when we encounter these men and women, the people who seem to exist for the sole purpose of getting in the way, we see them as obstacles, 'others' who could never possibly share the dimensionality of a regular human being. *Papers, Please* is a game that "judges us, for in asking us to judge others through its designs we are given an indirect opportunity *to see ourselves*" (Schenold). This game is the elephant applied to the real world—of politics, race, and economics. Lucas Pope illuminates the human inability to grasp the 'other' as part of the same whole as the rest of us. The immigrants in line are the blind men. Each makes a decision about the player based solely on the single interaction at the passport checkpoint. And so one man who is rejected concludes that you are an "imbecile," while another man who is separated from his son concludes that you are "heartless" (*Papers, Please*). Only the player, the elephant in the glass booth, understands the whole picture, but unlike the elephant in Donshu's painting, it is difficult to hold on to any smugness in your omnipotence among these particular blind men.

3.

Francisco Cantú had just graduated from college when he made the decision to join the U.S. border patrol: the real-life equivalent of the agent in the glass booth. In a passage from *The Line Becomes a River*, the yet-unpublished memoir of his experiences, he recounts Robles, his training officer, decreeing that "your body is a tool" (qtd. in Glass). Robles then told the story of two men, one whose life he took when he "kicked him over the edge of [a] canal into the water," and one whom he "battled to keep . . . afloat" in the rushing Colorado River (qtd. in Glass). Both men were illegal immigrants who were backed into a corner. One chose to fight while the other chose to jump. While both ended up in the water, Robles made drastically different decisions based on his unique position and his sense of morality and duty. As Robles told his story, Cantú "wondered if [Robles] thought of his body as a tool for destruction, or one for keeping people safe" (qtd. in Glass).

The liberal opinion of the border patrol, and thus the opinion that we often see reflected in art and the media, seems to be one of dehumanization. Officers are the obstacles, the draconian 'paramilitary' in the way of poor immigrants seeking peaceful asylum in the U.S. They are the faceless others whose bodies are "tools" to be wielded by the amalgamous mass of social xenophobia. But Cantú, the college educated son of an illegal immigrant, "had his reasons for stepping up," as did his classmates at the academy, "nearly half [of whom were] Hispanic." (Glass; qtd. in Glass). He told his mother, "I'm not going to become someone else." He was going to retain his humanity, even if others refused to see it. He bluntly testified that the agents would "slash [border-crossers'] bottles and drain their water into the dry earth [and] dump their backpacks and pile their food and clothes to be crushed and pissed on and stepped over, strewn across the desert floor and set ablaze" (qtd. in Glass). He did not deny the severe and seemingly unhumanitarian tactics of the CBP, but he paints the whole picture, the rest of the elephant that the mainstream narrative often refuses to acknowledge: "The idea is that when they come out from their hiding places . . . they'll realize their situation . . . That it's hopeless to continue. And they'll quit right then and there" (qtd. in Glass).

Michael Warner might explain this social inability to see the 'other' as the disconnect between "personal identity" and the "public" (415). In his essay "Publics and Counterpublics," he asserts that "personal identity does not in itself make one part of a public," but rather that "[p]ublics differ from nations, races, professions, or any other groups that . . . saturate identity" (415). In other words, although our identities are not dictated by the publics we are a part of, we are nevertheless colored, at least in the eyes of others, by the publics we choose to associate with. Because "we navigate a world of corporate agents that do not respond or act as people do," we then assign those inhuman qualities to the people who subscribe to those publics—in this case, the agents of the border patrol (415).

Warner also warned that it is easy to forget that the "public [is] capable of comprehension or action," and that continued denial of "people in minor or marginal positions . . . [will result in] a blockage in activity and optimism, a disintegration of politics toward isolation, frustration, anomie, forgetfulness" (415). Sound familiar? This philosophy is directly in line with that of Wallace, right down to the consequences of willed ignorance. The only difference is that, while Wallace calls for an exhaustive and perpetual understanding of every human that we interact with, Warner believes in the importance of keeping some people at the level of strangers. To him, "strangerhood is the necessary medium of commonality," because "the modern social imaginary does not make sense without strangers" (417). In response to Wallace's awareness, which demands the recognition of every minor character that protrudes into our lives, Warner would counter that "a nation or public . . . in which everyone could be known personally would be no nation or public . . . at all" (417). Without strangers, we can find no commonality in contrast. So, then, maybe the key is to find the 'other' and simply acknowledge that we see it as the 'other.' Maybe we don't need to exhaust ourselves with seeing the whole elephant; we only need to acknowledge that other parts of the elephant exist beyond the appendage currently being groped.

Cantú didn't join the border patrol out of a sense of patriotism or duty, or any binary sense of right and wrong. He had "spent four years studying about the border" in college and joined the CBP because he wasn't satisfied with the part of the elephant he was groping. He "[wanted] to see the realities of the border, day in and day out" in a way beyond what any books could tell him. And it was that pursuit that broke him. He began having "nightmares, visions of [men] staggering through the desert . . . and [he] was powerless to help them, powerless to keep them from straying through the night" (qtd. in Glass). Cantú joined the patrol to pursue a Wallacian awareness, only to come out trembling at the realization that he "hadn't learned anything" (qtd. in Glass). The elephant proved to be far too big for one blind man to grasp.

[epilogue]

Blindness is generally irremediable, just as unconsciousness is inexorable. There will always be strangers in our way, amalgamous and looming. Ungraspable. Our minds are far too small to see everything with awareness, so we do the best we can. We grope. We argue. We grope some more. Maybe it's inelegant—crude, even—but it's life. And it makes for a hell of an entertaining story.

WORKS CITED

Donshu, Ohara. *Blind Men Appraising an Elephant.* Early 19th century, ink and colors on paper, Brooklyn Museum, New York.

Glass, Ira. "613: Ok, I'll Do It." *This American Life,* from Chicago Public Media, 31 Mar. 2017, www.thisamericanlife.org/radio-archives/episode/613/transcript.

Koenig, John. "Sonder." *Dictionary of Obscure Sorrows,* 2013, www.dictionaryofobscuresorrows.com/post/23536922667/sonder.

Papers, Please: A Dystopian Document Thriller, created by Lucas Pope, 3909 LLC, 2013.

Schenold, Terry. "Critical Exemplars: *Papers, Please.*" *Critical Gaming Project,* 1 Feb. 2014, depts.washington.edu/critgame/project/critical-exemplars/.

Wallace, David Foster. "This is Water." Kenyon College Commencement Address, 21 May 2005. *Metastatic.org,* www.metastatic.org/text/This%20is%20Water.pdf.

Warner, Michael. "Publics and Counterpublics (Abbreviated Version)." *Quarterly Journal of Speech,* vol. 88, no. 4, 2009, pp. 412-425.

MERCER STREET

CONTRIBUTORS

Sandra Burlaud, '20, studies Computer Science at the College of Arts and Science. Originally from France, she moved to Miami, Florida, in 2011. Her essay "Your House Is Not a Home" encouraged her to explore the concepts of home and familiarity as they evolve over a lifetime. The subject became thought-provoking and surprisingly relevant for a readership distanced from family and home for the first time. Sandra enjoys traveling and learning languages, as well as writing fiction and claiming to know how to play the piano.

Mark Chen, '20, from Syosset, New York, is a Mechanical Engineering major at the Tandon School of Engineering. A fond and lifelong interest in science and technology has inspired his many pursuits, including writing. The increasingly important role of technology can be seen in his essay, "The Duality of Intelligence," which highlights the current state of artificial intelligence and its potential impact on our future lives. In his free time, Mark enjoys reading science fiction, lounging around on the Internet, and looking forward to his next travel destination.

Mary Colussi, '20, studies Dramatic Writing at the Tisch School of the Arts. Born in Australia, she moved with her family to the Boston area in 2001. At Tisch, she has been encouraged to test the boundaries between the artist as an individual and as a member of a larger public. Her essay, "Searching for Solace in a Lemon Peel," stems from this investigation. It asks what the objects we choose to surround ourselves with say about us and our communities. Mary hopes to write for television and the stage.

Andrew Galanter, '20, is pursuing a double major in Film and Television at the Tisch School of the Arts and in Linguistics at the College of Arts and Sciences. Originally from Tappan, New York, Andrew counts among his interests language and humor. The intersection of the two inspired his essay, "Humans and Dogs and Fishes! Oh My!" In it, he asks what makes something "lifelike." He insists that writing it constituted the most time he has ever spent thinking about mackerels. In his free time, Andrew enjoys praising the compositions of Stephen Sondheim and William Finn, reading the work of Philip Roth, and arm wrestling anyone who disputes Noam Chomsky's Theory of Universal Grammar.

Milo Hudson, '20, from Portland, Oregon, majors in Politics and minors in Economics at the College of Arts and Sciences. His roots in Quakerism and in the recreational enjoyment of silence led Milo to critically explore sound, sense, and spirituality in his essay, "That We May Hear." Milo espouses brevity (sometimes forgoing it) and disdains grandstanding (occasionally practicing it). A black man from America's whitest city, he has come to appreciate diverse communities and challenging perspectives. Beyond his studies, Milo is an avid news reader and television connoisseur.

Jaehyoung Ju, '20, is a rising sophomore in the College of Arts and Sciences. His essay, "On Dog Meat Consumption and Regulation," proposes a plan to address the inhumane conditions of Korea's dog meat industry.

Charlotte Kahan, '20, is a Public Policy major from Ridgewood, New Jersey. She is drawn to the way law and political decision-making can be used to alleviate poverty, reduce crime, and improve educational opportunities for underserved communities. Her essay "The Poverty Link" shows how local public school funding plays such a major role in exacerbating a critical education gap between wealthy and poor students. Charlotte hopes that her focus on the far-reaching consequences of underfunded schools will offer a more nuanced explanation for why poverty seems so inescapable. Charlotte volunteers at Rikers Island, helping incarcerated individuals with their academic assignments and public speaking skills. She intends to study law in the future in order to further her passions for debate and public service.

Audrey Larson, '20, is a Film and Television major at the Tisch School of the Arts. Hailing from Sharon, Massachusetts, Audrey started her own youth filmmaking organization as a teenager and has written and produced multiple award-winning short films. She has studied ballet, piano, and acting, and has performed in community theater and in various films. Homeschooled since the second grade, Audrey considers herself a lifelong learner. Her passions also include antiques, history, geography, and a dream to travel the world. "Playing with People" was motivated by the desire to unravel the many themes in Charlie Kaufman's work: perspective, the self, and human connection.

Christina Louder, '20, from Queens, New York, studies Applied Psychology at the Steinhardt School of Culture, Education, and Human Development. After only a short time at NYU–a predominantly white institution–Christina began to fully understand the importance of black voices, especially young black voices. Therefore, when given the opportunity, she decided to use her writing course as a platform for speaking about something that meant a great deal to her: being black in America. The passion she channeled to write "We Gon' Be Alright" is the same that fuels Christina's dedication to finding a way to combine all of her interests into a fulfilling academic experience at NYU.

Alice Lu, '20, grew up in Philadelphia, Pennsylvania, and later moved to the suburban parts of New Jersey. Now she lives in New York, where she studies Computer Science. Alice has a profound interest in Integrated Digital Media and Cognitive Science. As a web developer at the Stern School of Business and as a freelance graphic designer, Alice has cultivated a passion for learning how technology plays a role in the arts and human cognition. This curiosity inspired her to write "The Language Spoken by All," an essay focusing on photography and its influence on society.

Amelia Milne, '20, is a rising sophomore in NYU's College of Arts & Science. Her essay, "No Longer a Passive Subject," explores how modern photography can empower female self-representation.

Martina Pagliari, '20, originally from Rome, Italy, is a Film and Television major in the Tisch School of the Arts with a minor in Russian and Slavic Studies. Although mainly focused on pursuing a career as a filmmaker, Martina has an abiding interest in the study of foreign languages, her gateway to different cultures and modes of understanding. Social and political issues also play a main inspirational source in her work. The urge to address such issues inspired her to write "The Tragedy Underneath: Satire and Reality," which examines satire as an instrument of social critique.

Nick Panoutsos, '20, is a Jazz Studies major in the Steinhardt School of Culture, Education, and Human Development's Department of Music and Performing Art Professions. Pursuing a minor in Media, Culture, and Communication, Nick is also fascinated by the process of crafting and consuming news media. He seized the opportunity to investigate the public dialogue surrounding the Keystone XL Pipeline in his essay, "This Land Is Your Land." Through his research, Nick discovered the news media's role in establishing corporate accountability. As a freelance musician and magazine writer, Nick hopes to continue balancing his musical aspirations with journalism, both in his hometown of San Jose, California, and here in New York City.

Anthony Parks, '17, grew down in Brewster, New York. At the Gallatin School of Individualized Study, he built a concentration in "Queer world-making practices with nonfiction writing and Spanish literary translation." Maggie Nelson is among Anthony's favorite thinkers, and his essay "And On and On" came pleasurably, without pause. The essay was written for Professor Bruce Bromley's "A Spectrum of Essays" course, which profoundly impacted Anthony's undergraduate studies. Anthony enjoys slasher films, well-lit rooms, and exaggerating. He hopes for a future filled with delicious food, sharp prose, and redistributed wealth. He also hopes you have fun with his essay.

Emma Patton, '20, is in the College of Arts and Sciences studying Sociology. She was born and raised in St. Louis, Missouri, where she attended an all-girls Loretto high school that ignited Emma's passion for feminist issues and led her to explore the writings of Leslie Jamison at NYU. Jamison's essays reckon with the concepts of female pain and empathy. Topics that resonated with Emma's feminist and sociological interests and inspired her to write "Blood, Ink, and Pain: An Excavation." Emma is a College Leader, a Writing Tutor in the Expository Writing Program, an intern for Loretto at the UN, and a member of the CAS Student Council, serving as interim CAS Sophomore Class President.

Duc Minh Pham, '20, often finds himself in peculiar positions between different ideas and perspectives. He is pursuing a Computer Science major at the Tandon School of Engineering. He is also interested in politics and history, and participates in the NYU Model UN Club. Growing up in Saigon in conservative and traditional Vietnam, Duc sees both the importance of exploration and curiosity, as well as the promise of how different and even conflicting views can elevate each other. Thus, he tries to give his essay, "For the Vietnamese Youth," nuance in order to see the world through alternate standpoints. Duc is inspired by classroom discussions and influential instructors.

Elijah Scott, '20, is a rising sophomore studying Global Public Health/Nutrition and Dietetics at the Steinhardt School of Culture, Education, and Human Development. Elijah grew up in the Washington, DC area and has also lived in Beijing, China. Her love for city living played a huge part in her decision to attend NYU. She loves film and its ability to illustrate human behavior and expose societal fault lines. In her essay "A Network of Lies," she analyzes the sociopathic news stringer Lou Bloom from the film *Nightcrawler*.

Her essay compares the antagonistic role of the fourth estate to other figures in media-critique films, like *All the President's Men* and *Network*. Today's "fake news" controversies are not hard to recognize here.

Gabriela Serpa, '20, was born in Miami, Florida, but has been a New Yorker since she moved to Manhattan at the mere age of 30 days old. Gabriela's parents are from Bogotá, Colombia, where her family lived as of 2011. There, she received her high school degree and discovered her passion for the visual arts. Gabriela's expansive interest in mediums of self-expression brought her to NYU, where she is a student in Gallatin's School of Individualized Study. Her preoccupation with the relationship between imagination and reality—particularly in the realms of fairy-tales and theater—often resurfaces in her sculptures and written pieces. Writing "*Birdman*: Where Reality Takes Flight," was thus a very intriguing and personal endeavor.

Saianna Solomon, '20, studies Neural Science on the pre-dental track at the College of Arts and Sciences, and hopes to one day provide free dental care to refugees and in third world countries. Born and raised in Trinidad, West Indies, she brought with her to NYU an undying spirit of volunteerism and zeal for social justice. Spending an NYU alternative spring break giving aid in refugee resettlements in Clarkston, Georgia, Saianna met people from what seemed like entirely different worlds. This enlightening experience, coupled with her innate curiosity, challenged her to undertake a journey into these foreign worlds. Her essay explores the possibilities and limitations of empathy, and was inspired by her realization that empathy should not be reserved only for special occasions, but can be just as worthwhile as a daily practice.

Brennan Spector, '20, is a Drama and Musical Theater major in the Tisch School of the Arts' New Studio on Broadway. An actor from a young age, Brennan would spend his mornings in his hometown of Skillman, New Jersey, before going to Manhattan for rehearsals and auditions later that night. His essay "Reflections" arose from a deep fascination with art that blurs the lines between real life and performance. Weekly outings to museums and the theater have proven to be his most valuable research.

Aidan Stanley-Coughlan, '20, from Rochester, New York, is pursuing a degree in Social Work at the Silver School of Social Work. In "Sex Work and Social Welfare: Anti-Oppressive Social Work Practice," he seeks to examine those schools of thought which have shaped the services that social workers provide to New York City sex workers. It concentrates on how contemporary social work and scholarship perpetuate oppressive systems. Driven by a passion for radical politics, his essay was written in an effort to contextualize critical consciousness, and to do this within social work practice with a historically at-risk and frequently silenced population. In his free time, Aidan likes to read, teach health classes in public schools, and explore the colorful neighborhoods of New York City.

Phionna Teo, '20, is an Anthropology major in the College of Arts and Sciences. She hails from sunny Singapore. Her interest in social justice and cultural constructs drove her to Anthropology, and inspired her piece "A Writer's Occupation," an essay that questions the line between occupying and liberating. As a hopelessly irreligious individual, she found herself drawn to the study of Medieval Mysticism in hopes of understanding the driving forces behind extreme behavior inspired by religion. "The Significance of Food for Mystics in the Middle Ages" was the result. In her free time, Phionna can most often be found on the road, in pursuit of new places and passions.

Chloë Thorburn, '20, from Lexington, Massachusetts, is a Drama major in the Tisch School of the Arts. From babysitting in her teens to working as an America Reads literacy tutor in NYC, Chloë has been captivated by the way children often think far more critically and maturely than they are given credit for. "Dr. Seuss, Leader of the Resistance" stems from Chloë's belief that the autonomy and wisdom of children are too often undervalued. She seeks to analyze and challenge how our culture strives to raise children as successful future citizens while simultaneously suppressing their freedom to develop as free-thinking individuals. A child at heart, Chloë used this essay as an excuse to revisit some of the most beloved picture books of her childhood.

Benjamin Wang, '20, grew up in the lovely town of Northfield, Minnesota. He studies Drama at the Tisch School of the Arts. His writing process blends all the dubious earnestness of your philosophy major uncle with the gung-ho, loose-cannon courage that can only be riled at 3am the night before the deadline. He has long struggled to understand why people are so susceptible to anger towards strangers. His essay, "Wrestling Blind: Groping an Elephant in Three Acts," is not meant to be an "answer" to this problem, but rather a representation of his thoughts on the subject. Mr. Cohrs and Mrs. Mucha may be surprised to find a refreshing lack of snark in Benjamin's writing, a feat which has just been thoroughly betrayed.

Taylor Whitehead, '19, originally from San Jose, California, is an Applied Psychology major in the Steinhardt School of Culture, Education, and Human Development. She was driven to write "Boys Who Cry Saint" by an enduring interest in feminist theory and social psychology. Maggie Nelson's *The Argonauts* was also a strong influence. She is interested in how binary thinking can limit interpersonal relationships, and seeks to reconceptualize these notions through her writing. In her free time, she volunteers as a health educator for Peer Health Exchange and enjoys watching sitcoms.

Xiaolu Wu, '20, from Shanghai, China, is an Art History major in the College of Art and Sciences. Her interests include art and literature, religious studies and philosophy. Rebecca Solnit's essay collection, *A Field Guide to Getting Lost*, therefore attracted Xiaolu. For her, writing "A Digressional Guide" was a process of peeling away the complex layers of thought in Solnit's literature and putting these scraps of evidence together to create a literary theory of her own. "A Digressional Guide" also expresses Xiaolu's own belief in the meaning of life through Solnit's language. Besides literature, Xiaolu is deeply passionate about art, and loves going to museums.

MERCER STREET

NOTEWORTHY ESSAYS